GRE,

Born in Cambridgeshire in 1949, Phil Clarke left school 'essentially' at 14, was a factory electrician for 3-years, a scientific instrument technician for 6-years, then a full-time student for 4-years. After an incongruous year as a maths teacher, he spent a decade in the broadcast industry as a technician/engineer then operator before heading out around the USA (driving 16,000+ miles) then Australia and New Zealand for the best part of a year – since when he's ended up in Hastings UK where he was briefly a BT telephone operator. More recently he's driven around the EU a few times in a beaten-up old Jag, hostelling and camping, and otherwise cycles, walks (with the occasional sprint), sea-swims and generally idles about. In spare moments all through this, he's been dipping into all kinds of books. Some of these have inspired the making of notes for reflecting on and as reminders of the writers and works that seemed most impressive at the time. Now, with websites and self-publishing, comes the possibility of passing on these notes as in this little volume, maybe with one or two extras added. See also: zoneidle.co.uk

BY THE SAME AUTHOR

Tales of the Abnormal
Essays and Sketches
The First 40 Years (memoir)
The Coming Nuclear War

Phil Clarke

GREAT WRITERS

- Powerful Books -

A Personal Appraisal

ISBN: 9798398185676

CONTENTS

-

Note

If you read a book about a journey around Europe, say, you'll get the author's mostly unique experiences of countries, districts and towns, the flora, the cuisine and so on. The route taken will also be individual and unique. Such a book won't be comprehensive or focused on one country or aspect, as an academic study might, but will give an individual general impression. In that way, this book could be regarded as a kind of travel book around my own unique experience of writers and books. My route, too, has been almost random, with no set procedure for what I've read or in what order.

There's no academic research here either, and I'm no expert, so although I trust any objective details to be correct, don't bank on it. Other 'REAL' writers have already produced excellent biographies, studies and analyses on all the authors and books I cover.

So despite the Inevitable deficiencies and distortions of imperfect recall, this book is intended as a memoir of books and reading, with a bit on my experience of writing too. To illustrate what has attracted or impressed me I've included quotes and extracts: short excerpts are italicised and indented, longer ones are in appendixes.

I've read most of what's available from several of the authors I look at, but my knowledge of the majority is from rather less - so the appraisals remain essentially superficial and limited as well as possibly one-sided and even naïve in some instances.

Most of the articles were written over a period of years so there are occasional thoughts and perspectives I've since evolved from, and doubtless will further evolve - so I hesitate to update. As with my other books when I finally hold a copy in hand, I'm sure to notice with regret what I've failed to include, change or delete. Maybe a new edition will be forthcoming, which would also address the fact that If I'd given more time to the project I could have expanded significantly on several of the writers, certainly ones I've written less than a page on, as well as adding a few more.

Unfortunately, I lack the required industrious disposition for a more comprehensive appraisal. On top of which I have no proof-reader or reliable critic, nor can I afford to pay someone. So I have to conduct the dubious task of checking and editing my own work. I'm already aware that titles as in 'contents' are not always consistent with actual contents, and that names sometimes appear where they strictly don't belong. Plus, especially in *More Writers of Note*, many excellent writers of less significance *to me* are crowded together somewhat haphazardly. Even so, despite all these issues, and a few others besides – like inevitable typos - I think this book could be very worthwhile for anyone interested in the kind of literature that's grabbed not just my interest but many other people's too. And not just interest but more to the point: appreciation.

.
.
.
.
.

Introduction

'Kiss my arse or I'll kick your head in'

... said Nobel laureate Harold Pinter, genius playwright, master of concise dialogue, describing US foreign policy since the end of WW2.

Alas, my own skill for this kind of succinct wit, or for grasping vast concepts in a brief sentence, is lacking. Despite which, together with deficiencies the work of writers I've most enjoyed didn't suffer, I nevertheless persist in writing an occasional story or essay, and even writing about writing.

I trust it's also understood that the title refers not to writers considered by general consensus or expert opinion to be great, but to my own subjective judgment - though in some instances these might concur - whatever the current trend, fickle as that is. Nor can I claim any kind of expertise or qualification in assessing and analysing literature of any sort, or that the amount of my reading - though maybe more than most people's - is other than quite limited.

I guess I can only justify this book in that I regard myself as a more-or-less average guy who represents a more-or-less average reader but who places speculation on the future and glimpses of existential philosophy above romance, crime or other more popular genes - and who might be capable of presenting an even-handed, if also superficial, appraisal of authors he's enjoyed and been impressed by.

Since my education was deficient, certainly with regard to literature, what I've read throughout the years has depended as much on chance as choice. There are many authors, including the most famous, whose work I haven't read. There are also less popular ones I've stumbled on perchance and found outstanding. Besides which, we are all subject to bias from our innate attributes, idiosyncrasies and experiences - including chance unearthing or failing to unearth certain authors, being informed or failing to be informed, or more crucially: being gripped or failing to be gripped. Hardly to mention the level of lethargy or enthusiasm we have for reading, due to negative or positive experience with books, and an abundance of alternative options these days.

But other than those fluke lucky discoveries of mine, how many, I wonder, great obscure books have I failed to unearth when traipsing around dusty second-hand bookshops? How many have I returned to their shelf unmoved? On the other hand, how many when noticed in an Amazon review of a different publication have triggered a spark of curiosity for further investigation?

As I progress through life and reflect, I gain new angles on writers whose work for whatever reason lingers in mind and remain relevant - as I say, perspectives evolve. Some writers I value highly I've written little about, other's I value less have inspired more reflection and analyses. And I often dwell on how I'm affected by what I read, how it relates to other aspects of life - I'm frequently as intrigued by a writer's life as by their work.

Until I was about 40 my background was almost exclusively scientific, so I'd written little other than technical-reports. Then my friend X, on the strength of a few long letters I'd sent him (pre-email days and I guess regarding my prolonged trip around the US), almost persuaded me that I could write well enough to interest people other than him, and should write more. Unconvinced, I went ahead anyway. I guess by then I'd reached that point Colin Wilson describes in his 'Below the Iceberg' – that is: I enjoyed the writing process, so kept at it:

As a writer, I am aware of the "feedback" process. My right brain produces the intuitions, my left has the task of turning them into words. When I was a beginner, I did it so clumsily that I usually killed the intuitions, and when I read it later, the words seemed dead and empty. Then I got better at it, until the left could catch the intuitions like a good fielder. Sometimes it did it so well that the right would get enthusiastic to see itself so well expressed; and then the left would be spurred to still greater efforts by the approval of the right and the whole process would build up until I felt positively "inspired".

That kind of feedback is one explanation for how practice can work. It's slow too, so one has to be fairly keen or attracted to the task, the 'art' – or at first not be too concerned about quality. This applies to any creative process: playing a musical instrument, learning another language, painting, sculpting... you start the slow process of creating inarticulate, stilted sentences that lack 'flow', then suddenly, just when you think you'll never get it: *voila* - you notice for the first time some kind of coherence and natural rhythm that was previously so elusive. This recognition spurs you on, like a pianist for the first time making the piano 'sing' with little melodies without conscious focus on their fingers. So you move onto the next stage, developing the skill on and on. The younger you start the greater the benefit. Practice shapes the mind and the shape sticks more firmly when young. If only I'd realised this as a youth – instead, when I began writing (about age 44) I was older than many great writers when they died.

I've read too that it takes about 10,000 hours, or 10-years, of practice to master a creative art. By which time you'll develop many subtle techniques, especially if you innately take to the art and are not pursuing it for reasons other than pleasure. I guess I'm approaching halfway, and will probably reach optimum when I'm about to peg-out?

So, as Wilson describes, I soon learned how the effort of *attempting* (whether or not achieving) to write clear, compelling prose, of revising, adjusting and perfecting and so on, could actually be both absorbing and rewarding. Though I'm never entirely contented with what I've written, I can't aspire to perfectionism, hence - as I guess readers will have noticed – a level of incoherence prevails.

One consequence of an obsession with perfection is illustrated by Camus from a character in 'The Plague':

> In his spare time, Grand polishes up his Latin, and he is also writing a book, but he is such a perfectionist that he continually rewrites the first sentence and can get no further.

Hemingway claimed he re-wrote the last page of 'Farewell to Arms' 39-times. Many aspects of life, especially art – in contrast to technical and scientific - involve compromise and improvisation. Any other approach, I contend, denies reality and presents obstacles as Monsieur Grand in Camus's novel found. As ever, though, there are exceptions – maybe Michelangelo took a perfectionist approach? Maybe most masterpieces are the result of an innate obsession for perfection - from a kind of madness of genius? Maybe it's just a skilled intuition for knowing when to stop - when as near as possible to perfection has been achieved?

The chief pleasure of creating any art, I contend, is from both the act of creating and of articulating to oneself what would otherwise be unlikely to enter consciousness – or if it did, then it would enter only at a superficial level. Yet although art allows one to evoke thoughts and ideas that might otherwise not surface, it is at the same time, with writing, impossible to relate in words more than a veneer of what floods through the mind while fathoming, exploring, experimenting... to articulate oneself - hopefully with clarity, and maybe a level of eloquence too.

From my own experience of reading, it's precisely through this veneer, assuming it's reasonably well-woven, that the reader's mind effortlessly (even unwittingly and unnoticed) constructs depth, meaning and empathy. The vast tapestry so formed from these monochrome hieroglyphics is dredged solely (where else?) from the reader's own unique reservoir of experience. After all, it's only squiggles on a page that we decipher and that has the power to evoke whole universes of feeling and thinking, of pictures, emotions and understanding. But it is through this consciously effortless, yet intensely creative, mental activity on the part of the reader that the real enchantment is found – one is, in a sense, creating what one reads. Maybe it's a bit like this computer I'm writing on receiving a few meagre codes from which it generates all the rich textures and colours I see on the screen - according to software already present without which the codes would mean nothing.

Now imagine an absorbing game in which every moment is original yet curiously familiar like waves on the sea, and which - unconscious of the slightest exertion - you play not only with keen anticipation, but with absorbing passion too. I'm talking about the most gripping and realistic literature here, texts one can closely relate to, where you forget you're reading; whereas the content of most books these days, I reckon, is light and shallow and can be dropped or placed aside at any point with little or no sense of loss. A lot is virtually impossible to get involved with in the first place; it is so banal, trivial and badly or boringly written - that's my subjective view of most contemporary books I dip into these days.

One explanation for why I find the quality of modern literature inferior, while most of what I prefer and describe in this book is older than I am, their authors long dead, is that these days most great writing never gets published. True, some does, but the market is swamped with popularist work that might be very good and highly entertaining, deep too even, but not great like Kafka, Hesse or Dostoyevsky, for instance.

And this is because publishers and agents as much as retailers are more than fully occupied with authors whose writing they know will sell. They're not interested, as Victor Gollancz famously was, in publishing or displaying great work that risks financial loss. Despite original aspirations and a 'love' of books and literature, most if not all publishers are in publishing to make money. Obviously, they have to make a living, but shouldn't more of them, like Gollancz, balance the profitable against the non-profitable?

I recently came into possession of a fine book called '*Why Don't You Fly? – Back Door to Beijing by Bicycle*' (2005) by Chris J A Smith. Chris has a website (cycleuktochina.com) where he describes the monumental effort to get his book published. Even when he managed to find an agent then a publisher to read it, which was a feat in itself, they invariably responded with solid genuine praise. Yet, they refused to publish because they estimated that it wasn't going sell enough to make serious money. This was pre-2005 when 'vanity' publishing – paying to get your book printed yourself - was for most people prohibitively expensive.

Now, with developments in computer and printing technology, print 'on-demand' has become the trend and vanity publishing is affordable. Amazon's kdp service means I can upload this book, as with my '*Tales of the Abnormal*' or my little book '*Essays & Sketches*', etc., and these appear on the Amazon website alongside millions of other books, with the great and famous too, and given the same kind of presentation. What's more, the entire process costs nothing – unless I buy a copy, which is about £5 for a 320-page book – perhaps less than a new book that size from a bookshop. As for publicity and advertising... that's another issue.

So now it all depends on publicity. How much is an author willing or able to afford? How much trouble are they prepared to go to? How certain is the author that their work is of sufficient merit to be worth advertising? Will enough buyers be attracted to justify the expense? Or will only 'populist' readers with a short attention span venture to 'look inside' and find the work dull and uninspiring or – despite the writer's high opinion through what he half-suspects could be his inevitable 'rose-tinted' glasses, and likewise of friends? Yet without some kind of publicity no-one will know of the 'masterpiece's' existence.

Another reason for the lack of great literature, or the invisibility (through populist swamping) of it - might be the nature of the present era, fashions and education, the general milieu? I, though, suspect it's there, almost under my nose, but out of sight, swallowed by the vast ocean of populist books, and it's the failure of the system to unearth it that's to blame?

One might imagine writers' groups could help. I've learned to steer clear of these. After attending an occasional open meeting of several I've invariably found members, especially who've had their book published, interested in nothing but plugging their own little 'masterpiece', as if the whole set-up is a mere marketing ploy – like so many radio & TV programmes that feature books these days, magazine programmes above all. Attending a writers' group is a quite boring experience too when 'successful' (ie, published) writers take turns to read-out their efforts. Maybe I'm just not into the stuff they write – which sets me wondering how readers will find the choices I describe in this book?

Powerful Books

This chapter was written back in 2002

About five years ago, because I'd been impressed with many excellent books, I wrote an account of the experience - with the intension of passing on a few details that might inspire readers to proclaim, "At last, that's just the book/author I was looking for!".

Until ten years ago I'd accumulated roughly 500 books. I was then 41 [ie, 1990], so that's an average of 20 a year since the age of sixteen. There are now around 1800 on the shelves, which means an average increase to 130 a year over the past ten years. What happened to spark such an upsurge? And why so sudden?

To write about the books that have influenced me might be seen as pretentious: why should anyone be interested in books that are important to *me*? But to write it for myself is another matter. For one thing, I'm obliged to revisit those books that unleashed to me the pleasure and surprise of new ideas and perspectives – and to take a fresh look at what those books had to offer, which together with experiences and events of everyday life have helped shape my thoughts, opinions and outlook. And for another thing, it gives me a chance to pick up fragments missed first time around. From all of which, presented in a chunk, as it were, I might assemble a more enlightened perception of life.

One of the difficulties in writing about books, particularly those that have influenced one's thoughts, is knowing what and how much to say: it calls for discernment and restraint (neither are strong points for me). And it's not always clear what has or hasn't had an effect or if so then how much effect. But the end result ought to give a fair guide to my personal philosophy and even personality, though this can never be more than superficial because as I say, chance has played as much a part as initiative in selecting what I've read. Many times I've stumbled on a book or an author I'd never before heard of that has then had a marked effect on the direction of my thoughts, and some of these have in turn led to other important works or authors.

The quest seems endless – it's part of the joy of visiting junkshops. Sometimes I've wondered if I'll run out of authors, which of course is impossible: often, I've finished all a writer's work and thought I'd never find anything I'd enjoy as much, or gain so much from, only to discover a few days or weeks later what seems like an even more striking author.

But of those hobbies that involve no obvious creative process, physical skill or exertion, it strikes me that losing oneself in books is hard to beat. I haven't always felt passionate about reading. Developing affection for books was a gradual process – despite that sudden increase in purchases back around the late 1980s, and has resulted in a pastime I now regard as an integral part of life.

What's more, reading is free – if you use a library – or, if you want to own the books so you can refer back, amazingly cheap either as kindles or second-hand paperbacks (which I prefer). Some of my most treasured volumes cost no more than a few pence second-hand (which is by far my greatest source) – and I leave the prices on as if they belong to the books, just as I always leave margin notes or underlining; so there's not merely an author's work but a mysterious layman-critic's too. Such notes can be enlightening, useful, amusing or silly and naive, but rarely irrelevant or dull. One can glimpse into the minds of some beguiling individuals. I've often regretted that these margin-fillers haven't included an email address so I can discuss the work that so inspired their scribbling. On several occasions I've bought a book purely for its abundance of notes, when without them I'd have left it on the shelf.

To read a book is to gaze into an author's mind, to see what he or she thinks about life and the human condition, as much their subconscious as conscious. But what compels an author to go to the enormous trouble – because that's what it is (I've tried it) - of writing it all down? Money is frequently a motive certainly, but if that were all then every author would strive only to produce Mills & Boon, pulp-detective or some other popular 'disposable' genre. A few exceptional writers have undoubtedly done this, and their work has survived the ages because of some special quality in how they relate, for instance, the simple age-old yarn about girl meets boy, rags to riches or a standard whodunit. And the reason for this quality – quite apart from the need to earn a living - is probably a combination of ingenuity, meticulous attention to detail and real joy in the creative process. Plus, frequently, a life solid with experience, usually traumatic or in some way difficult. You can see precisely the same aspirations in a painting; a mere glance is often sufficient to tell whether it was created with love, sweat or genius, or dashed out for a swift profit by an amateur.

When I reflect that the books on my shelves represent untold hours, years even, of concentrated toil by some of the greatest minds that have ever lived, I feel a curious warmth - probably like a millionaire when reflecting on his fortune. And these books are everyone's for the reading, whenever the mood takes us.

The Beginning

I can't remember much of what I read before I was 15. There were the usual children's classics: Enid Blyton's *'The Faraway Tree'* and Alan Milne's *'Winnie The Pooh'*, followed later by Henry Rider Haggard's *'King Solomon's Mines'*, Arthur Conan Doyle's *'The Lost World'* and Jules Verne's *'20,000 Leagues Under The Sea'*. Obviously, I read others, but since I can't remember them I guess they were few.

Until I was about 12, Mum and Dad used to read to my brother and me almost every night before we went to sleep. If it was a ploy to get us to bed it worked well. Unfortunately, I can only recall a few of the stories they read. I especially liked Dad reading those gripping *'Five Minute Tales'* which most people are familiar with. Like parables, they can be tremendously thought-provoking - a valuable experience for a growing mind: Aesop's *'The Wind and the Sun'*, *'The Axe in the Ceiling'*, *'The Man, His Son, and the Donkey'*, *'The Old Woman in the Vinegar Bottle'*, and many more.

I also remember him reading that masterpiece of satire: Swift's *'Gulliver's Travels'*. He seemed to prefer stories with a deeper meaning than a kid would normally be conscious of but whose messages would reveal themselves as the mind matured. Mum, on the other hand, went for adventure stories that were less introspective but were just as exciting: ie, Stevenson's *'Treasure Island'*, Marriat's *'Children of the New Forest'*...

Curiously, none of this encouraged me to read (I'll speculate on the reason for this in a moment). All I remember is Collodi's richly illustrated *'Pinocchio'* and Charles Kingsley's *'The Water Babies'*, and easy short stories like Andersen's *'Fairy Tales'*. Then nothing - until I discovered the mind-blowing worlds of science fiction.

That initial excursion into science fiction – alongside science non-fiction – was to last initially till I was 24. Then at 28, after four years of study (polytech) that allowed little time for reading more than a sprinkling of fiction, I finally had the opportunity to read normally again. But now I felt oddly disinclined to even glance at a fiction book. Apparently, I was out of practice and had lost the habit. I could only surmise that in those four years I'd reverted to the curious mental lethargy that had gripped me during secondary school... until (at maybe 16?) I was woken by Asimov's *'The End of Eternity'*.

This lethargy for reading continued for perhaps a year until I was almost 30 when my sister handed me that famous political treatise: Robert Tressell's *'The Ragged Trousered Philanthropists'*. But the 'lethargy' I experienced, happens to many people. Maybe it depends on the imagination, though less on how developed it is than on how it is accessed. That is, accessing the imagination is not the same when listening to a story as when reading it – as if there are two distinct routes, either of which can only be fully opened by frequent use. And the listening route is rather more active for most of us than the reading route – we listen all day, but read in snatches.

In addition, the parts of the brain that process sight are probably not the same as those that process sound, so perhaps it's not surprising that listening and reading are not interchangeable when it comes to imaginative wherewithal. The path to my imagination, as it applied to reading, needed to re-establish connection. Could this really be why I found it hard to return to reading after an extended break?

On top of this: we know, as I've said, how draining TV can be - because the imagination falls dormant we can feel kind-of uninspired, in need of mental refreshment. Eventually, if we go on watching TV, those links to the imagination seem to vanish altogether and the effort of reconnecting them increases – it can only be achieved by the most gripping text. Well, that's my theory.

The Writer

One of the key points I'm trying to make here with this book is that I think people should ask themselves what they are alive for and what they should be doing with their lives. These, of course, are the questions that most of the philosophers and writers I mention were addressing in their own special way.

Einstein said: *'The most beautiful thing we can experience is the mysterious. It is the true source of all art and science.'* And then he set out to destroy as much as he could of it - knowing, of course, that for every mystery solved several more would spring up to replace it - like the multi-headed mythological hydra: cut off one head and two more grow in its place. So instead of creating mystery where none really exists, wouldn't we do better to seek only clarity and truth as Camus, for instance, did?

In a letter written shortly before he died (prematurely from a chance infection), Kazantzakis (author of *'Zorba the Greek'*) wrote:

> *'What purpose? What do we care? Don't ask, fight on! Let us set ourselves a purpose... We must conquer the last, the greatest of temptations - that of hope... We sing even though we know that no ear exists to hear us; we toil though there is no employer to pay the wages when night falls. We are despairing, serene and free. This is true heroism...'*

Compare this with Sisyphus who famously, over and over, spends eternity pushing a rock to the top of a hill only to see it roll down again - and whose predicament, which can be seen to parallel our own, Camus examined in detail in his great philosophical work 'The Myth of Sisyphus'. Any mention of Zorba, incidentally, reminds me of his announcement: 'Life is like chamomile tea, but you've got to drink rum!' Is it possible to idle and 'drink rum'? Kerouac seemed to manage it, both literally and figuratively - neither, perhaps wisely (yes, wisely), in moderation.

But even at the advanced age of 74, I can still experience to an extent those delights Camus describes so lucidly (see section on Camus), ie: of days spent diving in the sea, listening to the kiss of the waves, communing with the 'melody of the world'.

Twenty years ago I wrote: I last swam in the sea on 11th October, less than a week ago. That was the day of the torchlight parade here at Hastings, and the burning of effigies – these days always politicians. And this week, immersed in the radiance of sun, wind and sea, walking the promenade, the wild beach beyond the town, the cliffs and woods... the same sensations - diminished by age, I know, but reinforced by memory. Dostoyevsky:

> "You are told a lot about your education, but some beautiful, sacred memory, preserved since childhood, is perhaps the best education of all. If a man carries many such memories into life with him, he is saved for the rest of his days. And even if only one good memory is left in our hearts, it may also be the instrument of our salvation one day."

(This resonates well with my theory of the importance of nostalgia). A childhood that gleans firm memories of the sights and scents of nature is invaluable, priceless: Where else this life affirming nostalgia? For me, though, my 'pseudo wanderer's' life is compromised by a ridiculous addiction to home comforts - (how much more free and happy I felt in the antipodes with nothing in the world but a small rucksack). But how superior is even this to the endless commuting and daily grind that so many of us choose - as I once did - or are forced to endure by circumstances we have unwittingly created or have had shoved down our throats.

A few days ago, in a little book of short stories, I found this – little gem taken from William Saroyan's *'The Barber's Uncle'*.

> *'It was a warm winter day and the world was sleeping. It was very still everywhere in the world. Nobody was rushing round in an automobile and the only thing you could hear was the warm and cool, happy and sad silence of reality. The world. Ah, it was good to be alive somewhere. It was splendid to have a small house in the world. Rooms and tables and chairs and beds. Pictures on the walls. It was strange and wonderful to be somewhere in the world. Alive, able to move through time and space, morning, noon, and night: to breathe and eat and laugh and talk and sleep and grow. To see and hear and touch. To walk through the places of the world under the sun. To be in the world. I was glad the world was there, so I could be there too. I was alone, so I was sad about everything, but I was glad too. I was so glad about everything that I was sad. I wanted to dream about it: the places I had never seen. The wonderful cities of the world: New York, London, Paris, Berlin, Vienna, Constantinople, Rome, Cairo. The streets, the houses, the people alive. The doors and windows everywhere. And the trains at night, and at night the ships at sea. The dark sad sea. And the bright moments of all the dead years, the cities buried under time, the places rotted and ended. Ah, in 1919 I dreamed a dream one day: I dreamed the living lived for ever. I dreamed the end of change and decay and death.'*

That last sentence has ambiguous implications unless one is aware that it reflects an innocent moment for an 11 year old kid. But here Saroyan begins to touch the core of what it means to be alive. It's not easy. Like Hesse, he comes within a whisker of mawkishness. This is a great skill. It looks so simple - assisted here by the occasional brush of juvenile semantics. It's like looking at a great painting where a few deft rough-looking brushstrokes reveal and tell all.

In an article on writing, Kurt Vonnegut said:

> *'The great masters wrote sentences which were almost childlike when their subjects were most profound: "To be or not to be?" asks Shakespeare's Hamlet... It may be that you too are capable of making necklaces for Cleopatra, so to speak. But your eloquence should be the servant of the ideas in your head... Our audience requires us to be sympathetic... ever willing to clarify - whereas we would rather soar high above the crowd, singing like nightingales.'*

There's nothing here of trying to hoodwink the reader. Quite the contrary. It is about expressing as closely and as accurately as possible, precisely the sensations the writer feels and strives above all to convey. With the inevitable limitations of the written word, writing as art usually requires some talent and much effort. Attempting to aspire to this end presents an awesome challenge to a novice like me - and is probably a pointless quest anyway (which is why I don't even try - when I have, I've always ended-up with mushy drivel). But as with all art, dedication to practice - and perhaps some innate ability too - can produce the most durable and rewarding results. For every Dostoyevsky, J.M.W. Turner or Mozart, there must be millions who, regardless of any audience, discover huge pleasure in creating for its own sake. Some achieve recognition, some - who, me? - achieve nothing. It matters not; creating is its own reward.

-
-
-
-
-

Writing

My experience trying to write fiction

Writing short stories is a strange experience. You have an idea, a scene is set, and off you go. You can, for instance, just launch into it as if enlightening someone to something you witnessed, and let things develop naturally as events take place, one thing leading to another. Sounds easy; and occasionally it is - in fact it usually is if one's imagination is working well. But without certain qualities your story can turn into a dull succession of trivia that would fail to grip even the most determined reader.

So, quite apart from the mystery of 'what happens next' you have to surreptitiously weave in a kind of enthusiasm, as though it really mattered to the person writing it. This means, for me at any rate, that one needs to be in the right frame of mind. Most days when I sit in front of the computer doodling at this and that, trying to start a story, nothing comes of it. Everything I write peters out after a page or two, or else becomes so much drivel. Occasionally something begins to turn into a plausible story, and then after several pages the imagination dries up - or the original idea suddenly begins to evolve into something ludicrous. But when a reasonable story does emerge and take shape and eventually conclude satisfactorily, then I regard it as a lucky strike. Even then, the chances are that when I go back and read it I find fault after fault. It could be problems with logic, boring sections with unnecessary or excessive description, or merely the rhythm of sentences. There could be too frequent use of banal words, which dull the effect; or too many adjectives, an excess of passive words... many things can be wrong. So I start correcting, cutting, augmenting, etc. And when I go back and read it a second time, it's lost all spontaneity - that sparkling quality which often comes from simply spilling out a story in one burst, so to speak.

On those extremely rare occasions - rare for me, that is - when a story seems to write itself, apparently straight from the imagination and out onto the screen so that virtually no correcting can improve it, then one gets a taste of that unique warmth which is the true reward of creating. But even that can be an illusion. The story has to appear equally good the next day, and again the next week. How often I've written a story and felt that sense of accomplishment, only to discover when I read it the next day that it's tosh! But if that doesn't happen, then it's ready to show around, so then it has to grip others too - even if that showing is just one person who has the patience to give your story the time of day. And if *they* like it: Eureka!

A few details I try to remember

If a story starts going in a different direction to that intended, then pause and make a decision: convey the intended story/message *OR* just tell a good story - usually you have to be lucky or probably well-experienced to get both at the same time.

The direction of a story when you let it develop naturally (without trying to steer it) is a 'right' brain phenomenon - it's where creative energy originates... whereas to steer it is a 'left' brain act – the conscious, and the intellect. So you have to decide: do I make a good story *OR* write of what I consciously prefer? Both, as I say, are probably only possible after years (maybe decades) of practice, including, ideally, the teenage years.

It's a great feeling that natural flow which emerges when you let a story carry you along as if you're mesmerised and are watching events as they unfold unexpectedly even to you as you write. I think that's the secret to writing creatively)!

Some of the most successful creative writers have, I reckon, experienced trauma or intense loneliness maybe, especially during childhood because their stories are often horrible – which, curiously, attracts most readers (I guess it's the exaggerated drama and shock that jolts people from routine humdrum lives?). My childhood, in contrast, was relatively pleasant/easy - except school (which I can't say was in any real sense traumatic) so writing of scary or abominable events like murder or war or monsters doesn't come naturally to me. Weird things are more my line - for some obscure reason - like sci-fi or the peculiar kinds of events as in my 'real' stories. So I don't try to write what's not in my head.

I say to myself

Set (and people) the scene, and just see what happens. If it goes on an unintended tangent every time, then try adjusting the initial scene, or maybe introduce a powerful character who steers things the way you want.

To write a good yarn, though, you have to practice being a good liar - unless your life is unusually 'interesting' and you can generate some gripping autobiographical tales (many writers' work consists of variations on autobiography... and waking dreams of what could be or have been). Pretend, too, you're telling just one person who knows you and would detect any artifice or attempt to tart-up the language or story. That way it should be more natural. Don't worry about errors or weird sentences till after you've written the story, because then you won't interrupt the flow and you can go back later to smooth out the faults and make a good first paragraph (easier once you know the whole story) - so the reader gets hooked and carried easily along. Sometimes writers work out a story by tracing back from a final key dramatic scene or clever twist, then inventing a first dramatic gripping event that leads to that preconceived conclusion.

* * * * *

Does literature, fiction at any rate, lose its copyright 50 (or 70) years after the death off the author? There's websites that have published some of the best literature available: ie, online-literature ...And if you go there you'll find, for instance, more than 200 Chekhov short stories. Some of these are amongst the most outstanding short stories ever written. '*The Bet*' and '*The Black Monk*' are superb and have both been on radio. '*The Steppe*' is really a novella, but is excellent in every way. My favourite of those I've read is '*On the Road*' (not to be confused with Kerouac's much longer masterpiece of that name) which when I first read it almost 20 years ago had been translated as '*On the Way*' (a more apt title, I thought, due to the ambiguous slant in the word '*Way*'). This for me is the perfect short story. As I start to read, before I know anything, I feel present in the room at the tavern, sitting in a corner watching, the wind howling outside and roaring down the chimney of the stove, snowflakes chasing wildly around the window - the whole atmosphere, everything. Then once the characters are presented to us in no more than a few key details (so telling yet so elusive to my own imagination when I attempt a story), we are dished up with a gripping life-history of the co-protagonist, which is set out with such perfection that only a true genius could do it.

However, if you then take a look at '*A Blunder*' (672 words) or '*A Chameleon*' (1393 words) or '*A Classical Student*' (1178 words) - to pick just the first three stories, you'll see that even the great master Chekhov did not always shine. We are lucky to have these 'inferior' pieces to give us the feeling that if that's the work of a genius writer, then there's hope - just a glimmer maybe - for us normal folk who aspire to amuse others with little stories.

But those 'attempts' by Chekhov are perhaps equivalent to the 'hurried' pencil sketches of Turner, for example, and actually contain elements that in my ignorance I'm unable to recognise? One key reputed quote from Chekhov that helped inspire me to attempt all these weird stories and essays and so on, is:

> '...only he is an emancipated thinker who is not afraid to write foolish things.'

I might add: *'Or is afraid to write badly.'* As I've said, sometimes the ability to write a worthy story eludes one like money eludes the habitual gambler. But at those wonderful exceptional moments when one's frame of mind is perchance in tune - and one can never know beforehand how it will be - a story will fall almost perfect from your fingers in a brief couple of hours, as if - clichés aside - by magic. Effortless, simple and delightful, like making a good cake. If only it worked every time, like the cake.

But I guess that's the unpredictable nature of creativity (however inferior): infuriatingly elusive but poised to spring out unexpectedly at any time. And the law of reversed effort applies as much here as it does to other activities in life that demand spontaneity: ie, sex, sneezing and yawning - to name three.

I don't pretend I can ever hope to create stories good enough to sell. Apart from technical reports I wrote nothing before I was forty-something, so what can I expect? It takes years of practice, like playing a violin well, not so much to learn technique as to mould the brain.

But there's always a chance for amateurs who after just a scrap of experience can, when they're on form, beguile a moderate audience. When I reflect on the fact that I first tried to write stories when I was older than Chekhov when he died (of TB in 1904 at the age of 44), I realise with resounding clarity that I'm starting some 30 or 40 years late. The 'wiring' in my brain is no more oriented to creative writing than to playing a violin - because I did neither in my teens or early 20s. There are two keys, though: First - as I've mentioned before - is Hemingway's 100% shit-detector; and second, the ability to cut. Also, the determination to give it a go. As for motivation -

that's another issue … and I have to say I'd never have attempted any of it without X's nudging – so if you don't like my stories, blame him!

.

.

.

.

.

Short Stories

After thanking X for emailing his praise of one of my short stories – ie *'Zen Among The Asteroids'*, he replied thus (among other things):

> *"Your stories are a bit like a naughty kid who pretends and plays along to the teacher that he is thick, but actually he is showing the teacher up for not seeing his skills!"*

Although I could well do with a few criticisms – from which I might learn something – this kind of comment does have a definite warming effect: to realise that at least one person notices and enjoys the merits (deliberate or otherwise) in one's effort... though maybe the word 'effort' is inappropriate here because the kind-of effort involved more resembles that of taking a dip in the sea on a hot day in August. Which doesn't make positive responses any less welcome – especially when I'm inclined perhaps to be excessively self-critical, dismissing much of what I write as trash (which all too often it probably is).

Besides which... due to concentrating on other issues, I've failed to respond to an important question X has put to me several times:

> *"Do you ever have the effect that a story you read from another author consumes you and is on your mind all the time?"*

The answer is YES, frequently, at least to a moderate extent. What's important to me, as much as being quickly gripped or finding some weighty meaning or other, is 'tone of voice', which can be the most compelling quality of a story, and of which there are many variations. Dostoyevsky's '*A Strange Man's Dream*', for instance, and his deeply introspective '*Notes From the Underground*', are both profound existential first-person narratives, though in quite different tones. Hesse's little tale of an aspiring artist '*The Wicker Chair*', his perceptive '*Iris*' and his autobiographical '*A Guest at the Spa*' and '*The Interrupted Class*' are all fables of a kind, but also contain Hesse's unique 'voice'. So too for his deeply reflective '*The Day at Karino*' and its poignant sequel '*The Music of Doom*' (see Appendix 10) - these subtly lure and disarm the reader with an inviting jocular 'tone', which quite apart from the poetic harmonies Hesse weaves into his prose - these two brilliant pieces are so outstanding to me that I decided to include them in this volume as an example of genius and (see section on Hesse). On the other hand several of Tennessee Williams' short stories spell out some stark realities with understated insight - '*The Malediction*' for example, or '*The Angel in the Alcove*', while Gogol's '*The Overcoat*' - of which Dostoyevsky is reputed to have said, "*We have all come from under* The Overcoat." blends humour with '*symbolic humanitarian messages*' (ie, Belinsky - leading critic of the time); or how about Lermontov's earthy '*Taman*' which begins:

> *Taman is the foulest hole among all the sea-coast towns of Russia. I practically starved to death there, then on top of that someone tried to drown me. I arrived there late one night by....*

These have very different 'tones of voice' yet all are gripping and linger in the mind, those specifically mentioned have remained with me for decades - as others mentioned below. And you can never beat actually READING (or hearing) a story. This is because, in contrast to watching a film, the kind-of almost unconscious self-created images that accompany reading and hearing seems, curiously enough, to remain more firmly in memory than anything you might view on a screen...

at least, it does for me. With Chekhov's evocative '*On The Way*' (sometimes translated as '*On The Road*') - in my view, among the best ever short stories.... even surpassing, I reckon, his intellectually masterful '*The Bet*' - Chekhov's 'tone of voice' seizes you instantly so you get the sensation of being suddenly in the scene, and drawn along as though you're watching everything from a dark cupboard through a spy-hole... rather like the protagonist in Barbusse's 'The Inferno' (or '*Hell*'). This is from the translator's preface:

> *Observation of humanity in its most private moments and secret activities has been a popular theme with writers and artists for thousands of years, but it has rarely been carried to such lengths as in Henri Barbusse's novel Hell.*
>
> *A young man staying in a French hotel finds a hole in the wall above his bed, through which he can see and hear the occupants of the next room. Before long he has become obsessed with the study of the hidden lives of his neighbours, and he spends long hours and days at his spy-hole, not as a voyeur but rather as a seer. He sees in their naked reality childbirth, first love, marriage, adultery, lesbianism, illness, religion and death; and he hears the voices of his fellow humans whispering, screaming, pleading, arguing, exulting and dying. Only when he has explored every circle of the hell of human life does he pack his bags and return to the everyday world of pretence.*

Then there's the weird allegorical '*Andersen's Fairy Tales*' - some of which are simplistic, while others are impressively artful and, like Chekhov, Hesse and Dostoyevsky in particular, but many others too, they have the power to affect your mind for weeks or even years afterwards. Some can permanently alter your whole outlook and direction in life. Hence, presumably, the old maxim that '*the pen is mightier than the sword*'.

Though what better to shake the brain awake than those two great yet absurdly brief parables from Kafka: '*Before The Law*' (taken from '*The Trial*') and '*An Imperial Message*' – I've included these in this volume (see section on Kafka) because although each covers hardly more than a page, even after several decades my brain still reverberates from them...

* * * * *

I could list perhaps more than a hundred excellent short story titles that have set me thinking for some while afterwards. The one's mentioned above came instantly to mind. There are several greats from Scott-Fitzgerald and Dorothy Parker. There's a brilliant one I recall: '*A Letter and a Paragraph*' from Henry Cuyler Bunner (1855 – 1896), and there's Thurber's '*The Secret Life of Walter Mitty*', Saroyan's '*The Daring Young Man on the Flying Trapeze*' and his best of all, I reckon: '*Seventy Thousand Assyrians*' - all these are gripping. Moravia's weird erotic tales present another angle, and of course Asimov with his astounding Robot stories... the list goes on and on: Giono, Bukowski, Borges, Pirandello, Brecht... the outstanding Raymond Carver – ie, '*Where I'm Calling From*'... and many by obscure authors like Russell Banks and William Hauptman, or those not especially renowned for their short fiction: Henry Miller and Richard Ford... etc., etc.

If one cares to search the Net then most of the best stories can probably be unearthed... if not now then after their author's death and when copyright ceases. GOOD HUNTING......

Finding a Book

A BIG advantage of having loads of books - I have ~3000 at a rough guess (ie 2023) - is to be able in a dull moment to browse around and pick one out... at random, maybe, or at a whim, from an attractive spine or title, or from suddenly noticing anew some long neglected subject or author. Then, searching around, there's always a chance of locating several related tomes... novels, biographies, critical analyses... revealing a further masterpiece or gem of inspiration to dig into... or just dig.

This can be done on the net, of course, and to much greater extent - the range these days is massive: sites like Guttenberg for example, or 'online-literature'... as mentioned above in *'Writing'*. Plus there's always wikipedia, and who-knows how many other excellent sites...

How I write stories, though, and how professional writers write them is a quandary for me. Quite probably I and they have nothing in common - I say this because despite telling a few people about these books of mine, I know only a couple of people who like my books, or say they do. And it was one of these 'X' who put me up to this mad writing stunt in the first place, which I've come to enjoy doing – whether I do it well or not is beside to point.

So much for 'self-education', I conclude, when I reflect on my random whimsical approach to reading over the decades. But who gives a rap? The truth is, altogether it's been pretty sensational, a great little 'arty' diversion from the rest of life... and maybe better than any kind of structured course...

because 'random' to me means free and spontaneous - or as spontaneous as it's possible to be under the numerous limitations one finds oneself landed with: of background, chance encounters - or failures to encounter - of knowns and unknowns... etc.

-
-
-
-
-

Provisional List

So now to the first list I made of what I've read over the years…. or *some* of it… because there were loads of arbitrary tomes and authors soaked-up in my brain that made less impact at the time of reading. The list is from some years back in response to a request from my friend X of what I'd recommend. I can't say what I don't recommend because being an idler means I'm also a giver-upper; if I start something and find after a couple of pages that it's a trudge, then unless there's some overriding reason to continue, I just give up - why bother if it's no pleasure? I've given-up on several books that I've tried again and discovered to be fine, even outstanding as with Nabokov's *'Lolita'*. For de Bernieres' *'Captain Corelli's Mandolin'* I was luckily advised that it actually began around page-50… for Fowles' *'The Magus'* it was page-20… otherwise I'd have missed those exquisite descriptions of Greece evoking images that make you feel really there, smelling the flora, the earth. It's well known that an author needs to get into the atmosphere of a story, which means very often the first few pages or so need to be re-written or cut. An experienced author will usually do this, but occasionally they don't.

Which partly explains why I prefer short stories: the time investment is small. I once tried Tolstoy's *'War & Peace'* - because it's spoken so highly of, and is extremely well written… but it dwells almost exclusively - up to page-238, at any rate - on the hassle and turmoil of war and the weird manoeuvrings between upper-class 19th Century Russians with all the ritual and rigmarole and other trivia… which to me was irrelevant pap about as removed as it's possible to be from what I enjoy reading about or wished to know. Who hasn't done this with TV: just letting the programmes glide through your brain because they're reasonably well made but are actually tripe, or at least of no interest to you - yet there you are caught-up, wasting several hours that could have been spent on things you positively enjoy or maybe would benefit from.

The list below of stuff I've read also indicates that YES, I read it so it must have been OK - *at the time I read it*! Which means I have a positive memory of it. What particular aspect of a work kept me reading is another issue: gripping style, great knowledge to be gained, weird events.... any one of numerous attributes can make a work compelling or worth reading. Some works, though, have been outstanding, and I'll explain later what's impressed me.

I could include some not in the list below, such as 'Greene's '*The Honorary Consul*', Webb's, '*The Graduate*', Levin's '*Rosemary's Baby*', Segal's '*Love Story*'... the last three purely for the intimate style, even if the content was not especially interesting - in the case of '*Love Story*' I even detested the characters.... yet was still gripped. That's what I call: skill in technique - the worst reader-response is indifference! Then again, Doctorow's '*Ragtime*' shone like a beacon above those aforementioned *merely finely-written* works.... as did James Vance Marshall's '*Walkabout*' or the astounding, unique, mind-blowing '*The Dice Man*' by Luke Rhinehart. And there are others... many others... including some impressive (auto)biographies like Stephen King's candid memoir '*On Writing*', Michael Crichton's '*Travels*', Ken Kesey's '*Demon Box*', Robert de Ropp's '*Warrior's Way*', Carl Jung's remarkable '*Memories, Dreams, Reflections*', or even Daniel Farson's various (eccentric) observations... all have/had their particular impact.... as with numerous other fine works now lost (yet still absorbed) in *a* lifetime of memory...

...because unless it's jogged, a memory may never be recalled. Just take a walk; notice the multitudinous unimportant details: a bit of discarded orange-peel, someone's name chalked on a wall, a broken red biro.... a micro-sample of all the trivia we normally ignore... then if someone asks: *'Did you notice a broken biro?'* you'd think and reply, *'Umm, I don't think so.'* But walk back the way you came, and there are the hundreds of insignificant little things you forgot you'd seen, and probably a few major items too, but on seeing them again recall them all perfectly.

Had I been one of those journal fiends who keep a record of everything, like what they read and when, then this would all be easy. But the only record I have is in my head, jogged awake when perusing the bookshelves here - which don't contain all the tomes I've read or dipped into: before the internet and Amazon, I was a frequent library borrower; a year or two ago I threw out a BIG wad of slips each containing the title and author of books I'd ordered, which in those days could take months to arrive from another library, and might have come from Kingston-on-Thames, York, Inverness or Eastbourne...

So the list below indicate just some of the authors and titles I've read, am familiar with and judge as great reads (tiles in brackets I've only part read). There are many other books I've devoured and enjoyed too but haven't listed here. Many are mentioned elsewhere in this book. And in the sections following I expand on some of the authors and titles. If life was longer I'd expand on them all and much more besides. Alas, unlike most of these amazing writers who spent - sacrificed in some instances - much of their short lives writing instead of, or as well as, living, I (luckily for me) lack both persistence and talent. At least, I have the insight to recognise and accept this, so may as well spend my time living, with just a small dose of writing - since writing is reward enough; it's matters not whether anyone will read what I write. And writing, as I say, frequently evokes surprising, even exhilarating thoughts and ideas that might otherwise never surface... as though one is tapping into some deep and mysterious crevice of the brain.

The asterisk * against titles in the list indicates what I'd rate especially highly. So, in alphabetical order, here's the most significant works - *to me at the time, and remembered* - that I indulged in over the decades... which by alphabetic coincidence starts with my first *REAL* encounter, without which maybe I wouldn't have bothered to pick-up many of what follows:

Isaac Asimov
The Rest of the Robots (short stories)*
I, Robot (short stories)
Asimov's Mysteries (short stories)
The Naked Sun
Foundation trilogy
Foundation's Edge *
The Robots of Dawn
Building Blocks of the Universe - non-fiction *
Plus many more novels, stories and non-fiction.

Roberto Bolaño
Last Evenings on Earth (short stories)
The Return (short stories)
The Insufferable Gaucho (stories + essays) *
The Secret of Evil (short stories)
Between Parentheses (essays) *

Heinrich Böll
The Train Was On Time
What's to Become of the Boy *
Irish Journal - non-fiction
(The Clown)

Paul Bowles
The Sheltering Sky *
Too Far From Home (short stories)
Their Heads are Green - non fiction *

Ray Bradbury
Zen in the Art of Writing *
Several short stories

Charles Bukowski
Tales of Ordinary Madness (short stories)*
Post Office
Factotum
Ham on Rye

Albert Camus
Lyrical & Critical Essays *
The Stranger
The Plague
Exile and the Kingdom (short stories)
Short stories
(The Rebel)

Truman Capote
Other Voices, Other Rooms *
Music For Chameleons (short stories)
The Dogs Bark - but the Carnival moves on...
Answered Prayers
Breakfast at Tiffany's (short story)
The Grass Harp (short story)

Raymond Carver
Many short stories *

Raymond Chandler
All the novels
Some short stories

Anton Chekhov
The Steppe *
The Black Monk
On The Way *
The Kiss
The Bet *
Many other short stories

Fyodor Dostoyevsky
Crime and Punishment *

Poor Folk *
Notes from The House of the Dead *
Notes from Underground *
The Idiot
The Insulted and the Injured
Netochka Nezvanova
The short stories, inc
A Strange Man's Dream *

F Scott Fitzgerald
The Great Gatsby *
The Last Tycoon *
The Crack-up (non fiction) *
Many short stories

Max Frisch
Homo Faber
(A Wilderness of Mirrors)
(I'm NOT Stiller)
(Sketchbook 1966-71)

Eduardo Galeano
(Voices of Time)
Upside Down *

Gabriel García Márquez
One Hundred Years of Solitude *
No One Writes to the Colonel
Love in the Time of Cholera
+ short stories

Nikolai Gogol
The Overcoat (short story)*
Dead Souls *
Diary of a Madman (short stories)
The Nose (short story)
The Carriage (short stories)
(Village Evenings Near Dikanka)

Maxim Gorky
Fragments from My Diary *
(My Universities)

Gurdjieff
Meetings with Remarkable Men *

Ernest Hemingway
A Farewell to Arms
A Moveable Feast - non-fiction *
The Old Man and the Sea
various short stories

Donald Henderson
Mr Bowling Buys a Newspaper
A voice Like Velvet

Eugen Herrigel
Zen in the Art of Archery (1953) *
The Method of Zen

Hermann Hesse
Knulp
Steppenwolf
The Glass Bead Game
Journey to the East *
Siddhartha
Narziss & Goldmund
Peter Camenzind *
Beneath the Wheel *
Demian *
Gertrude
Klingsor's Last Summer *
If The War Goes On (non-fiction)
A Guest at the Spa   .. ditto
Wandering *
+ many essays and short stories in various titles:
Strange News from Another Star

Pictor's Metamorphosis
Autobiographical Writings
Stories of Five Decades

Victor Hugo
Les Miserables

Eugene Ionesco
The Hermit
Fragments From a Journal *
Notes & Counter Notes

Franz Kafka
Amerika *
The Castle *
The Trial *
All the short stories, inc:
The Metamorphosis

Jack Kerouac
On the Road *
Big Sur
Desolation Angels *
The Dharma Bums
Satori in Paris

Laurie Lee
As I Walked Out One Midsummer Morning *
Cider With Rosie
A Moment of War

Mikhail Lermontov
A Hero of Our Time (short stories)

David Lindsay
A Voyage to Arcturus *
The Haunted Woman
Sphinx

Arthur Miller
The Crucible

Death of a Salesman
I Don't Need You Anymore (short stories)

Henry Miller
The Tropics *
The Colossus of Maroussi *
The Rosy Crucifixion
The Air-conditioned Nightmare
Many essays and a few stories...*

Alberto Moravia
The Woman of Rome *
The Conformist *
Two Women
A Ghost at Noon *
The Empty Canvas
Two Adolescents
Most of the short stories

Vladimir Nabokov
Lolita *

Pyotr Ouspensky
The Strange Life of Ivan Osokin *
Talks with the Devil *
(In Search of the Miraculous)
(A New Model of the Universe)

Harold Pinter
The Birthday Party
The Caretaker
(The Dumb Waiter)

Luigi Pirandello
Henry IV
Short stories
Essays

Robert Pirsig
Zen and the Art of Motorcycle Maintenance

Lila

Alexander Pushkin
The Queen of Spades (short stories)
The Station Master (short story)
The Snowstorm (short story)

Jean Rhys
The Wide Sargasso Sea
Good Morning, Midnight *
Short stories *

Carl Sagan
Cosmos
Contact (fiction) *
Billions & Billions *
The Demon Haunted World *
The Dragons of Eden

William Saroyan
Little Children (short stories)
The Daring Young Man on the Flying Trapeze
Seventy Thousand Assyrians *
The Human Comedy
I Used to Believe I had Forever...
Plus many other short stories and essays *

Jean-Paul Sartre
Words
Nausea
(Saint Genet)
No Exit
(Being and Nothingness)

Rod Serling (& associates)
Many short stories from 'The Twilight Zone' *

Aleksandr Solzhenitsyn
One Day in the Life of Ivan Denisovich *
Short stories

John Steinbeck
The Grapes of Wrath *
The Moon is Down *
Working Days *
East of Eden
Journal of a Novel *
Tortilla Flat
Cannery Row

Leo Tolstoy
The Death of Ivan Ilych *
 various short stories
(War & Peace - to page 238)

Robert Tressell
The Ragged Trousered Philanthropists *

 Ivan Turgenev
(Sketches From a Hunter's Album).

Voltaire
Candide & other stories

Kurt Vonnegut
Slaughterhouse 5
Several short stories

R H Ward
A Drug Taker's Notes *
A Gallery of Mirrors *

Alan Watts
The Wisdom of Insecurity *
In My Own Way (autobiog)
The Way of Zen
The Watercourse Way
Does it Matter?

H G Wells

The Time Machine *
The War of the Worlds

Nathanael West
Miss Lonelyhearts
The Day of the Locust *

Colin Wilson
The Outsider *
The Occult
The Craft of the Novel *
Mysteries *
A Criminal History of Mankind
Religion & the Rebel
Below the Iceberg
Frankenstein's Castle *
The Strength to Dream
Poetry & Mysticism
The Books in My Life
Adrift in Soho *
The World of Violence (fiction)
Man Without a Shadow (fiction)
Ritual in the Dark (fiction)
+ a few others

-
-
-
-
-

In Summary

Probably my assessments reveal more about me than the authors and books they're intended to illuminate. All is subjective - even when it seems otherwise. Yet I think most of what I describe tells enough about the subject to offer at least an introduction. Whether this inspires further investigation or merely forms a (hopefully) lucid, if unusual, account of one person's (my) reading experience, is less important, I think, than if it raises issues the contemplation of which have the power to enrich and improve our lives in some way - because isn't that precisely what most if not all the authors cited here were probably attempting to do?

We'd have to be a bit stupid, insular, or arrogant to brush the efforts of these remarkable people aside without a thought. And if we do that, then who loses? There's enough we miss out on anyway - through our failure to unearth stuff or through not being informed - without deliberately perpetuating such deficiencies by avoiding new ideas, new vistas for the mind.

When I reflect on what's been missing for me at crucial times in my life, as touched-on in the first item below regarding one key instance, I feel a bit sad. I've made-up for that since, just a little - as scrolling down this page shows - but there remains a huge list of books I've never even begun to look at: the so-called Classics, Homer, Shakespeare, most of the great philosophers... much fine contemporary work too which may not be so immediately gripping, though contains profound observations on life. It's a hell of a list and life's just too short... this is a problem...

Kafka's solution might seem a bit polarised:

> *'Altogether,' Kafka writes in 1904 to his friend Oskar Pollak, 'I think we ought to read only books that bite and sting us. If the book we are reading doesn't shake us awake like a blow on the skull, why bother reading it in the first place? So that it can make us happy, as you put it? Good God, we'd be just as happy if we had no books at all; books that make us happy we could, in a pinch, also write ourselves. What we need are books that hit us like a most painful misfortune, like the death of someone we loved more than we love ourselves, that make us feel as though we had been banished to the woods, far from any human presence, like a suicide. A book must be the axe for the frozen sea within us. That is what I believe.'*

From Alberto Manguel's *'A History of Reading'* 1996, p-93.

And up to the word *'painful...'* I can see his point - too many books are flabby with pap. In fact, I agree with all Kafka says here, except I would broaden it to include books that are emotive in ANY sense. Why restrict such vicarious experience as books provide to just pain? But already, as we know, this very bias is precisely the problem with literature. Nearly all of it these days is either 'Crime' fiction, which involves pain, or 'Horror', which evokes fear, shock or panic - aspects of pain; and even 'Romance' can stir certain people to painful tears... when the heroine dies, for instance.

So apart from the power, the thrust and punch... if it's ever possible to so load words on a page that the reader will feel them like a brick in the face... I think Kafka's wishes have been largely met. It is precisely this that the masses seem always to demand - to be thrilled, shocked, distracted somehow from the monotony of life they've chosen in favour of risk and adventure - ie, of safe enslavement (as corporate propaganda so subtly sews into young brains). For the few who perchance avoid or circumvent that insidious net of conformity that keeps for social order, this kind-of '*painful*' escape literature probably has few attractions.

As for me, I tend to go for jolts from being hit in the left-brain. I relish the jolt of discovery (or failure to discover): overcoming a technical problem against the odds (or failing to overcome it), the resolution of some weird philosophical impasse (or the failure to resolve it)... and then, so informed, embarking on new quests, and in new directions. But literature that demolishes firmly held beliefs or opinions, is to me the most delightful and valuable of all. That's what I seek and treasure most - to be challenged, to be forced to think, to revise and replace old mistaken or primitive ideas. For some people that would mean intense pain, I know. But literature is about enlightenment.... about being woken-up... having your brain purged of garbage... being psychologically refreshed... sensing the joy of self-evident reasoning... it means homing-in on TRUTH, which can only lead to a closer affinity with the world, reality and with oneself.

True, there's no shortage of dross out there, but there's also an inexhaustible wealth of all kinds of brilliant experience to be gained from books, and below is a little sample of what I've stumbled on over the decades - stuff, quite often, to really make you THINK:

* * * * *

Needless to say, digging into books has been a consistently uplifting pastime. I've been doing it for decades. I guess the seeds were sewn when I was a small kid from the books I've mentioned that my parents read to my brother and me at bedtime. But it wasn't until in my early teens I stumbled on Asimov and especially his robot stories when my passion for books really began. I wondered too about the amazing guy who wrote those remarkable tales.

Years later, after discovering '*A Strange Man's Dream*' and '*Poor Folk*' - among other great stories from Dostoyevsky - I learned of the bizarre events following his arrest for 'subversion', when facing a firing squad he was reprieved at the last minute and sent to Siberia for 7- years - which he later described in gripping detail in 'Notes from The House of the Dead'.

Subsequently, I unearthed much more from a range of sources about these and other characters - mostly writers, though also artists, whose work (or more likely some aspect of their life or lifestyle) caught my interest. The more eccentric or controversial, the more attracted I was.

One recent find, Anthony Burgess, I remember from way back in the 70s. Always drawn in by what he had to say on any issue - in the rare TV appearance, radio discussion or interview - I'm mystified now at why I never dipped into his work... maybe I did (in a bookshop or library) and have forgotten. His fiction isn't quite the kind I'd have chosen in those days. Back then my fictional interests resided solely in sci-fi... until I discovered Dostoyevsky... then Hesse... Kafka... Camus... Kerouac... etc; but even regarding those, it seems to me now, the subjects of Burgess's fiction would have struck me as... not abstruse exactly... but what I suppose I'd call 'compelling trivia', like popular TV, which after a few minutes (or even hours if you're not careful) you wake-up from and wonder why the hell you're reading or watching such pap - though the judgment 'pap', at least in this instance, would be entirely subjective and, as I say, apt to change over the years. As for the non-fiction, however... that's definitely more cerebral and like hearing him speak; so you get a sense of the familiar eloquence, culture, edification... uplift even.

So I regret failing to examine Burgess's non-fiction in the 1980s when I was absorbing the work of those other great authors. I make up a little for that omission now. One impressive publication is 'Ninety-Nine Novels - the best in English since 1939' (1984) with its 99 perceptive, concise analyses in just one page.

Occasionally, these days - not too often - I check the local £-shop for remaindered books, which unlike many items, retain the original £1 price-tag. A month or so ago I found there

Jonathan Raban's 600-page '*Driving Home*' (2010): essays and reviews first published between 1993 and 2009. I recalled how - back in the 80s when I worked near Shepherds Bush and could afford new books (and before I went travelling around the US) I'd picked-up his '*Old Glory*' in the local bookshop, dipped-in (as usual), found it gripping on each dip so bought it. Raban is a skilled travel writer and that book describes his trip down the Mississippi on a small boat. The guy serving in the bookshop told me, as I paid him... together with payment for another equally thick volume... that he wouldn't recommend either of them; adding, while waving his hand at a big display, "what about Carl Sagan's '*Contact*'?" ('*Contact*' is an impressive sci-fi that I read a year or so later).

Stubbornly, I declined his advice at the time - and was glad I did, for the other book was Steinbeck's '*East of Eden*', which I too wouldn't recommend, but still it's a great book and of all his work was Steinbeck's own favourite. His '*Grapes of Wrath*', on the other hand, is a masterpiece, while '*The Wayward Bus*' and '*The Moon is Down*' are fine,... and stand out as what I'd recommend from several others of his I read back in the '80s.

Among the reviews in '*Driving Home*', though, was a reference that led me to another tome on my non-fiction shelf: Martin Amis's 500-page '*The War Against Cliché* ' - also reviews, but which unlike Raban's book, has an index. And then I spotted a section where Amis examines several of Burgess's books.

Youtube, I should add, has many clips of Burgess from as far back as the early 60s, soon after '*A Clockwork Orange*' was published. Not all are complimentary; he was a controversial figure, which as I say makes him all the more interesting.

What struck me especially - perhaps partly because of where I live - was that during this key early-60s period Burgess lived just up the road from here in Etchingham; what's more, his seminal novel was inspired from the summer of 1960 when he and his wife Lynne took a day trip to Hastings. It happened to be the day when Hastings was famously invaded by vast numbers of 'mods' with their highly-polished, multiple-mirrored motor-scooters, and similarly vast numbers of motor-biking 'rockers' in studded leather jackets. The Burgesses witnessed some violent clashes that day - and as ever, like with just about every event in his life, Burgess began to cook-up a new novel. Realising that contemporary slang would be too short lived for a novel where slang was essential if the dialogue was to 'sound' authentic, and failing to work-out some alternative, he briefly shelved it.

A year or so later, however, during a short holiday by boat to St Petersburg (then Leningrad), he was struck by the sound of certain Russian words, and decided these, with modification, could form the basis of the 'slang' required for 'A Clockwork Orange'.

Somehow - I guess I'll find out how as I look deeper into the details - the novel fell into Stanley Kubrick's hands and the rest is history, as they say.... But Kubrick's film only used the first section of Burgess's book... the violence and youthful excesses. The rest of the novel shows the protagonist as he mellows and comes-good. So although the film made Burgess rich and famous he hated it - it was incomplete, and showed its author as if glorifying violence. Several years later Burgess wrote a sequel 'The Clockwork Testament' as if, it seems to me, a rebuke to Kubrick, a kind-of 'letter' in the form of a novel.

In his 'You've Had Your Time - being the second part of the confessions of...' (1990 - three years before he died), Burgess describes events around a conference he attended in New York in early 1966 where:

> '...a delightful dynamic girl, fizzing with the champagne of the February Manhattan air, who took a fancy to the author of 'A Clockwork Orange', the only work of mine that had made any impression on the fractional percentage of Americans who read books. She, like many others, and not only in the United States, had expected its author to be acneous, brutal, coarse, in strange garb, burbling nadsat [the unique slang] or slavering over

Ludwig van, swinging a bicycle chain. She was delighted to find a soft-spoken man growing grey and old.'

So I continue dipping into Burgess's work - there's far too much to do more than dip here and there... while reading leisurely his excellent *'You've Had Your Time'*... maybe I'll sometime get around to Part-1 of his autobiography: *'Little Wilson - Big God'*, (1987) which Gore Vidal advised him should have been *'Big Wilson - Little God '*.

It's a great hobby though, researching eccentric or controversial writers (and other characters)... until I get bored or have read or learned enough to feel that I understand something of how their minds worked, their motivations, the significance of their achievements, etc. Burgess was, though, impossibly (for me) prolific. He covered an enormous range, gaining a reputation that was perhaps unique: always ready to write anything on any issue for anyone who cared to fork-out, and invariably producing good gripping copy that was, crucially, on time - a publisher's dream.

See Appendix 1: Burgess - Paris Review Interview 1973

The Paris Review has been publishing interviews like this with prominent writers since around 1957. These are available in a series of books, each containing about 15 in depth interviews that focus chiefly on the writers' process and experience of writing. Most are more 'in-depth' than the example I've placed in Appendix 1: *'Writers at Work – the Paris Review Interviews'*.

I own about five of these that came from Clive Linklater's little second-hand bookshop 'Bookman's Halt' that was in Bohemia Rd Hastings until Clive retired several years ago. He wrote a couple of splendid books himself, about book selling and a few other aspects of everyday life, all light-hearted and in a splendid friendly tone.

.
.
.
.
.
..

Sci-Fi

So first came Sci-Fi. I was 16. I'd escaped from dreaded
compulsory 'education' a couple of years earlier - first as a
truant (the halcyon days), then as a factory-dogsbody (sheer
horror)... so now I needed a new kind of escape. I'd owned a
couple of 'Space' books several years before then - even they
were frowned on at school - but crucially they'd got me
thinking about the future, space rockets, robots, etc. Then I
found Asimov. What a revelation! It was like stumbling into a
new universe...

At last literature that was readable, palatable, instead of the
dreary establishment mush we all got dished up with in those
days of tedium and intellectual deprivation - from teachers,
radio, TV, even the library - here was a whole new realm of
existence, a whole new angle on life.

It's hard to believe in 2012, but 1950s (and early 60s) TV was
solid with turgid highbrow, conventional humbug and
drudge... or else tripe for numbskulls, (or, to be fair,
infants)...ie, *'Toy-Town'*, *'Muffin the Mule'* etc. This flat, lifeless
monochrome two-channel window on predictable pap was
about as gripping as a wet banana skin. Since no-one in the
adult world around me was going to reveal such 'subversive'
gold as Asimov provided - either it was alien to them or they
regarded it as harmful nonsense, like jazz or rock... *would
anyone believe, these days, that such weird views could ever
be held by anyone?*... since that could never be a source, to
unearth this amazing new literature from Asimov off my own
bat was a monumental breakthrough: you think you're the

only person on the planet who's disillusioned with everything around you: the drab, boring, pointless, absurd, irrelevant... the ordering and conforming and discipline (spurious and irrational, frequently involving violent assault), solid with traditional dogma and all in the guise of 'education' (*how could ANYONE believe such 'Upside Down' propaganda?*) - then suddenly you discover a chink of light, dazzling at first, but coming into focus... a kindred soul out there with imagination, with a mind (though far superior) like yours! And this guy wasn't just some amateur hack feebly attempting to create improbable futures; his work was reasoned, finely crafted and calculated, philosophical and technical, was wide-ranging and inspiring. It examined issues which (to me) had never been tackled before. This 'new' literature involved intellectual digging and enquiry by its readers; it had depth and relevance: we were, after all, moving towards the mysterious futures it portrayed. Above all, it was fresh like nothing else.

That writers like Asimov - and musicians like Bill Haley and Elvis Presley - were dismissed and rejected by traditionalists, the establishment: teachers and so called 'intellectuals' (who in fact were anything but: these days the word 'dimwits' would be more appropriate), just boosted tenfold their attraction. Anyone with more than half-a-brain was in no doubt that these innovators were geniuses, while the staid old pricks who condemned them, and who were in charge, belonged (at best) in the nut-house.

I'll never be free of the venom I have for those years - the '50s especially - when, consigned to a straightjacket of enforced ignorance, and at such a crucial time of maximum brain potential, being prevented from developing.... and then to hit on Asimov around '65... age 16: too late then, the brain is pretty-well formed by 16. It was like someone bursting with energy, for years itching to leap and run, but all the time being chained to an immovable rock. *How cruel is that?*

But the key issue this page is supposed to be about.... is those green-flagged Sci-Fi tomes, which I discuss on a dedicated page: ASIMOV... So I won't continue on Sci Fi here - except to note that around the time I discovered Asimov, someone working in the TV industry must have discovered something similar (or maybe for them it was several years earlier). Suddenly, from the USA, our screens were ablaze with '*Lost in Space*' and Serling's '*The Twilight Zone*'. Then, presumably nudged by these major successes, the Beeb launched its own Sci -Fi productions with '*Out of the Unknown*' and '*The Outer Limits*'....

At long last the world was waking-up. The staid old pricks were dying off and a new breed of literature, drama, music... etc., was elbowing into the limelight, for instance '*The Beatles*' in '63... and soon, people couldn't get enough... a new era of enlightenment was being inaugurated... Henry Miller's marvellous books were published... homosexuality ceased to be illegal – I wonder, can anyone imagine anything more ridiculous or intrusive than outlawing same-gender relationships? What kind of irrational retards were they who made the laws in those dark, backward days of ignorance and prejudice?.... pocket radios were less than a fiver.... TV converted to colour... it was all happening, and I was in it.... *Yowwweee!*

The late 60s was certainly exhilarating. And glancing back in 2012 the optimism wasn't entirely misplaced... yet somehow, although technology advances, taboos fall away and certain absurd restrictions are lifted - less by legislation, than by progressive and intelligent social acceptance - cruelly managed (unregulated) capitalism, which is merely another term for 'legalised corruption' (and who, I wonder, makes the laws?), continues to be an overriding curse, and even increases in vigour.

We live in a jungle; dinosaurs rule. No fiction here - these are facts: solid detestable facts. And the dinosaurs have never been more ravenous and driven. Fathoming where this might lead presents a rich arena for the Sci Fi genre as well as documentary speculation: technological advance alongside social decadence is a contrast that's spurred (at least parts of) several great stories/films: Spielberg's 'AI' for one.

Sci-Fi & Science

So I only seriously began to read when I was 16 - more than a year after leaving school. When I was 14 (my last full year at school - I played truant for most of the final year), a supercilious teacher proclaimed that science-fiction was trash and that sensible people read Shakespeare and Dickens. Considering the 'education' I'd been landed with, it's not surprising that these authors bored me out of my head; it was a struggle to get past a first page. So, naturally, sci-fi gained top place in my 'lazy' mind. In any case, who wants to be 'sensible'? Better to be crazy and have a good time than be 'sensible' and bored to death, I thought.

I imply that I came to science-fiction by choice. The truth is that I came upon it by accident. One day in Boots in Cambridge, passing a small display of books, my eye was caught by Isaac Asimov's *'The End of Eternity'* - the author's name seemed almost as attractive as the title. I was so intrigued that I bought it on the spot. What kid could ignore a title like that - or name? Later, I saw an Asimov book with the word 'Robot' in the title. So *'The End of Eternity'* was promptly followed by *'The Rest of the Robots'* and *'I, Robot'*.

Soon I was hooked on Asimov, and went on to devour his famous *'Foundation'* trilogy and many more until over the next ten years I'd covered 30 or so of his books. Then I'd eagerly await new work, which he obligingly churned out for a further 27 years until his death in '92.

Much earlier, I developed an interest in what turned out to be 'electronics'. Since the age of about four I'd been intrigued by radio and was keen to solve the great mystery of how it worked. They didn't teach electronics at school so my continuing interest was assured - nor, luckily, did they teach physics (that is, real physics like relativity and quantum mechanics), because soon after discovering Asimov I bought, on another strange impulse, Milton Rothman's little paperback *The Laws of Physics*', and instantly there opened a whole new universe. Oddly enough, I've never been the impulsive type, so these uncharacteristic purchases were truly auspicious.

A few months later - it was the summer of 65 - whilst waiting for a train to go on holiday with a friend and his family who lived opposite (the 'intercom' remember?), I decided to scan the station bookstall. Expecting to find nothing of interest I suddenly noticed a magazine with a futuristic train on the cover. I took it down and when I saw the title my brain seemed to glow. It was just as though a light had been switched on in my head. I had discovered '*Science Journal*' - and from that day I collected monthly every issue until it ceased printing (for economic reasons) in the early '70s. In fact, I still have every copy stored in a box under the stairs. After that I turned to '*Scientific American*', which was similar in style and presentation but unlike the Journal was often a bit over my head.

All this science-fact served as a perfect complement to Asimov's fiction. Unknown to me at the time Asimov was in fact a scientist with a PhD in biology and had written considerably more fact than fiction. Perhaps that was why his fiction, however farfetched, seemed so realistic; I regarded it as a fair prediction of what might one day come true - which left me feeling curiously optimistic.

Occasionally '*Science Journal*' would examine, for instance, the future in space or robots - and this was serious stuff - but for me fact would merge with fiction to create almost limitless scope for the imagination. In addition, the great electronic revolution was beginning: micro-miniaturisation was already underway, and integrated circuits loomed on the horizon. These developments were accompanied by an avalanche of related innovations that seemed to occur by the day.

From '67 to '73 I worked in Cambridge for a scientific instrument company. I spent my last four years there as a technician in a laboratory where scientists worked at the forefront of technology; and at college I met other technicians and engineers who were employed in all kinds of technical industries that were also pushing at the frontiers of science.

In those days, contentment didn't seem to depend on how wealthy you were. Money was scarcely considered or mentioned in the circles I moved in. Even so, I and my peers all hovered close to the breadline; and if anyone owned a car (as I did) it was invariably an old wreck (the Ford, remember?). Alongside this was a growing libertarianism and tolerance in almost every aspect of life: clothes, music, relationships, lifestyle, etc. An altogether liberating experience - as the 60s is famous for.

So to be directly involved with advancing new science and technology, and all taking place amidst a vibrant new social scene, provoked a keen sense of engagement - perhaps akin to Sartre's political engagement of the 40s - and a feeling that the future could only get better and brighter.

I've often since wondered whether this constant 'high' of the late '60s/early '70s, which seemed to be experienced by virtually all those I associated with, was something generally experienced by youth, or - as I'm inclined to believe - was peculiar to that period.

By now I was 19 and studying electronics at college. In addition to various social activities (ie, going down the pub), I often went along to evening lectures at one or other of the universities; these concerned new discoveries and inventions (ie: lasers, holography, fluid logic etc) - so reading science-fiction was already beginning to get displaced, if not by related events then from lack of time.

Isaac Asimov
(1920 – 1992)

During the 80s, however, I read several new Asimov sci-fi books which were strangely different from his earlier work - they seemed aimed at a younger readership and contained hints of 'new-age' philosophy which shifted them about as close as they could get to fantasy without actually becoming it; they lacked his former economy and the gripping raw ultra-science and realism of earlier times. In a way, he'd 'gone soft'. Curiously, though, so had I, and I rather enjoyed this new angle on his work, even if it did lack those earlier qualities of sharp logic and invention.

I have occasionally read science-fiction by other authors, though usually it failed to seize my interest like Asimov (perhaps I have a particular affinity for his style and ideas?). The most recent alternative that I found impressive was Carl Sagan's 'Contact', but because Asimov had such an influence during a fairly crucial period in my life, I'll try to explain what it was about his early work that struck me with such force.

I'm amused now to think of that time when, amidst the bustle of lunchtime crowds, I lifted *'The End of Eternity'* from its rack expecting to learn what lay at the end of time itself. In a flicker of satiric humour I remember wondering if such an important discovery had been announced on the news. I forget why I went into the shop, but clutching this little paperback I hurried to the checkout and a few minutes later in a nearby park (Parker's Piece?) I sat on a bench and read:

Andrew Harlan stepped into the kettle. Its sides were perfectly round and it fitted snugly inside a vertical shaft composed of widely spaced rods that shimmered into an unseeable haze six feet above Harlan's head. Harlan set the controls and moved the smoothly working starting lever.

The kettle did not move.

Harlan did not expect it to. He expected no movement; neither up nor down, left nor right, forth nor back. Yet the spaces between the rods had melted into a grey blankness which was solid to the touch, though nonetheless immaterial for all that. And there was the little stir in his stomach, the faint touch of dizziness, that told him that all the kettle contained, including himself, was rushing upwhen through Eternity.

He had boarded the kettle in the 575th Century, the base of operations assigned him two years earlier. At the time the 575th had been the furthest upwhen he had ever travelled. Now he was moving upwhen to the 2456th Century.

Immediately realising I had been deceived by the title, I could still hardly fail to be gripped by this astonishing opening.

Asimov wrote his first story in 1937 at the age of 17 because he thought he could do better than the stories he read in pulp magazines like '*Amazing Stories*' and '*Astounding*'. That first story was called 'Cosmic Corkscrew' and centred on a time traveller. It wasn't until 1939 and nine rejected stories later that he had his story '*Ad Astra*' - 6,900 words about a trip to the moon - accepted as his first for publication. He gained his war-delayed PhD in 1948; eleven years and many stories later '*The End of Eternity*' appeared in the bookshops.

There was one enthralling incident in that book which I mulled over for several years. Harlan was a technician in 'Eternity' - the name Asimov gave to a parallel existence whose inhabitants had engineered a method of travelling backwards and forwards in time. In this way they could enter and exit our world at whatever date they chose. On one occasion Harlan leaves something behind in our world by mistake and to prevent someone else from finding it and possibly upsetting the course of history he has to return to the precise moment he was previously in that location to retrieve it - or not quite precisely, because he hadn't met himself before. (Or had he?) So how could he meet himself when he returned - without violating causality and placing the very existence of 'Eternity' at risk?

In fact when he did return he froze in fear when someone opened the door to the room he was in - the implications, of course, were colossal; but before that someone entered, to Harlan's relief, they retreated. After that he quickly recovered the item and returned to 'Eternity'. It was only then, reflecting, that he realised it had been himself who had opened the door when he had first been there, but had sensed that someone else was in the room so had swiftly retreated and closed it again - meeting people was a particular hazard... though there was one special person...

The situation, though, conjures a range of possibilities and ample opportunity for paradox. The obvious question is: What if he had met himself? I remember hoping, at the time, that this would happen, and wondering how Asimov would resolve it. If anyone could handle such an event then Asimov could. So why didn't he?

Over the years I've read several biographies of sci-fi writers, and one characteristic that's emerged is that when they've come across something such as what I've just described, they didn't simply shrug disappointedly, as I did, they would sit down and work it out for themselves and create their own solution - if necessary writing a whole novel. Was Asimov failing to address or confront the problem because it was too difficult, or did he include the incident merely as an aside to jolt the reader awake and maybe into chewing over the implications - as I did?

He was certainly one smart guy. Michael White, in his biography of Asimov, describes the episode when Asimov's IQ was discovered. In November 1945 he was subscripted in the army which he hated and:

> *A few days after arriving at Fort Meade, the recruits had to undergo a series of psychiatric tests. One of these was an army intelligence test, called the AGCT. Asimov stunned everyone in the barracks by getting the highest score ever recorded by the psychiatrists assigned to the Fort - a rating of 160... The average was a little over 100.*

Much later Asimov became a friend of Carl Sagan. They had much in common, sharing a wholly rational outlook on life, a love of science, space and all it entails, a keen social conscience verging on pacifism (and liberal socialism), and an unquenchable but realistic optimism for the future of humankind. They were men of compassion (what else with an IQ of 160?).

When I opened '*I Robot*' and read the page facing the Introduction I felt that I had discovered the ultimate:

> *The Three Laws of Robotics*

> *1 - A robot may not injure a human being, or, through inaction allow a human being to come to harm.*

> *2 - A robot must obey the orders given it by human beings except where such orders would conflict with the First Law.*

> *3 - A robot must protect its own existence as long as such protection does not conflict with the First or Second Law.*

> *Handbook of Robotics,*

> *56th Edition, 2058 A.D.*

Here was a fiction writer who took real science and logic seriously. It was only a matter of time, I reasoned, before 'U.S. Robots' (as Asimov envisioned it) would become a reality. Even the Introduction was a convincing spoof; like a comedian who can never revert to being serious, Asimov was true to form. Many of the stories in that book scrutinise and fault these seemingly infallible Laws. The robopsychologist, Susan Calvin, became perhaps Asimov's most famous character after Hari Seldon of the early 'Foundation' books. It was she who was called upon to solve the curious mysteries of eccentric robot behaviour caused by ambiguities in the Laws.

The First Law alone generates a possible multitude of odd responses. My first thought was that perhaps this Law should apply equally to human beings. But precisely what, for instance, constitutes harm? And to what lengths should a robot go to adhere to this Law? The scope for dichotomies and conflicts in logic were enormous, and Asimov exploited them thoroughly.

Next came that classic trilogy: '*Foundation*', '*Foundation and Empire*' and '*Second Foundation*'. The story concerns a period in future-history when humankind is in the process of populating the galaxy, finding and settling worlds, establishing administrations and working towards a Galactic Empire. Each of the five parts in the first book, as well as several chapters at the beginning, start with an extract from the 116th Edition of Encyclopedia Galactica which provides a synoptic introduction to key characters and events.

The story begins with mathematician, Gaal Dornick, who has just arrived on Trantor to join 50 other mathematicians working under Hari Seldon, the first and most brilliant psychohistorian.

Psychohistory may well one day become a real science - or so I'd like to believe. By observing an individual over a period of time one might stand a chance of predicting their behaviour in particular circumstances. That's about the most one could say, because there's a strong possibility they may do something out of character. Such is the nature of the individual human psyche. Apply this to a crowd, though, and the accuracy of prediction increases. For a nation it is more accurate still; a whole world, and your probability becomes almost a certainty. But apply it to a galaxy and you can hardly fail - assuming your starting information and calculations are not at fault; ie, from the beginning of chapter 4:

> PSYCHOHISTORY - ... Gaal Dornick, using non-mathematical concepts, has defined psychohistory to be that branch of mathematics which deals with the reactions of human conglomerates to fixed social and economic stimuli...

> ...Implicit in all these definitions is the assumption that the human conglomerate being dealt with is sufficiently large for valid statistical treatment. The necessary size of such a conglomerate may be determined by Seldon's First Theorem which... A further necessary assumption is that the human conglomerate be itself unaware of psychohistoric analysis in order that its reactions be truly random...

> The basis of all valid psychohistory lies in the development of the Seldon Functions which exhibit properties congruent to those of such social and economic forces as...

> ENCYCLOPEDIA GALACTICA

Hari Seldon predicted 30,000 years of galactic barbarism, and like any conscientious citizen he set out to see what could be done to eliminate it. All he could do was shorten it to 1,000, which was quite an achievement - but it would only work if he could somehow guide the Foundation at each point of crisis he predicted it would face. To achieve this, Seldon made his calculations and recorded himself giving the appropriate advice as he had calculated. He would use his reputation for genius to forestall political attempts to defeat him by not depending upon personal successors. (He also set up in the secret location of a key planet 'Terminus' the foundation for a new order to replace the old Empire.) After his death, when a so-called 'Seldon Crisis' arose, his recording could be consulted for the most appropriate action. Two problems emerged from this: First, how to recognise a 'Seldon Crisis', and second, whether to adopt his solution when it seemed outrageously misguided - for how, the politicians asked, could he have predicted this unique event?

At the same time Seldon set up the Foundation to create the 'Encyclopedia Galactica' which had to be complete before the onset of decline - calculated to begin five hundred years hence. Copies would be distributed to all parts of the galaxy so that once stability returned the knowledge gained over the previous twelve millennia would not need to be re-discovered, and civilisation could re-emerge and continue from where it left off - though now much fortified like a phoenix risen from the ashes. A whole planet and nearly 100,000 people was commissioned for the project - the creation of the Encyclopedia.

So the 'Foundation' books immediately introduced several remarkable new concepts that I racked my brains over for quite some time. Quite apart from the fabulous backdrop of supercomputers, leaps through hyper-space, planets and galaxies and so on, there were these constant confrontations with logic and probability and how it applied to human populations. It was science, psychology and sociology in a single package, working together for the benefit of humankind.

A further concept that emerged (I'm sure among many others I can't now remember) was of a planet secretly controlled by it's larger neighbour. The method of control, via priests and religion, was an idea that had once occurred to me as actually happening. What can be more rewarding than to read something like that in a book? It is an idea, though, which symbolises reality: The Pope; the Bible... and all the other powerful indoctrinations that take place - and have similar effects of control on its victims. Could these be merely the ambassadors of something much larger or more malevolent?

'Foundation's Edge' - a sequel to the trilogy - contained no special ideas that could compare with its forerunners, but it was one of Asimov's best reads, and it links the Foundation books with his Robot saga. This began with the Elijah Bailey detective novels. Together with his intriguing robot assistant R Daneel, Bailey shuttles back and forth around the galaxy solving crime mysteries - which to me were strictly a pretext for all the special background detail.

The first of these novels was 'The Naked Sun' (1958) which is the story of a planet where the population is maintained so that every individual lives in luxury on a vast estate, with a throng of robots at their command. The fact that Bailey and his fascinating companion were called from Earth to investigate a murder seemed to me beside the point: the story for me resided in the backdrop and how logically Daneel responded to events.

In the 477-page 'The Robots of Dawn' (1983) - what a title! - a much updated Daneel is fully equipped to make love to a sensuous woman named Gladia. But there's nothing sentimental or tacky here. Though more simply written - as became Asimov's work as he aged - it does not deviate from his consistently professional approach. In this novel another even more sophisticated robot, Giskard, is introduced, who, in the final 505-page robot novel 'Robots and Empire' (1985) - whose back cover has the caption: Can two conscience-stricken robots save the galaxy? - Giskard becomes mortal and on the last page dies hand in hand with Daneel:

> Daneel kneeled at the side of the seated Giskard and took the unresponsive metal hand in his own. He said, in an agonised whisper, 'Recover, Friend Giskard. Recover. What you did was right by Zeroth Law. You have preserved as much life as possible. You have done well by humanity. Why suffer so, when what you have done saves all?'

Giskard said, in a voice so distorted, the words could barely be made out, 'Because I am not certain. What if - the other view - is right - after all - and the Spacers will - triumph and then themselves decay so that - the Galaxy - will be - empty. - Good-bye, Friend - Dan -'

And Giskard was silent, never to speak or move again.

Daneel rose.

He was alone - and with a Galaxy to care for.

Even here Asimov tussles with the ambiguities of his Three Laws. But inspired by this extract let me digress briefly:

One of the greatest enigmas to confront science is: What is it that gives rise to consciousness? From where, exactly, does it originate? For me, this is the kind of question these stories of humanoid robots evoked. Would it ever be possible for a machine containing no living material to experience consciousness - or, for that matter, experience anything?

There seemed no doubt that robots, even ones far in advance of those portrayed by Asimov, would one day exist. Nor did I doubt their potential for apparent consciousness - ie, so it would be impossible to show in any practical situation that they didn't actually possess it.

Also, using themselves as a model, robots would some day spontaneously design and build even more advanced offspring - leaving humans far behind, and evolving at a rate that would astonish the most fanciful romantic. No longer would a mere human be capable of intervening (except, presumably, to halt or adjust the direction of progress); the technicalities would be beyond the most brilliant technician.

The conclusion that we, humankind, who has been around for maybe 10 million years, will one day be overtaken by our own creation as masters of at least this sector of the Milky Way seems a fair prediction to me. And it will be they who engineer the vehicles with which to pioneer space, establish settlements and spread through the galaxy.

Not that we are likely to be overtly dominated - after our initial period in charge, I'm sure we could adapt to their pampering. And in the light of such stupendous intelligence we will probably resign contentedly to the role of observers or just playing on beaches and tinkering with trivia. So real evolution, which as a kind of catalyst we will have set in motion, will take place; and for the robots both time and space will essentially have no end.

But the question remains: without a living cell, can a mere machine ever achieve consciousness? Considering levels-of-simulation at the core of synthetic thinking devices, my answer in those days was a resounding, optimistic yes. Now, though, I'm not so sure, and would guess that the likely answer is no. This is because consciousness probably emanates from somewhere within the molecular structure of cells, possibly in the nucleus. Like gravity, a grain in space would measure zero, as would a boulder the size of a house. Only when the cell-mass reaches a certain very large size perhaps does consciousness begin to show.

A living cell is a unit. A computer is a unit. Both can exist alone and function - assuming an external energy supply. But take part of either away, and function will cease. Now supposing we could use nanotechnology to construct millions of powerful computers each of comparable size to a living cell or bunch of cells, and we interconnect them so each can communicate with all the others, and that in their design we have hard-wired programmes (as in DNA) for particular functions... etc, etc... Even then the whole will still not be any more conscious than a pebble on the beach. It makes no difference if the hardware is based on layers of semiconductor (as it is now) or, say, slithers of quartz (optical guides and components have been envisaged for their speed, size, and immunity from interference and energy loss). The fact remains that this sort of hardware consists essentially of blocks: blocks of plastic, blocks of silicon, blocks of quartz - albeit that the scale of thickness is atomic.

And it seems highly improbable to me that blocks, inert in themselves, can, purely on a basis of size or quantity, somehow give rise to consciousness - any more than an old mechanical calculating machine as big as a planet could become somehow conscious merely on the basis of size.

This digression is, at best, wild speculation; but it illustrates the kind of thinking that can be provoked by writers like Asimov. And one doesn't have to fly into realms of fantasy as I have; imagination can operate at any level - for instance, to build a humanoid one requires not just the technology but also the dream. It goes without saying that every human action, every artefact ever made, began as a figment in a human mind. Who would argue that imagination is not the most powerful tool in the universe - so far?

But after that emotional final scene in 'Robots and Empire' it seemed inevitable that 'new-age' sentiment would be a major influence in Asimov's concluding fifth volume of the Foundation saga, 'Foundation and Earth' (1986). I keep this 510-page epic on a shelf where it seems more to belong: with books on spiritual philosophy and Zen. Sufficient to say, it has symbiotic planets and robots, and a general air of pathos throughout. It was an impressive, unique piece of work, but was not vintage Asimov - though I'm certain some readers would prefer it.

If I had read no other author I would not be perturbed, perhaps I would be a lot wiser - because, as well as much else, he even wrote several volumes analysing the bible (scientific angle, of course) - and I'm sure that to this day I wouldn't have exhausted his prolific output.

This brief account of how I interpret a mere fraction of Asimov's magnum opus is unavoidably incomplete. But it would also be one-sided if I didn't include a mention of what is a far greater portion of an astonishing 470 books he produced.

In his non-fiction his tone is always friendly and combines a deeply serious approach with a hint of joviality. He is one of the most articulate authors I've read, and there's little in his non-fiction that an intelligent child wouldn't understand, yet it is certainly not childish. He tackles some difficult scientific issues and makes them both compelling and simple. Such was his genius.

In *'Building Blocks of the Universe'* Asimov treats each atom in the atomic table in turn, each with its own chapter, describing it, how it was discovered and named, what its uses are, and so on - all in compelling tones. He has covered, in the few books of his that I have, virtually every aspect of the universe, maths, physics, chemistry... and examined them to beyond the limits of what was known at the time he wrote them: *'Extraterrestrial Civilisations'* (1979), *'X Stands for Unknown'* (1981), and *'Counting the Eons'* (1983), are a sample.

So I wonder, but for that chance discovery in Boots on a sunny lunchtime in Cambridge... I may never have peered into the brilliant mind of what must be one of the greatest authors of the 20th Century - and what direction might my inner mind have taken then?

* * * * *

The Oct 68 special edition of 'Science Journal' subtitled *'Machines Like Men'* featured robotics.

The last item in the edition was appropriately authored by Isaac Asimov. In this, summarized by himself, version of his own short story Asimov says more about the universe than about his 'supercomputer AI 'Multivac' (which he calls 'ac' for short... standing maybe for Asimov's Computer or Analogue Computer?), and his speculations are about the most extreme in both depth and in time I've ever encountered in science fiction. Maybe H G Wells came close in a different sense with his outstanding *'The Time Machine'* that describes so brilliantly the last days of our World before it being engulfed by the sun. And maybe Douglas Adams came close too with his fabulously satirical *'Restaurant at the End of the Universe'*? These, of course, were entertainingly juggling with serious concepts.

See Appendix 2: *'The Last Question'*

-
-
-
-
-

James Baldwin
(1924 – 1987)

THE BURDEN OF RITUAL, RELIGION & PREJUDICE

I think my friend X had been watching the '*Family Guy*' episode with the circumcision joke where Peter asks the surgeon if he makes much money from it, and the surgeon replies: *'No, but I get to keep the tips.*' Because a few weeks back he asks me to write a poem on the subject for Christmas in the style of Blake. Always willing to oblige, this is what I came up with:

If you were lucky and born a boy,
Intact with a fabulous penis toy,
Beware the surgeon, your protection to snip,
And wreck the ecstasy in the tip.

Not brilliant, but OK for an idler who's not into poetry... and I'm neither Muslin nor Jewish nor Catholic or anything else.... most definitely not when it inspires the mutilation of defenceless infants - as appropriately warned in my little verse for 1st Jan.

In addition to absurd and primitive disfiguring ritual, there's the monumental indoctrination problem, ie:

> *"It is worthy of remark that a belief constantly inculcated during the early years of life, whilst the brain is impressible, appears to acquire almost the nature of an instinct; and the very essence of an instinct is that it is followed independently of reason." - **Charles Darwin***

Millions of hapless victims are shackled for life by these burdens - imagine that: your whole life muted, blunted, second-rated, unable to experience the freedom of thought, the range of sensual pleasure, the full essence of being alive that even most people born into poverty take for granted - just as white people have taken for granted the lack of racial prejudice against them due to skin colour.

Lucky for me I escaped all these horrors, but I don't feel particularly smug about it. My feelings are the same as when learning of any brutality that goes on in the world - which is relentless these days with huge corporate interests in the military, dirty energy, keeping the poor enslaved, crushed, disenfranchised (hollow choices, like the Monty-Python 'spam' menu). What a pointless farce this irrational humbug all is.... How easily people could escape - if only they knew it (they only have to open their eyes) - so many of us, blinded by the culture we're brought-up in and its relentless propaganda, its crazy prejudices, so we act like dumb caged animals who if they just had the imagination to lift a simple psychological latch could free themselves for the rest of their lives.....

Wake-up.... is anyone there?

All this is brilliantly clarified in the life and work of James Baldwin. His '*Go Tell It On The Mountain*' illustrates how insanely swamped by religion the lives of black people in the USA deep south became as a means of coping with their repression and enslavement - all greatly encouraged by the white slave-owners.

Even when they were no longer enslaved in that way, and moved north, still their lives were entirely dominated by religion and associated rituals - even the most banal conversations, everything was steeped in it, distorted and corrupted by it. Baldwin captures the dialogue perfectly.

I prefer above all Baldwin's excellent short stories. But for poignant truths his essays are outstanding - as in the 700-page '*The Price of the Ticket*' (Collected non-fiction 1948 – 1985)-

these essays shine with such energy and vivid reality that reading the most well known of them left me feeling like I'd been born black inside but with white skin. With piercing insight the essays address religion and race, but much more than that. I've been to New York, though not to Harlem - nor would anyone need to because Baldwin presents his experiences there in a universal context so that anyone can relate to them. The horror of events that befell him is all too palpable in those essays.

With a keen eye for prejudice, Baldwin pulls no punches in describing the sordid truth of his observations and experiences. As one reads, his words become self-evident - western society is solid with prejudice. We find prejudice on several fronts, not only according to skin-colour. Just as the Nazis under Hitler discriminated against gypsies, gays, non-white, non-blond.... etc., the class system in its various forms discriminates everywhere too. Even in Paris in 1948, though Baldwin did not experience colour prejudice himself, he noticed that Algerians were victims. Subsequently, he came to realise the phenomenon as an aberration of every society he lived in, whether France, Turkey, or the USA - and probably applies almost everywhere in the world.

There's some fine interviews/discussions, etc., on youtube. He was as courageous as he was perceptive, and we're lucky he survived to write the truths that most people seem to prefer not to acknowledge. If I get around to re-writing my Heroes page, then he'll certainly feature near the top - but I hadn't even heard of Baldwin when I wrote that; and I'm not in the least surprised: he belongs among those prophets and geniuses who establishments of all kinds would like to erase from history. I could select several of Baldwin's short essays that I think everyone could gain from reading as an eye-opening part of their education. Ie:

See Appendix 3 - '*Notes of a Native Son*' (1955).

.

.

.

.

.

Roberto Bolaño
(1953 – 2003)

Roberto Bolaño is unique. He escaped Chile when Allende was assassinated and 'the West' installed their Fascist Pinochet, as they've done since WW2 with any country that elects a socialist president and fails to obey Washington neocon diktat. Who could fail to be deeply affected by the kind of horror and fear that prevailed at the time. But Bolaño, who for most of the latter part of his short life lived in or near Blanes, Spain, writes freely about anything: politics, sex, zombies, other writers, especially of South America and Spain. His style is refreshingly 'open' and often poignant, even bizarre. His prose-poetry is sometimes a bit incoherent, but if you imagine his life, from as he describes it – both inner and outer - then its coherence recovers significantly. There's much autobiography including of the writing experience and jousting with fellow writers who he always speaks of with reverence and affection, as Henry Miller did of his. There's some great essays and stories, especially in his 380-page indexed '*Between Parenthesis*'. Not sure if he could speak English, but Bolaño is someone I'd really like to have met.

There's a real gem of a biography by Monica Maristain that's actually a collection of conversations from people who knew Bolaño. The wealth of admiration and respect they show for him is impressive. Alas, like many great writers, Bolaño died so young, age only 50 - same as Raymond Carver. I didn't discover him until well after his untimely death in 2003.

A fine example from '*Between Parenthesis*' is the short story JIM. Who knows how autobiographical that is? It has energy, unlike his *'Last Evenings on Earth'*, which is a favourite of mine. His essays, though, and stories are sometimes almost indistinguishable from one another. A truly fascinating guy.

See Appendix – 4: *'Jim'*

Heinrich Böll

(1917 – 1985)

I found Heinrich Böll only quite recently, around 1995, while fumbling around one of several dusty chaotic second-hand bookshops in Hastings Old Town. I'd read a couple of his short stories, partly because they were in books I had, and partly on account of him being a Nobel laureate. Then I bought his autobiographical '*What's to Become of the Boy*'. Mostly about his childhood, it reveals the kind of tough existence he had during the Nazi era, and how, regardless of consequent hardships, he was never tempted to cave-in to the propaganda or other pressures. The image I had of him as a very fine human being was enhanced when I read his 'Irish Journal'. His fiction is what he's famous for, though, because of its subtle angle and observations on the Nazi regime which he survived against the odds. He writes lucidly, though in my view not grippingly - yet is well worth a look, I think.

Paul Bowles

(1910 – 1999)

Paul Bowles has written some fine essays and other work. An American living in Tangier, he produced one magnificent book.

'*The Sheltering Sky*' 1949, was many years later made into an excellent film (in which Bowles appears briefly, wizened old man that he was by then). Was it just the skill of the narrative, or that the director shared precisely my own imaginative range? Either way, watching the film was a bit like déjà vu.

The quality of this book is not simply its compelling style and its sense of authenticity, but more than anything it is the way it reveals the underlying frailty of human values and what we like to call 'civilisation'. By contrasting Western and Eastern perspectives on how we live, it addresses the question of how much our lives and minds are formed and bound by the culture we come from. It forces the reader to contemplate the bare bones of what is human, what is existence. Mostly taking place in a desert, stripped of flora (both real and symbolic), losing grip on one's very sense of autonomy to the extent that the concept itself becomes lost, even meaningless and irrelevant, what is there left to cling to? The conditions in the story are bleak and desperate, yet resonate with these fundamental questions: who or what really are we inside, how much are our perspectives governed by the society we grow-up in, and how would we handle, if we could, having this soft comforting rug of culture suddenly pulled from under us?

You, a lone Earthling, crash-land your spacecraft on a planet populated by aliens whose society is about as foreign to you as you can possibly imagine. The aliens regard you either with abject indifference or as an object to exploit. This is the metaphorical essence of this deeply philosophical treatise - of self-examination, of seeing your and other cultures in a new objective light. The more I reflect on it, the more brilliant and unsettling this book is.

.

.

.

.

Ray Bradbury

(1920 – 2012)

Ray Bradbury is fairly prolific - and although not particularly lucid or articulate, somehow, through creative leaps I guess, manages to lure one along in his work. His famous '*Fahrenheit 451*' - a title emulated by Mike Moore in the film '*Fahrenheit 9/11*' - placed his name firmly on the list of literary immortals. His short stories can be worth reading, a few are superb, and he has a perceptive view on many intriguing Sci-Fi issues. He has some excellent, if not outstanding, presentations on youtube - from his home and the lecture theatre. His little book '*Zen in the Art of Writing*' which I've flagged is a minor masterpiece - highly recommended.

.

.

.

.

.

Charles Bukowski

(1920 – 1994)

From The Independent:

> '*Bukowski thrived on spontaneity and aimed to capture in words what he called "gut-life". He disdained literary circles and academic discourse: "Those who have been writing literature have not been writing life," he says in one letter and elsewhere he claims: "(I) get more knowledge of life by talking to a garbage man than I could by talking to TS (Eliot)".*'

Bawdy, boozy, bizarre... Bukowski is like a feral beast that steps, now and then - just to give us his perspective - into the irrational world of culture and conformity with which most of us are so familiar. His work is fresh, plain and down to earth like that of few, if any, other authors. He's a natural rebel, and his writing emanates a freedom one rarely finds. An intellectual vagrant who exhibits a candour and uninhibited openness, a lack of shame or remorse, like no one else, Bukowski has a sharply practical approach to life, bawdy and basic, yet often uplifting and optimistic. He has no ambition, no avarice, few scruples. Living somewhat simplistically in the moment.... observing, a bit like a Buddhist, events around him, letting what doesn't affect him directly take care of itself... and just writing out the grit of it, harsh experience.... with a fine yet obscured sense of humour. At least, that's how I read it, especially the short essays/stories in '*Tales of Ordinary Madness*', which are obviously autobiographical, and quite probably without fabrication.

From 'FACTOTUM' (going home late from a 12-hour day at work):

>"... I always walked to my room, it was six or seven blocks away. The trees along the streets were all alike: small, twisted, half-frozen, leafless. I liked them. I walked along under the cold moon.
>
>That scene in the office stayed with me. Those cigars, the fine clothes. I thought of good steaks, long rides up winding driveways that led to beautiful homes. Ease. Trips to Europe. Fine women. Were they that much more clever than I? The only difference was money, and the desire to accumulate it.
>
>That was all a man needed: hope. It was lack of hope that discouraged a man. I remembered my New Orleans days, living on two five-cent candy bars a day for weeks at a time in order to have the leisure to write. But starvation, unfortunately, didn't improve art. It only hindered it..."

Indeed. As we well know: virtually every writer of note, and for that matter of no note, is either middle-class or Jewish - neither of which are renowned for their poverty..
Or, with rather less pathos, contrast that against -
From 'Nut Ward Just East of Hollywood' in 'TALES OF ORDINARY MADNESS' :

>"....They all came to see me. There's one guy with a last name like Ranch or Rain, something of the sort, and he's always coming by with his sleeping bags and sad story. He hits between Berkeley and New Orleans. Back and forth. Once every two months. And he writes bad, old-fashioned rondos. And it's a fiver and/or a couple of bucks each time he hits (or as they like to say, "crashes"), plus whatever he eats and drinks. That's all right, I've given away more money than I have cock, but these people have got to realize that I also have some trouble staying alive.
>
>So there's Mad Jimmy and so there's me.
>
>Or there's Maxie. Maxie is going to shut off all the sewers in Los Angeles to help the Cause of the People. Well, it's a damn nice gesture, you've got to admit that.

But Maxie, buddy, I say, let me know when you are going to shut off all the sewers. I'm for the People. We've been friends a long time. I'll leave town a week early.

What Maxie doesn't realize is that Causes and Shit are different things. Starve me, but don't cut off my shit and/or shit-disposal unit. I remember once my landlord left town on a nice two week vacation to Hawaii. Okay.

The day after he left town, my toilet stopped. I had my own personal plunger, being very frightened of shit, but I plunged and plunged and it didn't work. You know what that left me.

So I called up my own personal friends, and I'm the type who doesn't have too many personal friends, or if I have them, they don't have toilets let alone telephones ... more often, they don't have anything.

So, I called the one or two who had toilets. They were very nice.

"Sure, Hank, you can shit at my place anytime!"

I didn't take up their invitations. Maybe it was the way they said it. So here was my landlord in Hawaii watching the hula girls, and those fucking turds just lay on top of the water and whirled around and looked at me.

So each night I had to shit and then pluck the turds out of water, place them in wax paper and then into a brown paper bag and get into my car and drive around town looking for some place to toss them.

So mostly, double-parked with the motor running, I'd just toss the god-damned turds over some wall, any wall. I tried to be non-prejudiced, but this one Home for the Aged seemed a particularly quiet place and I think I gave them my little brown bag of turds at least three times..."

If you can recover from laughing, here's a short biog' from the net: The following note accompanied Charles Bukowski's first published story, in the March-April 1944 issue of *Story* -

Charles Bukowski was born in Andernach, Germany in 1920. His father was California-born, of Polish parentage, and served with the American Army of Occupation in the Rhineland, where he met the author's mother. He was brought to America at the age of two. He attended Los Angeles City College for a couple of years and in the two and one-half years since then he has been a clerk in the post office, a stockroom boy for Sears Roebuck, a truck-loader nights in a bakery. He is currently working as a package-wrapper and box-filler in the cellar of a ladies' sportswear shop.

In Bukowski's 1975 novel Factotum, he describes the experience of his frst publication (calling Story's Whit Burnett "Clay Gladmore"): "Gladmore returned many of my things with personal rejections. True, most of them weren't very long but they did seem kind and they were very encouraging...So I kept him busy with four or five stories a week." On the subject of his first sale, Bukowski wrote, "I got up from the chair still holding my acceptance slip. MY FIRST. Never had the world looked so good, so full of promise." Upon seeing the story in print, however, Bukowski's ebullience disappeared. "Aftermath" had been placed in the end notes, and he felt Burnett had published it only as a curiosity. Feeling humiliated, Bukowski never again submitted anything to Story, and he cut back on his writing. It wasn't until the late 1950s that he resumed writing for publication.

NOW FROM ME:

I stumbled on Bukowski - like most other 'GREATS' - by sheer fluke. It was actually a John Fante novel 'Ask the Dust' that hit me first. On the cover it said: "*Fante had a major effect on me. Fante was my God.*" CHARLES BUKOWSKI

I thought: who the hell's this Bukowski guy who was so impressed with Fante? So, I sought out his work. After devouring three of his books, it occurred to me that in its way this stuff was as important - admittedly from a less orthodox angle - as, say, Hesse or Camus.

In essence, Bukowski's writings are wild and free, scattered with the filth and dregs of the bohemian life, on streets and in flop-houses, in bars and with whores, drunken brawls, orgies etc... as so 'delicately' portrayed in his cult film 'Barfly' - which is quite tame: despite fights and other hassle, at no time does 'Bukowski' appear in the least angry (as too befits the temperament of his work).

Although other literature occasionally *touches* these more earthy aspects of the world, they habitually circumvent the detail: the raw, natural, plain portrayal of life as Bukowski relates it - and he does it so easily and spontaneously, so it seems, unperturbed by what a publisher might make of it. Henry Miller is an exception because he done this too - though, gritty as it often is, he did it in a more refined and sophisticated way. Hesse's writings, in contrast, was highly crafted and polished. His grit was less of the outer everyday earth, than of the id, the inner universe we each carry. The differences here are like that between Rimbaud and Betjeman, say, or - for a plainer comparison - between a fabulous old oak chiffonier from a 12th Century French monastery and a gleaming 21st Century sideboard from Harrods. Take your pick - both if you like, why not? I do. Life is short, but I'd say *glimpse what you can*.

Most literature, though it frequently seems otherwise when skilfully done, is fantasy and make-believe, unreal and fabricated. This is by necessity - since reality, when every trifling detail is examined, can appear dull even when the circumstances described involve dynamic and extraordinary events. Bukowski overcomes this dilemma by selecting, true, but telling it strictly as it is, plain and simple, no fancy work, no pap, just the way it is - *or so it seems!*

Two fine works of his (predominately autobiographical output) are the fairly comprehensive *'Ham on Rye'*, and the more famous *'Post Office'*. The short stories are similar, like disconnected chapters, as in the aforementioned *'Tales of Ordinary Madness'*. Then there's the clips he regularly submitted to 'OPEN CITY' - the rival paper to the 'LA Free Press'... ie, from the 'forward':

"...There was not the tenseness or the careful carving with a bit of a dull blade, that was needed to write something for The Atlantic Monthly. *Nor was there any need to simply tap out a flat and careless journalism (er, journalese??). There seemed to be no pressures. Just sit by the window, lift the beer and.... ...A bum off the road brings in a gypsy and his wife and we talk, bullshit, drink half the night. A long-distance telephone operator from Newberg, N.Y., sends me money. She wants me to give up beer and to eat well. I hear from a madman who calls himself 'King Arthur' and lives on Vine St in Hollywood, and wants to help me write my column... "*

So there we go. And now I'll end this little glimpse at good old CB and his fabulous wayward scripts - in order to bury myself in more of his wild humour and living-life-to-the-full, as they say of bohemian types. He didn't fight drink, he enjoyed it - unlike for me, alcohol didn't incapacitate his brain!

A clip from a fan

> *I first read Bukowski in the late 70's when I was 16 years old. He had a short story in Hustler called* "An Affair Of No Particular Importance", *a short piece from his novel* "Women". *It changed my life, and Bukowski's prose and poetry kept me alive for many, many years.*

> *This is* "The Genius Of The Crowd", *probably one of Buk's 5 most famous (or infamous, if you prefer) poems. He lays it out on the line here.*

> *I miss you, Hank.*

See Appendix 5: '*The Genius Of The Crowd*'

Albert Camus
(1913 – 1960)

World famed Nobel prize winner. His best work in my view was written in his 20s - lyrical essays on personal experience and reflections on life and the harsh yet idyllic conditions in Algeria where he grew up. He was a masterful humanitarian philosopher too - articulating and analysing in his work the key elements of any true civilisation, and those that can so easily destroy such an entity or concept: ie, *"It's the job of thinking people not to be on the side of the executioners."* His essays in *'The Myth of Sisyphus'* are a profound recognition of the human predicament and the personal choices we are ultimately presented with.

CAMUS, REVOLT, AND THE JOY OF LIVING

After occasionally practicing as a non-conformer up to the age of 15 (rules, I learned by then, were blindly obeyed only by idiots), I slid idly into conformity. I suppose it suited my various ambitions. For some years I followed this path of least resistance. But it was through that adolescent revolt that I discovered the pleasures and aptness of idling…. That's to say: non-conforming.

Perhaps it was from a new insight on 'work' that I leapt back into revolt (idling) - but this time a personal revolt, involving no overt subversion and no effort - in fact, the reverse: it was, ultimately, I suppose, a revolt against the inevitability of death.

Belated as this was, I now regard it as the only truly constructive move I've ever made; though to have made it sooner would perhaps have been pre-emptive:

From Herbert Read's 1951 Forward to Camus's *'The Rebel'*:

> *Camus believes that revolt is one of the 'essential dimensions' of mankind. It is useless to deny its historical reality - rather we must seek in it a principle of existence. But the nature of revolt has changed radically in our times. It is no longer the revolt of the slave against the master, nor even the revolt of the poor against the rich; it is a metaphysical revolt, the revolt of man against the conditions of life, against creation itself. At the same time, it is an aspiration towards clarity and unity of thought - even, paradoxically, towards order. That, at least, is what it becomes under the intellectual guidance of Camus...*

But has the nature of revolt changed radically in our times? It may have seemed so in the early fifties - or from a position of affluent isolation. But like the historic reality mentioned in the extract, my revolt was all three: beginning (as a kid) from 'slave against master', growing (as a 'youth' - a 25-year diversion) to include 'poor against rich', and finally taking-up 'Man against creation' - as Read puts it - or in my words: 'Man against his predicament'. All of these remain for me. And in spite of what Read says, I suspect all will remain in the world for a good time to come (the first two so long as capitalism thrives).

But in spite of our 'gloomy prospects', as Camus makes clear, there is nothing inconsistent about experiencing 'joy of life' at the same time as rejecting a deity; in fact, as Camus makes equally clear, any other combination would not only be inconsistent, but would fail to reflect (and seize) the truth of our predicament.

While most people accept a prosaic everyday life, or else plunge into some absorbing activity or other, there's always a few - whether pauper or millionaire - who choose to idle their way through the days and years. We idlers amble along, void of all tangible ambition, preferring (when we can) to observe and wonder than do anything 'useful'. It's enough for me, it seems, to roam the cliffs and beaches, to dive into the sea in the summer months, visit dusty second-hand bookshops and idly commune with other pseudo-bohemians. It's enough to enjoy the bright clear mornings for what they actually offer, and the dazzling sunsets... never mind living on the breadline. Priority number one: No reluctant trudge to the office, no grudging days spent in the tedium of unwelcome toil. Who needs money, beyond subsistence, when TIME is so short? Who needs money when, tacky clichés aside, the best things really are free for the taking?

That ephemeral glittering palace, for which every fortunate youth is headed, looms with such breathtaking clarity that you can't possibly doubt its existence. Even when it finally begins to fade, when it dawns on you that it was all a delectable figment, you are still buoyed by what the delusion once inspired: the sense of purpose, the warming power of optimism, the hope and trust you once felt in the unexplored road. It is something you can look back on with a smile when you stumble on that next con-trick: the stormy skies and craggy precipice of looming middle-age... as so strikingly depicted in the paintings of Thomas Cole. Do they still hang in Washington's Smithsonian?

This must be a common experience. Less common, I imagine, is the awareness, as a youth, of both these visions at once. Hesse, for instance, demonstrates this duality in his early work. But it was elucidated most plainly, I believe, by Albert Camus. Alan Watts remarked that 'Salvation consists in the most radical recognition that we have no way of saving ourselves'. I'd rephrase it thus: 'Our only hope is to abandon hope.'

As the extract below (see Appendix 6) suggests, Camus would have concurred with this. I first read it some years ago, noting how Camus was particularly inspired by 'Les Isles' ('The

Islands') written by his professor, Jean Grenier. Camus wasn't so much a nihilist, I believe, as a seeker of truth, a realist who saw the rough and the smooth with the same youthful yet eminently perceptive eye. His palace was the very real present, while his precipice lay equally real just ahead and just as clearly. The extract anticipates the above appraisal by Read, and is an account of certain experiences and analyses recorded in Camus's early work. It is refreshingly uplifting - though also perhaps disquieting:

See Appendix 6: '*THE MAKING OF A WRITER*' - 'Albert Camus 1913-60' by Philip Thody pp 21-25.

... from which, evidently, Camus learned early the ecstasies of what I call idling. But for it to work properly, he realised, one must have a clear conscience: the certainty that it is a sacred pursuit, which requires absolute honesty - no metaphysical riddles, no heaven or hell or other supernatural clutter.

Camus's '*The Outsider*' (1942) - sometimes called '*The Stranger*' - fits well in the existentialism that was beginning to dominate intellectual discussion when under German occupation in France. Its enduring quality I guess is that it focuses on the protagonist's indifference to what's happening around him – until he ends-up in prison awaiting execution for committing a senseless murder, and for the first time in his life wakes-up.

'*The Plague*' has a strange haunting atmosphere, but despite some interesting observations of humanity under stress, and I don't at all regret reading it, it isn't a book I enjoyed.

One excellent little story of Camus's I cannot forget is '*The Guest*' where a schoolmaster who lives alone beside his school on a hill at the fringes of a town is requested by the authorities to guard a foreign prisoner found guilty of murder. The circumstances present both the schoolmaster and his captive with dilemmas, which Camus almost leaves the reader to resolve, but ambiguity aside is essentially resolved.

Truman Capote
(1924 – 1984)

In '*Other Voices, Other Rooms*'. the reader is plunged immediately into the atmosphere in the first paragraph. Although the story becomes increasingly surreal and mysterious, the prose remains supremely articulate and easy to read, and is consistently gripping to the end. A brilliant first novel that took two years to write - I believe - which recreates a world Capote would have known as a kid living free in America's deep south during the '20s & '30s. Also, it addresses an angle on life that at the time in the West (and up till the '70s or '80s) was sidelined and taboo: ie, the protagonist, a boy of ~13 or 14, is gay (though implied from the start, this is not made explicit till the end), a detail that was directly relevant to Capote.

Curiously, his contemporary of about the same age (early 20s), Gore Vidal, was at around this time writing his own version of the same issue in '*The City and The Pillar*' - which also turned out to be a masterpiece, and made Vidal famous too, though he (unlike Capote) was born into great wealth and the status of the American (political) upper-class. So Vidal began with a big advantage - yet by publishing this novel he precluded any chance, so it seemed at the time, of a career in politics.

These two intellectual geniuses were later to become rivals who, in an attempt to discredit each other, fenced with publicly-made derogatory statements - often of great wit and humour. Maybe someone will write a book on the conflict one day - if they haven't already? It would certainly make great reading.

Raymond Carver

(1938 – 1988)

Dip into any of Raymond Carver's little stories and you'll be trapped, compelled to keep reading to the end. As if the plainest prose is the most compelling, he holds you gripped by what appears on the surface as everyday domestic trivia. It looks so simple, yet I've still to fathom how he does it. Pure magic.

Raymond Chandler
(1888 – 1959)

Raymond Chandler I remember so well, not just from the film noir back in the 60s when as a teen I worked part-time at an old cinema, but from the lucky day I picked-up a tatty second-hand copy of his *'The Little Sister'* in Huntingdon market and began reading page-1…. which opens:

> *The pebbled glass door panel is lettered in flaked black paint: 'Philip Marlowe… Investigations'. It is a reasonably shabby door at the end of a reasonably shabby corridor in the sort of building that was new about the year the all-tile bathroom became the basis of civilization. The door is locked, but next to it is another door with the same legend which is not locked. Come on in - there's nobody in here but me and a big bluebottle fly. But not if you're from Manhattan, Kansas.*

Gripped? How can anyone resist reading-on? The story, via all kinds of hard-boiled intrigue and protagonist Marlowe's incisive humorous wit, turns into a subtle exposure of the Hollywood myth… reflecting Chandler's ambiguous jaded experience with the place, and with his 'eccentric' co-writer (and director) Billy Wilder. This fits well alongside Fitzgerald's *'The Last Tycoon'* and Nathanael West's *'The Day of the Locust'* in their brilliant renditions of the now-infamous tarnished image of 1930s Hollywood.

I remember the summer back in 1992 when sitting a couple of hours a day in my garden in Bexhill reading all Chandler's novels in the order he wrote them - apart from *'The Little Sister'*.

According to Frank MacShane in his *'The Life of Raymond Chandler'*, Chandler would frequently force himself to sit in front of his typewriter all day - even if he ended up writing nothing. He reasoned that boredom would spark the creative impulse. For him it worked - occasionally.

Before novels, Chandler wrote many short stories. They strike me as mostly a bit dull, but learning from his hero Hammett – creator of the hard-nosed detective Sam Spade – he later cannibalised and integrated many of the short stories to make several outstanding novels.

Variations in this procedure are often adopted by novelists. They start writing what they expect to be a mere short story, but it develops and expands as they write to become a novella or even a long novel. This happened to Hemingway, apparently, and Sartre who on writing what was to be a short introduction to Genet's famous autobiographical treatise *'Prisoner of Love'* (my copy of which has an intro by Edmund White, an accomplished writer himself), ended up with such a large volume (my copy has > 600-pages) that he published it as a kind of philosophical study as *'St Genet'*.

Anton Chekhov
(1860 – 1904)

There can't be many who don't appreciate Chekhov on one level or another. Some of his simplest and apparently most banal (though still compelling) stories are his best and demonstrate most clearly his immense skill as a writer. For instance, within just nine brief pages in '*At Home*' or '*Home*', he demolishes any justification for the irrational horror the mere act of smoking by a kid evokes in many adults: a lawyer, presented with this choice, soon yields to his innate wisdom rather than to the pernicious trap of the status quo as voiced by the governess. Gently, humanely he reasons and finally fails to effectively reprimand his 9-year-old son for stealing and smoking his cigarettes. Part of Chekhov's skill is that instead of offending a detracting reader he educates them.

Most of Chekhov's work stands out from several angles - such as those I've asterisked on page 42. It's revealing to find how his '*The Lady with the Dog*' resembles in essence that famous old film '*Brief Encounter*' (written after Chekhov's story) AND ends with the opposite conclusion. Like Saki, Saroyan and others, Chekhov consistently opposed a moralising status quo, though did so in a style that enlightens and liberates, so that perhaps his readers will learn to approach the world in a more mature, progressive and intelligent way than before. And it's this, especially, I think: to perceive his philosophy, often woven between the lines rather than starkly explicit, that presents the reader with a challenge to look deeper, which enhances the pleasure of reading - as if every story contains a riddle that offers an authentic glimpse into the mind of its creator.

From a quite young age Chekhov was charged with the necessity to help take care of his family, so hardly experienced childhood. Yet he retained an intimate understanding of children, how they thought and what it was like to be a kid. This is evident in much of his work, '*The Steppe*' is a supreme example. At the same time, unlike most people, he was highly rational, competent and composed. Like other Russian writers, he also liked to explore - though in his case tangentially - fundamental aspects of life, what REALLY counts, what motivates us, what do we REALLY seek? '*The Bet*' is a fine analysis of profound philosophical questions about life. He forces his readers to think hard on these issues: of childhood, how they should treat children, what direction their life is taking, how corrupt and wasteful we are.... how we fail to appreciate the crucial details that make life so worthwhile.

'*On the Way*' is an eavesdrop on two people expressing the passions that make us who we are. Confined in the parlour of a remote forest inn during a violent snow-storm two they unfold their lives to one another in explicit detail. This kind of situation has happened to me several times when travelling....

In most of the stories Chekhov freely gives the more perceptive among us his political and ethical persuasions, sometimes with subtle restraint, sometimes openly. An example of the latter is clear in this little extract from '*A Doctor's Visit*':

> There is something baffling in it, of course . . ." he thought, looking at the crimson windows. "Fifteen hundred or two thousand workpeople are working without rest in unhealthy surroundings, making bad cotton goods, living on the verge of starvation, and only waking from this nightmare at rare intervals in the tavern; a hundred people act as overseers, and the whole life of that hundred is spent in imposing fines, in abuse, in injustice, and only two or three so-called owners enjoy the profits, though they don't work at all, and despise the wretched cotton. But what are the profits, and how do

they enjoy them? Madame Lyalikov and her daughter are unhappy -- it makes one wretched to look at them; the only one who enjoys her life is Christina Dmitryevna, a stupid, middle-aged maiden lady in pince-nez. And so it appears that all these five blocks of buildings are at work, and inferior cotton is sold in the Eastern markets, simply that Christina Dmitryevna may eat sterlet and drink Madeira.

But how warming to realise that - although they don't all shine like those mentioned here - there are more than 200 stories from this giant of literature and theatrical drama.

.

.

.

.

.

Fyodor Dostoyevsky
(1821 – 1881)

Talking of giants...

See Appendix 7 for an amazing account of the drama that inaugurated Dostoyevsky's first publication '*Poor Folk*' back in 1845.

Dostoyevsky observed that the most important quality for a writer is the ability to cut. At the age of 24, two years after 'Poor Folk', Dostoyevsky produced 'The Landlady' in which he reveals a growing self-realisation in Ordynov, the protagonist (how much of this is autobiography?). Here's an extract:

> "...*never, not even in the present instance, was there any order or preordained system in his solitary studies; all he knew now was the first ecstasy, the first fever, the first delirium of the artist. He was creating a system for himself; it had obsessed him for years, and little by little the vague, obscure, but somehow wonderfully gratifying outline of an idea was taking shape within his soul; the idea was embodied in a new, lucid form, and this form cried out to be released from his soul, tormenting it; he was as yet only timidly aware of its originality, truth and distinctiveness: the creative achievement was already announcing itself to his energies; it was forming and establishing itself. But the day of creative realization was as yet far off, perhaps very far off- perhaps quite unattainable!*"

This, I imagine, is precisely the sensation experienced by Dostoyevsky himself. Who can fail to admire the extraordinary skill of Dostoyevsky (and a few others)? Do I envy their talent, their ability to express themselves in such gripping and clear original prose? I have no right to envy them. I've made virtually no effort. Quite probably they slaved at their desks for years; whereas I, instead of applying myself, have chosen to amble through woods and fields, drive dreamily around the USA, Australia or Europe, and generally laze about. I wrote not a single thing in those crucial teenage years so long ago when the brain is fresh and learning by practice is so effective. But I have good memories and I aim to add to them. The truth is, though, I'm an indolent, self-indulgent loafer, an irredeemable slacker, an aspirant to perpetual contentment - a 'folly' acutely bulldozed by some. Yet, to me, doing nothing is a fine pastime, and is only inappropriate when I'm confronted with an obvious need to act. It is said that helping others is a way of losing yourself. If that's your primary aim, fine. But it's not mine if I set out to help someone. And the 'helping-hand' of the inept can strike hard, be very severe and is frequently unwelcome.

But I've experienced no such creative inspiration as Dostoyevsky illustrates in the above extract. And it seems impossible to induce artificially: no amount of self-motivating tactics appear to work. Perhaps it emanates unconsciously from deep within - a bit like being love-struck. Maybe this is what happens when a kid knows, with spontaneous certainty, what to do with their life. Are they the lucky few? Probably they are. Whether or not we are aware of the truth in Shaw's maxim: 'Make sure you do what you like or you'll end up liking what you do.' - most of us are inclined to drift and get stuck in whatever hole we perchance fall into. I was lucky in a different way because for a few years I experienced that passion for knowledge that Colin Wilson speaks of in his *'Beyond The Outsider'*:

> *'For those who have experienced it, the hour of the awakening of passion for knowledge is the most memorable of a lifetime... in that moment, man glimpses*

the possibility of becoming truly human, and recognises that the instruments required in this new existence are not weapons and tools, but intellect and imagination.'

I remember above all the strong sense of engagement. This wasn't creative energy or the consciousness of innate potential for originality - as infected Dostoyevsky's Ordynov. Rather, it involved a yearning to understand certain details of physical reality. Perhaps this corresponds to the creative impulse to the extent that such passion removes you from yourself, you are gripped by the thrill of the moment and the anticipation of great things to come.

I was more than 30 years old before I first read Dostoyevsky. Although I'd heard of him years before, I'd also heard of many other authors, so how - as a mere casual reader - could it have occurred to me that his work might be in any way special or even worth glancing at?

What first alerted me was a masterful series of biographical documentaries on channel 4: *'Ten Great Writers'*.(see section below).

With some regret, I confess to still not having read what are considered to be Dostoyevsky's greatest works, his last two epic novels: *'The Devils'* and *'The Brothers Karamazov'* of which I persisted through part-1, almost a quarter of its 900-pages, and still failed to get hooked.

On page 157 of *'The Outsider'*, Colin Wilson describes these and *'The Idiot'* as "*...surely the sloppiest great novels ever written; this must be qualified by adding that they are also among the greatest novels ever written.*" Great they may be; easy to read (that is, compelling) they are not - at least the two I mentioned are not.

In my view, however, *'The Idiot'* is fine. Although it becomes tired towards the end, it is in places outstanding: most notably all of Ch6 (which brought to mind Giono's *'The Man Who Planted Trees'*), p45 (where Myshkin muses on the guillotine and what must go through the victim's mind at the very instant before the blade cuts through their neck), and at the opening of part 3 where the author leaps onto a tangent and attacks the Russian railway system.

'*The Idiot*' (and probably other works too) also contains a few gems that apparently came from Dostoyevsky's habit of scouring the newspapers. After writing late into the night, he would get up late each morning and read the newspaper sitting outside at his favourite café. One of these 'gems' tells of a man in a first-class railway carriage who refused the request of a lady sitting opposite with a lapdog to extinguish his cigar. The lady promptly snatched the cigar from his mouth and tossed it through the window - whereupon the man snatched up the lapdog and sent it out too. This is one of very few instances of humour - if the lapdog will forgive me - in Dostoyevsky's work. Though perhaps 'humour' is the wrong word because even that example contains an element of horror.

His '*The Insulted & the Injured*'' his clear elements of autobiography – a character discusses his, Dostoyevsky's , earlier work, which to me was fascinating whereas his sharply poignant '*Notes from the Underground*' has been described as reflecting a decadent Russian society of the time. These, together with his first story '*Poor Folk*' (1845), written when he was 23, '*Netochka Nezvanova*' (1849) which translates as 'Nameless Nobody', and '*A Strange Man's Dream*' (1877), are among the most gripping and revealing stories I've read.

For me, though, there's no doubt that his most brilliant achievement was '*Crime and Punishment*' - a masterpiece of psychological ingenuity: gripping, penetrating, gruesome and intense from start to finish. In addition to the grit and weave of the story, much of which takes place in the deep psychological musings of Raskolnikov, the protagonist, Dostoyevsky analyses the curious phenomenon of how certain high-status individuals in elevated positions can commit horrendous crimes like genocide, with virtual impunity and apparently no stain on their conscience, whereas an ordinary individual who commits a single, perhaps even socially beneficial, crime - such as murdering an evil old money lender - will suffer guilt, anguish and remorse for the rest of their life. This was the fate of Raskolnikov in the novel. Dostoyevsky, though, leaves him effectively on the brink of a precipice at the end, from where he has the option to retreat and begin his repentance. He has learned a great lesson and has already reformed before his exile begins.

In 'The Idiot', in contrast, Myshkin arrives by train from a sanatorium in the country to 'enter the world' as a kind of saint. But it emerges through the course of the novel that he is entirely out of place and seems only to exacerbate discordances he attempts to ameliorate. Finally, disheartened, he 'slouches' back to the sanatorium.

Using an entirely different technique, Dostoyevsky distils the essence of this remarkable novel into his 'A Strange Man's Dream' - the very story, in fact, that inaugurated my adventure with perhaps the greatest writer the world has yet known. I'll relate briefly below a significant event in Dostoyevsky's life (from Geir Kjetsaa's biography), and then reproduce a few of what I see as worthy extracts from his work.

In 1849, at 28, Dostoyevsky, was accused of subversion and with several others became victim to a mock execution by firing squad. It was an experience that changed his life:

> The priest mounted the scaffold and faced the prisoners, quoting from the bible...

> 'Death was not to be avoided,' Dostoyevsky recalled years later, 'If only it would come as quickly as possible... And then I was seized by a profound indifference. Yes! Yes! Yes! Indifference. I cared not for life or those around me. Everything seemed meaningless beside that terrible moment when I would pass into the unknown, into darkness...'

Three platoons, each with sixteen men, were lined up fifteen yards from those who were to be executed. With loaded rifles, the soldiers took aim. Half a minute of excruciating, terrible suspense passed... Suddenly someone appeared waving a white cloth and the soldiers lowered their rifles...

At first there was no joy over the pardon. All of them were gripped by indifference... Many of the spectators wept.

A Danish historian wrote much later: '*...he survived and became one of the giants in world literature.*'

Shortly after the mock execution Dostoyevsky wrote to his brother:

'*...When I look back at the past and think of all the time I squandered in error and idleness, lacking the knowledge needed to live, when I think of how often I sinned against my heart and my soul, then my heart bleeds. Life is a gift, life is happiness, every moment could have been an eternity of happiness! If youth only knew! Now my life will change; now I will be reborn...*' *Before leaving for exile in Siberia, his brother was granted permission to see him: 'Don't cry, dear brother,' he said, 'This is not a funeral. I am not to be laid in my coffin. They aren't beasts in prison. They are men, perhaps better than I am, perhaps worthier than I am...*'

That letter to his brother echoes what was, I believe, to become the final words of that small masterpiece '*A Strange Man's Dream*', one of the few stories I've read that continues to haunt me. Finally (for the moment), a few extracts from what struck me as some of his most eloquent work - first, from the last page of '*A Weak Heart*' (1848):

'*Dusk had already fallen by the time Arkady made his way home. As he approached the Neva he stopped for a moment and cast a penetrating glance along the river into the smoky, frost-deadened distance, which had suddenly flared with the last purple of a bloodred sunset that was burning itself out on the smudgy horizon. Night was descending over the city, and the whole immense clearing of the Neva, which had swollen with frozen snow, was being showered, in the sun's last reflection, with infinite myriads of sparks thrown down by the hoar-frost. It was minus twenty-degrees. Frozen steam fell heavily from horses which had been driven to death, from the people hurrying by. The taut air shivered at the slightest sound and, like giants, from all the roofs of both embankments columns of smoke rose into the cold sky and floated aloft, twining and untwining on their way, making it seem as though new buildings were rising above the old ones, as though a new city were being formed in the air... It was as if, at last, this entire world, with all its inhabitants, the shelters of the poor or the gilded palaces for the delight of the powerful of this world, resembled a fantastic, magical vision, a dream that would in its turn vanish in a trice and evanesce towards the dark-blue heavens.... He quivered, and his heart seemed in that instant to fill with a hot jet of blood which had suddenly boiled up from the influx of some mighty sensation hitherto unknown to him.... His lips began to tremble, his eyes flared with light, and at that moment his eyes seemed to open on something new.'*

I cannot read that without feeling almost present in the scene, the sensations rise in the imagination to make one completely forget one is reading. But how about this from the opening of Ch-6 of 'The Meek Girl' (1876)?

'Now that terrible reminiscence...

I woke up the next morning, at about eight I think it was, for the room was almost completely light. I woke up at once, fully conscious, and opened my eyes suddenly. She was standing by the table and was holding my revolver. She had not seen me wake up and was unaware that I was looking at her. And suddenly I saw that she had begun to approach me with the revolver in her hands. Quickly, I closed my eyes and pretended to be fast asleep.

She reached the bed and stood over me. I could hear everything; even though a dead silence had set in. I could hear that silence. At that point there was some kind of convulsive movement - and suddenly, against my will, I opened my eyes.

She was looking straight into my face, and the revolver was now at my temple. Our eyes met, but remained there no more than a moment. I forced my eyes shut again, and in the same instant took a mighty resolve neither to open them nor to move one muscle, no matter what awaited me...'

I would like to have included some extracts from the ultimate existential story *'Notes from the Underground*' but find it so full of powerful impressions that it is impossible to select one in preference to another. It belongs with the most penetrating and thought-provoking stories I've read. One is forced to identify with its author's paranoia - the 'sickness' of the time - because Dostoyevsky has observed an aspect of ourselves that, essentially, we probably all contain in differing degree, perhaps depending on our circumstances and how we respond to them, though in this instance it is so deep and out of sight that many people will - presumably through self-deception or misplaced pride, refute its existence - as in the 1950s regarding Kinsey's findings from research into human sexual behaviour. I confess a vestigial awareness of some level of all these unflattering characteristics in myself - some even since about eight years old, and am prepared to acknowledge truth whether palatable or otherwise. How else, except by such acknowledgements - such self-knowledge - can one understand, accept and live contented with oneself?

The great secret is: focus on what IS - not what you might wish... for that, I suggest, is the way to ultimate salvation. If nothing else, I learned that great detail from reading the world's (alongside Tolstoy, perhaps) greatest ever writer. But before concluding.....

A Crucial Question

I recently noticed in a book of quotations that Dostoyevsky had posed the question:

> *Imagine that you are creating a fabric of human destiny with the object of making men happy in the end, giving them peace and rest at last, but that it was essential and inevitable to torture to death only one tiny creature, and to found that edifice on its unavenged tears, would you consent to be the architect on those conditions?* (The Brothers Karamazov (1879, 80) bk. 5, ch. 4.)

This question is more far-reaching than it might at first seem. But how many of us would reply like all the rest throughout history, with an enthusiastic: Yes! Yes!

Unfortunately, human beings prefer not to think; they tend to view such questions simplistically. If they pause to reflect, they would notice that the detail is both incomplete: What if that insignificant creature were me? - and unrealistic: Could such a future be possible without humanity being reduced to an innocuous race of morons?

Maybe it is possible; one would hope so; but most people, I think, on assessing the problem when they might be chosen as the insignificant creature, would answer a very clear no. Who would forfeit their life in such a way even if that unlikely promise was a certainty?

To die is, for the individual, equivalent to annihilating the entire universe. Before we die we believe everything will carry on as normal without us, and so it will. But once you're dead, this is irrelevant - which means that nothing has greater value than life. And so on. As we reason through these kind of questions, we build a framework of provisional opinions and feelings - to be updated on receipt of new relevant information or by progression of thought. With the possible exception of suicide, life, then (my train of thoughts conclude), should therefore always be regarded as sacred, as if it is us, ie, me or you, whose life is in the balance. Which means the answer to Dostoyevsky's question must be an emphatic NO. Appropriately, I recently read on a Quaker notice board: 'The time is now, and now is sacred.'

What we fail to realise is that to analyse for ourselves hypothetical questions like this can have a marked effect on how we conduct our everyday lives. For instance, I have concluded above that life should be preserved at all costs, when previously I may have believed life dispensable in certain special conditions - not in others: ie, if it's mine. This will influence, perhaps, whether I support capital punishment - or even corporal punishment - or, ultimately, any punishment at all. It will affect the level of respect and concern I feel for other people - and perhaps also other creatures: whether I become a vegetarian, for instance. Together with a little imagination, this sort of thinking broadens the perspective, and can alert us to alternative viewpoints. This is important if people are to get along better because it will increase the respect we have and show for those we disagree with - or disapprove of, including dumb animals.

So, observing and weighing what the greatest minds in history have thought gives us an edge. And because reading happens at a controlled pace, one can pause for thought, reread, make notes, discuss with others, and even (as I'm doing here) consolidate thoughts by writing them - which forces one to focus and take greater care in analysing issues than might otherwise be the case.

"Ambition," said Proust, "is nothing more than a lust for power." I've yet to find reason to disagree. So when I say that I have an ambition, I'll have already assessed how Proust's lust applies to me. My ambition is to learn and experience. Among a few lesser things, I lust for power over myself. Left to myself I'm apt to laze around and waste time, become self indulgent in ways that if not restrained would certainly shorten my life considerably. But even if I do nothing but read time-tested books for the rest of my life, they can never make me wise - that depends upon me; books contain only knowledge.

F Scott Fitzgerald
(1896 – 1940)

Fitzgerald's key work is '*The Great Gatsby*'. There are many fine short stories too, which I'd recommend, but '*Gatsby*' is the masterpiece. His other interesting work '*The Crack-up*' - an autobiographical account of a nervous breakdown - is revealing of the consequences of his lifestyle, I think...

What especially impressed me about the Gatsby book was the tone and style of the writing and the intellect of the narrator who somehow manages to remain above the profligacy and dissolution of the characters and social events he witnesses. So to me, it wasn't so much what the story was about: the underlying decadence in 20s 'high society' America with the stock market boom and untold wealth and the vast consequent arrogance and waste of the time... the entire myth, in fact, of the so-called 'American Dream'... it wasn't so much that, as the way the story was told.

In truth, neither the subject nor history interest me much. But the way Fitzgerald grips you right from the first paragraph, and doesn't let go for a moment, keeps you there for more than 160-pages, is quite brilliant. He didn't achieve anything approaching it again.

And most of the books I discuss, have this same quality of drawing the reader in right from the first line, *and then keeping them there*. It doesn't have to be dramatic or startling or shocking.... often such openings can be dull, like a cliché. It's a quality that's hard to define, and is so variable that it can -

and I'd wager, frequently does - happen by chance. Apparently, my story '*Fired*' has this quality - so I'm told!

Here's the compelling first paragraph of Fitzgerald's 'great American novel' that justifiably won him so much acclaim:

> *In my younger and more vulnerable years my father gave me some advice that I've been turning over in my mind ever since. "Whenever you feel like criticizing any one," he told me, "just remember that all the people in this world haven't had the advantages that you've had."*

Another aspect of Fitzgerald's insight is clearly evident in the following extract from his 1934 novel '*Tender is the Night*'

> *With Nicole's help Rosemary bought two dresses and two hats and four pairs of shoes with her money. Nicole bought from a great list that ran two pages, and bought the things in the windows besides. Everything she liked that she couldn't possibly use herself, she bought as a present for a friend. She bought coloured beads, folding beach cushions, artificial flowers, honey, a guest bed, bags, scarfs, love birds, miniatures for a doll's house, and three yards of some new cloth the colour of prawns. She bought a dozen bathing suits, a rubber alligator, a travelling chess set of gold and ivory, big linen handkerchiefs for Abe, two chamois leather jackets of kingfisher blue and burning bush from Hermes - bought all these things not a bit like a high-class courtesan buying underwear and jewels, which were after all professional equipment and insurance, but with an entirely different point of view. Nicole was the product of much ingenuity and toil. For her sake trains began their run at Chicago and traversed the round belly of the continent to California; chicle factories fumed and link belts grew link by link in factories; men mixed toothpaste in vats and drew mouthwash out of copper hogsheads; girls canned tomatoes quickly in August or worked rudely at the Five-and-Tens on Christmas Eve; half-breed Indians toiled on Brazilian coffee plantations and dreamers were muscled*

out of patent rights in new tractors - these were some of the people who gave a tithe to Nicole and, as the whole system swayed and thundered onward, it lent a feverish bloom to such processes of hers as wholesale buying, like the flush of a fireman's face holding his post before a spreading blaze. She illustrated very simple principles, containing in herself her own doom, but illustrated them so accurately that there was grace in the procedure, and presently Rosemary would try to imitate it.

But the little treatise describing his mental breakdown *'The Crack-up'* reveals much more and is a great read. Alas, Fitzgerald was destined to join the many other great writers who died prematurely, in his case age 44.

.

.

.

.

.

Eduardo Galeano
(1940 – 2015)

Basically non-fiction, '*Upside Down*' illustrates in anecdote or parable form the gamut of circumstances in modern society where the logic, the situation, the design, whatever, is precisely 180° out of phase with how it should be ideally or rationally. In other words, it shows us where things are Upside Down - usually on purpose due to ulterior motives, hidden agendas, etc., (which Galeano excels in exposing), but frequently too due to sheer wanton ignorance, blatant stupidity or recklessness.

This is probably the most recent title in the entire list here. For some reason, most contemporary work, especially fiction, strikes me as dull, tedious, mundane, trite, everyday or else inauthentic and sensationalist.... I pick up many books in the library, especially on the 'For Sale' table, and am unable to get through a first paragraph, from the first page or dipping-in either randomly or at the start of another chapter. Yet this is definitely not the case with the books I've flagged green in my list.

Looking on the Amazon reviews I find this from Sarah Meyer dated 2005... which reminds me of the time and I reflect now on events of nearly 2-decades ago:

> *The 2005 G8 conference is over. Simultaneously, at least 60 people were murdered in London by bombs sown by the Bush-Blair "War on Terror," whilst more people die each day in Iraq from bombs, bad water, starvation. Nothing has changed for the poor people struggling under*

the yoke of trade laws in Africa and elsewhere. Nor has anything changed to help global warming melt down. The Corporate Crime Brigade and its PR machine are alive and well. Galeano's Swiftian understanding and dissection of the powers that are destroying us all is a MUST read.

NOTHING HAS CHANGED.... surprise surprise.. in fact our predicament is decidedly worse now, which I suppose stands to reason since none of the elites in control were ever philosophers or could claim any kind of wisdom, rather the opposite: just a mob of psychopathic murderous marauding dinosaurs – not only heading for self-destruction but determined to take the rest of us and the planet with them into oblivion.

And from Harinda Jadwani in 2019:
:

A must-read for anyone who wants to understand how the world really is....

Explains in clear, lucid, poetic prose - full of savage satire - how 'topsy-turvy' the reality of the world is compared to the illusion that is its presentation in the Western media. Read his preface comments on the 'crime' he and collaborators are committing against the West, by telling the truth about it, and how they are likely to be 'punished for their misdeeds'. A world full of propaganda by a West plundering the resources of the rest of it, certainly will regard its exposure as a crime.

Then, a few days ago appropriate to this, a primordial UK celebrates a coronation: 5th May 2023. After the obscene flaunting of the same medieval ritual as Jack London wrote of so evocatively in his masterful '*People of the Abyss*' (1903) – ie, the 1901 coronation - we witness again the elite asserting their position: the overwhelming power they have over the minds of the masses.

Julian Assange, incarcerated in Belmarsh prison for exposing many heinous crimes of the elite, wrote a letter to the king inviting him to visit his (the king's) prison. Not that anyone remotely connected with the king will even be allowed to see anything like that... or if they did see it they'd only use it to wipe their arses on, of course, with the same contempt they hold for the rest of their 'subjects', the enslaved plebs who they continually fleece and keep impoverished to fund their opulence and excesses.

Imagine the many thousands of rough-sleepers in London where Buckingham palace - just one of many homes of the king - has 775 rooms: 240 bedrooms, 78 bathrooms.

Gabriel Garcia Márquez
(1927 – 2014)

Reading '*One Hundred Years of Solitude*' was like falling into a weird amazing dream. Full of magic, poetic mystery and political intrigue - as well as complex domestic and social relationships and arrangements.... and all within a compelling, dreamlike fantasy-land, written in a form of language that could have derived from some alien yet beautiful realm of ancient art, this epic tale relates 100-years of events in a remote, isolated community deep in the Amazon jungle (or some such location). It is hard to describe precisely - one just has to read it to feel the atmosphere, the depth...

BANANA Land: Blood, Bullets and Poison....

Reading Gabriel Garcia Márquez's memoir '*Living to Tell the Tale*' where he mentions writing his first 'novel' (or novella) '*Leaf Storm*' around age 27, it occurred to me how little I knew of his motivation for writing what he did. I hadn't read '*Leaf Storm*' (though it sits on the shelf beside me - acquired, I notice, from an Old Town junk shop for 35p some years ago) but I remember well his masterpiece '*One Hundred Years of Solitude*' from when I read it way back in the 80s (it was published in 1967 when he was 40) and his reasons for writing it are described on wikipedia – briefly: as well as to symbolise 'western' policy towards South America in a massacre, it would also, from the brilliant hypnotic style he gave the novel, entice people into reading his other work, most notably '*No-one Writes to the Colonel*'.

Garcia Márquez was born just after the banana massacre that was so shocking to ordinary people they could barely talk about it, opponents of such corporate murder (instigated by the US govt on behalf of the United Fruit Company) formed alliances from which emerged the famous people's army FARC. It was this massacre that haunted Marquez and which he portrays in '*One Hundred Years of Solitude*'. As he implies in his memoir: If you want to exorcise what haunts you then write about it.

Publication of issues like this makes no difference, alas; the world remains dominated by greed and brutality, mostly derived from or supported by US politicians and the corporate outfits they support and represent, as with the banana massacre. But to become aware... to look deeper and question the true nature of the thugs we are expected to vote for every 4 or 5 years should be an obligation of us all.... only then might there be a chance that civilisation can prevail in the world.

In his 1997 memoir '*Palimpsest*' Gore Vidal dedicates a whole chapter to Guatemala where he lived during 1954 when the US bombed Guatemala City because workers resisted that same United Fruit Company's attempts to enslave them. Vidal later discovered that a 'kindly' millionaire uncle of his who was heavily invested in United Fruit (and was close to the US govt) had inspired the attack which led to the overthrow of the Guatemalan govt and the installation of a US compliant Fascist dictator. Vidal subsequently spent the rest of his life attacking the US establishment and its empirical ambitions.

Garcia Márquez eloquently denounces these and other atrocities in his 1982 Nobel Prize speech - but almost, I thought, as if they were a more or less inevitable part of a history of violence and massacres in Latin America. Even so, he declares his hope that such events remain in the past... yet 40-years later Western imperialists (the US, UK and Israel) have only increased their imperial ambitions, but not just in Latin America: see, for instance: William Blum's '*Killing Hope*' - scroll down through 56 chapters of invasions, massacres and plundering by the US alone between 1945 and 1992 - since when most notably there has been Iraq, Afghanistan, Syria, Libya... as well as continued attempts to overturn elected Latin American governments, esp Venezuela with its vast oil reserves like Iraq.

Another intriguing detail Garcia Márquez reveals is, as described above, that his favourite of all his work is his short 80-page: '*No-one Writes to the Colonel*' (1968) and that he only wrote '*One Hundred years of Solitude*' to attract attention so people would then read that little 80-page novel.
.

'*No-one Writes to the Colonel*' is an evocatively written story about a colonel who saved the nation by defeating the enemy and who was promised a small pension from the government he rescued. He lives with his wife in humble circumstances in a small village, just managing to get by with the help of friends and his ingenuity Every morning over the years he has walked down to the jetty to meet the mail boat. He is expecting a letter from the government pensions department. And every morning he is disappointed, yet he lives in hope. Of course, the letter never arrives – the war was won because of him, but he, along with the risks, his bravery, the tough challenges he faced, the losses he suffered, etc. etc., is now forgotten history. No-one is interested, least of all in fulfilling an obligation to keep a promise: a small pension.

I see two reflections here: Don't expect anything of other people, regardless of how well you've treated them; and don't lose hope - or don't lose trust in the good nature of others.

See Appendix – 8 for a poignant journal entry from another Nobel laureate José Saramago concerning the 2008 financial crisis and a New World Order that he envisaged and now 15-years later as I write this in 2023 is being belatedly forming. In a recent speech (Late May 2023) Vladimir Putin stated that quite separately from the Ukraine conflict, the formation of a New World Order was well under way already, but now spurred by the colossal international impact of that 'East-West' conflict, the expansion of BRICS nations from countries fed-up with being under Western domination, is taking place more rapidly so that in a decade or so the capitalist elite of the 'wild-west', the US/EU/UK fascists with their so-called free-market system, will no longer be free to rape and devastate the planet and its people.

Saramago is one of many academics and other commentators who are keen to promote the end of the disastrous hegemonic battles and slaughter described in William Blum's important book '*Killing Hope*'.

Nikolai Gogol
(1809 – 1852)

The first story I read of Gogol's was *'Diary of a Madman'* (and other stories - of which *'The Overcoat'* was the most outstanding). Later, after reading *'Dead Souls'*, I was in no doubt that Gogol was a true master of literature who shone above even his idol Pushkin. Of all the writers in my list I think Gogol displays the greatest sense of humour, as well as insight into social justice - maybe Bukowski comes a close second. *'Dead Souls'* leaves you with a sense of having traversed the whole of Russia, the expansive steppe and plains... and tasted a strange yet mouth-watering selection of foods on the way, met numerous eccentric characters: farmers, serfs (souls), the landowning idle classes at their most incompetent and absurd (and who relied on their serfs for everything from putting their boots on to growing crops), and encountered a few curious events and conversations too. The protagonist, Chichikov, with his two fabulous servants - without whom the novel would lose much of its humour - charge around that vast country visiting the various Excellencies who own the most serfs.... journeys that involve all the everyday detail of resting, eating, etc., being entertained, failing to be understood, getting stuck in mud... it's a hilarious jaunt and a profound social comment in one epic and breathtaking sweep.

•

•

•

•

•

Maxim Gorky
(1868 – 1936)

I haven't read a lot of Gorky, only 'dipped-in' here and there in various works - esp his '*Fragments from My Diary*' which is highly entertaining in places, when he meets Tolstoy, for instance, and his first-hand account of Chekhov, and the numerous amusing anecdotes. Some of his autobiographical '*Childhood*' is less gripping, though his sequel '*My Apprenticeship*' starts nicely:

> So here I am - an apprentice. I am the "boy" in a "stylish footwear" shop on the main street of the town. My master is a round little creature with a bleary face, greenish teeth, and bilge-water eyes. It seems to me that he is blind, and I make faces at him in the hope of confirming this. "Don't screw up your mug." he says to me quietly, but firmly.

It continues in the same vein... becoming even sillier, and in a tone and manner that I find compelling, and moreover which Nabokov had too, and Gogol, and even Tolstoy in some of his shorter works. It seems to be unique to Russia, this style, and captures (like no other authors I've read) those seemingly insignificant yet telling everyday trivialities that provide instant recognition - that is, on an intuitive level. And the way these details are expressed are frequently, and unintentionally so it seems, hilarious: 'The ball's gone under Grandma's commode.' in the first pages of Nabokov's '*The Gift*', or from Tolstoy's '*The Death of Ivan Ilych*':

As he sat down on the pouffe Piotr Ivanovich remembered how Ivan Ilyich had arranged this drawing-room and had consulted him about this very pink cretonne with the green leaves. The whole room was full of knicknacks and furniture, and on her way to the sofa the widow caught the lace of her black fichu on the carved edge of the table. Piotr Ivanovich rose to detach it, and the pouffe, released from his weight, bobbed up and bumped him. The widow began detaching the lace herself, and Piotr Ivanovich sat down again, suppressing the mutinous springs of the pouffe under him. But the widow could not quite free herself and Piotr Ivanovich rose again, and again the pouffe rebelled and popped up with a positive snap...

These Russian authors, apparently, have uniquely inherited this skill. It is most extravagantly demonstrated in Vaslav Nijinsky's famous diary, which he wrote (I believe) purely for his own eyes - possibly for one other person too. Yet there it is, this remarkable natural feature in its most touchingly childlike form, scattered throughout. This style of description, in Nijinsky's case, is as sad as it is amusing - so a sensitive reader might find themselves laughing and crying simultaneously. Dostoyevsky, on the other hand, doesn't quite seem to manage it - though it's not for the want of trying. In several of his works; '*The Double*', for instance, and even his impressive '*Notes From Underground*' and '*The Gambler*' you can see him striving for it, brushing it. It's an attractive feature, though, which I'd love to be able to emulate... and it looks so simple, like those masterful Picasso sketches! Ah, for the want of a more pliant brain....!

·
·
·
·
·

George Gurdjieff
(1866-77 – 1949)

Most of Gurdjieff's writing is said to be 'difficult', and I take other people's word for that - I guess they're right. But his *'Meetings With Remarkable Men'* is both lucid and compelling, and contains some intriguing thoughts and events. Gurdjieff was one truly authentic and hard-nosed eccentric. His extrovert manner increased as he aged - nothing was done 'by-halves'. What has been written about him and his teachings (especially by Ouspensky) is gripping enough in itself. Some of the latter is thought provoking and deep, but much is extremely weird and esoteric.... to the extent that you might wonder if he was relating his experiences of some alien planet, or else was a highly articulate lunatic whose brain was operating at the margins of normal comprehension.

Colin Wilson's biography *'The War Against Sleep'* paints a sober tribute to this inspiring genius who had a curious psychological grip on those around him, not necessarily of persuasion, but in the mere awe of his presence, his lofty expectations, outlandish discipline, frequently bizarre behaviour that kept everyone 'on their toes'. *"In his presence you always felt utterly alive - like a mountain climber at a precarious point on a rockface."*

•

•

•

•

•

Earnest Hemingway

(1899 – 1961)

Of the authors listed here, Hemingway is one who I wouldn't have chosen to meet - yet, he was said to be highly sociable, tolerant and friendly with those he didn't see eye-to-eye with. One has the impression, though, of someone impulsive, aggressively competitive, a bit obsessed like the protagonist in '*The Old man and the Sea*'.

But merely the stark plain tone of his groundbreaking and masterful '*Farewell to Arms*' gives the sense of a hard-nosed writer, fitted to the life of a soldier. His close friend Scott Fitzgerald (while in Paris in the 20s), on the other hand - though one might have an image of someone aloof - gives an entirely different impression. Yet there they were, together with James Joyce, Gertrude Stein, Ezra Pound.... who else? It doesn't matter, because Hemingway's best work - so far as I'm concerned (having not read most of his work) - was '*A Moveable Feast*', his autobiographical account of his years in Paris with those fellow writers, all struggling to create that elusive seminal 'Great American Novel'. Only Fitzgerald achieved it - brilliantly, and remarkably concisely with '*The Great Gatsby*'. While Hemingway, though not exactly producing the quintessential masterpiece, still hit records that a few decades later earned him the Nobel Prize.

Eugen Herrigel

(1884 – 1955)

I know nothing about Herrigel, except that his world famous book '*Zen in the Art of Archery*' introduced me to a completely new way of observing and approaching life. I've never even attempted archery - in the proper sense of the term - as a professional might. But this doesn't matter. The particular activity, to which Herrigel's philosophy and approach applies, is really irrelevant. It's maybe three or four decades since I read this little book - which can be devoured in one sitting (and contemplated for a lifetime) - but its key feature, as I recall, is that you are taken right into the very nub of the action... you focus down into the minutest detail of only what is immediate. And even then, it's not a question of concentration - but rather about poise, being relaxed, natural, at one with '*what is*'. At the point of the arrow's release, the archer doesn't even consider the target - which might seem absurd. Yet there's an invaluable lesson here. It's a lesson about observing, about becoming like plasticine, allowing your mind to shape around the situation, to exactly fit '*what is*': the 'true reality' in every sense and at that very instant. An analogy might be the way you let your eyes relax so they can find their own focus on those 3D computer pictures that are otherwise an unintelligible mass of repeating coloured patterns. I was convinced that as a philosophy Herrigel had cracked a great secret. And I'm reminded of the Zen story '*Is That So?*' (see below) in which, instead of resisting or attempting to fight as anyone normally might, the Zen master Hakuin knows better: he flexes and moves with the wind, the conditions, deflecting and adjusting... one moment this... next moment that... unhesitatingly according with circumstances...

precisely as illustrated by Alan Watts in '*The Watercourse Way*' and D T Suzuki in his '*Studies in Zen*'.

Unfortunately - like so much else in life unless one makes a great effort to embrace a thing - the practice of Zen is not something I've done very much. The times when it's been especially useful is at moments of impasse. Then, poised and focused, a new perspective appears which can be immensely illuminating - 'lateral thinking' becomes automatic, and everything falls into place as best it possibly could, or so it seems: as though decisions/actions are optimised.

A recent radio programme explained how people who suffer depression experience an excess of continual and unquenchable brain activity: (ie, random chatter). This can apparently be reduced by electro-therapy - which is a help to most, though not all, sufferers. Perhaps, instead, one could try deliberate poise and then focus as described above - ideally to focus on nothing, though a candle or any simple object or even a mantra could be used.

This phenomenon was touched-on - perhaps, in fact, much more than merely touched-on - in a Theosophy Course I attended some years ago. See also my '*Meditation*'.

Although I prefer his more his famous book, Herrigel's '*The Method of Zen*' (also about 100-pages) is a fine book.

See Appendix - 9 for the little Zen story: '*Is That So*?'

-
-
-
-
-

Hermann Hesse
(1877 – 1962)

'Pilgrim of Crisis' -is an apt title for Freedman's outstanding biography. Despite crises, Hesse eloquently articulated aspects of eastern philosophy in his stories, as well as challenging authoritarian establishments - asking, above all, 'Who should we obey?' and leaving no doubt of the answer.

> *"We kill at every step, not only in wars, riots, and executions. We kill when we close our eyes to poverty, suffering, and shame. In the same way all disrespect for life, all hard-heartedness, all indifference, all contempt is nothing else than killing. With just a little witty skepticism we can kill a good deal of the future in a young person. Life is waiting everywhere, the future is flowering everywhere, but we only see a small part of it and step on much of it with our feet."*

Some years ago I found a book containing biographical sketches by Hermann Hesse in which he eloquently levelled precisely the same criticisms of his education - more than a hundred years ago - as I had at mine. Discovering this was both warming and depressing. Warming because it challenged an issue that seemed almost universally unacknowledged: here was an esteemed Nobel laureate who wrote openly against the establishment (any establishment); depressing, since I lamented on how it would have boosted my confidence had I read this as a thirteen-year-old. Nothing ever changes, I thought, upon discovering this, in spite of the A S Neills of this world and now in spite of this celebrated author too - the tired old system drags on leaving ever more damaged lives in its wake.

> '*For those who have experienced it, the hour of the awakening of passion for knowledge is the most memorable of a lifetime... In that moment, man glimpses the possibility of becoming truly human, and recognises that the instruments required in this new existence are not weapons and tools, but intellect and imagination.*'
> ('Beyond the Outsider' 1965. Colin Wilson)

I cannot quote that extract too often (see page 103). What people fail to realise, I reflect whenever I hear someone explain how a particular teacher inspired them, is that for every positive event like that there are many thousands - perhaps millions - in which the opposite happens. For the fortunate few - for whom this passion for knowledge arises - it nearly always does so in spite of and not because of school. It was certainly so in my case. But this situation illustrates how the immense inertia of tradition overpowers reason, common sense and practical experience - or perhaps, to take a more cynical view, it reveals the determination of the Establishment to preserve its position, and to keep the masses ignorant and deceived, and in their place.

The truth is that there has been no significant progress in state secondary education in the UK in the past 50 years - except the abolition of corporal punishment, which was only achieved through pressure from European human rights laws. Secondary school for most children remains the same grim, joyless day-prison that's it's essentially been for more than a century. Delight in learning, zest for knowledge - these, should a kid somehow retain them into adolescence - rarely have any connection with school; for most kids school means long hours of sitting bored in oppressive rooms crowded in with other kids just itching to be free - each of them with their own unique interests and concerns, and, under threat of punishment, having to behave in ways that conflict with virtually all natural instincts. For them - or most of them - the entire concept of 'Education' is turned on its head, making it something to dread rather than relish.

Except perhaps in a few universities, there seems almost no awareness of the Neill or Hesse psychology or of the real needs of youth. Nor does there appear to be a genuine will to create a truly educational environment. In fact, from all appearances, 'education' remains a mechanism for preserving the status quo, for keeping juveniles off the streets, for producing factory and office fodder as required by the corporate regime we live under and for turning creative minds into ones that are sedate, unquestioning and conformist... minds that will generally obey almost any conditioning and accept, grudgingly or otherwise, a soundly embedded mediocrity and fate.

It wasn't necessary to read anything to be aware of the above, but it may well have drifted from my mind altogether and become relegated to a dead and mostly forgotten past - as doubtless happens for most adults once they are free from the compulsory reins of so called 'education' - were it not for the resurrection inspired by Hesse's autobiographical essays. This, though, is just one detail of many that emerge from Hesse's work. Hence there follows a slightly more comprehensive perspective.

> "*Remember, dear friends, now and then, just for a moment: how short life is.*" Hermann Hesse

What initially impressed me about Hesse was the way his work dramatically changed my attitude to books and even life in general - and I was well into my thirties when I discovered him. Chiefly, at first, it was his expression of intangible inner experiences that made the greatest impact. These seemed to match precisely what I felt but had not until then been aware of, even less been able to articulate to myself. His work was both new and familiar, and seemed to address remote yet important aspects of thought - subconscious thought. Science, politics and other conscious intellectual issues were things that one could take or leave according to circumstances.

Hesse's work, on the other hand, concerned all of existence - inner and outer world alike, and the curious relation between them.

With a wholly different perspective to that taken by existentialism, this new approach was not so much optimistic and intuitive - as compared with the predominately pessimistic, rationalistic overtones of existentialism - but was eminently artistic and beautiful despite its essential tragic component.

Such was my 'education' that it is a shameful and telling fact that I had scarcely heard of Herman Hesse until, as I say, I was almost 35 - even then, it was by sheer chance that I discovered him. The younger brother of a friend had begun a degree course in literature. This brother had lent him one the books on his reading list: Hesse's 'Knulp' (1915).

From the cover:

> 'Knulp is the eternal vagabond. Haunted by a sense of the perishable nature of everything, he keeps on the move. But, as for everyone, the sunny days of good health give way to illness and decline. Even an aimless life, he realises, has some purpose... erratic and irresponsible, yet always with warmth and fellow-feeling, Knulp followed his nomadic instinct to the last.'

This yearning for vagrancy preoccupied Hesse for most of his life. Perhaps we are all wanderers at heart, and like Hesse half-despise the dull comforts afforded by our normally settled lives which we cannot bring ourselves to relinquish but which we know can be suffocating. Anyone who has travelled abroad 'on a shoestring' will know the immense joy of being free from the cares and concerns, routines and attachments, that invade the settled life.

Living in the time and place that he did, Hesse's life was not free of despair, and was in fact a kind of sad fairytale (See Freedman's 'Pilgrim of Crisis'). But his work touches the heart as Dostoyevsky's touches the intellect. Together these authors demonstrate the pinnacle of human achievement in art. Yet literature, at least in their case, is more than art - the art is in the compelling form and structure, the skill of articulation, of clarity and apparent simplicity, of poignant philosophies interwoven into a strange beauty of language that flows from the sincerity of natural genius; but it also contains elements from within us, usually inaccessible and inexpressible, mysterious yet meaningful, elements which we instantly recognise and lock-on to, mesmerised, astonished, shaken, as by a lucid dream.

Most of Hesse's work is at surface simple and clear, but to the novice it is also strange and mysterious. It is tempting to believe, as I did while reading Hesse, that one is being guided along a divine path, a path that will ultimately lead to some wonderful realisation, some undreamt-of fulfilment - even nirvana itself. We are induced into believing we are moving towards a destiny in paradise, or at the very least a destiny that will reveal some glorious final solution to the greatest problems and questions of life and existence. We are buoyed-up and carried along like the children who followed the pied piper - we imagine ourselves transported from our mundane and chaotic lives into a landscape of untold beauty and ultimate inner peacefulness, and the promise of great beyonds... This is what happens for Anselm at the conclusion of Hesse's remarkable story '*Iris*'.

'*The Journey to the East*', though, is perhaps his most poignant treatise of all. And we can easily relate to it, for each of our lives is a journey, sometimes smooth, bathed in sunshine and adorned with flowers... sometimes rough and barren, festooned with stones beneath turbulent skies. But although he sets us going in leaps, one soon realises that Hesse's journey was exclusively his own, and can belong to no-one but him. Like Leo in the story, we suddenly realise we've lost our way, and just as Leo seeks to return to his lost 'path', so can we.

On the back of my copy of '*The Journey to the East*' is written:

"...is the story of a youthful pilgrimage that seemingly failed. As the book opens, the narrator is engaged in writing the chronicle of this remembered adventure - the central experience of his youth. As he becomes immersed in retelling the chronicle, the writer realises that only he has failed, that the youthful pilgrimage continues in a shining and mysterious way."

It's impossible to avoid falling under the spell, of believing that this is all our chronicles, that we all have failed, but that unknown to us, because of our adult blindness - caused by years of becoming increasingly lost, of unrelenting diversions from what we inwardly know should be our true course if only we had the courage to follow it - unknown to us, the great universal pilgrimage goes on; we have only to open our eyes... Luckily, the book is small, about 100 pages, because I confess that I had to read it several times before I began to sense its significance.

So Hesse's fiction is not always easy to penetrate fully, yet it is very easy to read and understand to the depth one needs to see, or is prepared to make the effort to see, which can be enhanced by relating one piece of his work to another. For instance, some of the poems attached to 'The Glass Bead Game' loom into clarity when one has read the autobiographical sketches: 'Childhood of a Magician', 'From My Schooldays', 'Life Story Briefly Told' etc. And the locations for 'Klingsor's Last Summer' (my favourite story – see Appendix 10) can be found on a map.

In contrast to the vaguely surreal aspect to most of his work, Hesse wrote many essays. Some examine particular subjects such as 'Notes on The Idiot by Dostoyevsky' or 'Happiness' or 'Interpreting Kafka' while others are of a more penetrating, critical nature. The latter are among his most incisive, containing none of the usual mystery. Here he was addressing the intellect and intended us to be in no doubt. They concern serious issues - of the moment: 'Letter to a Young German', 'World Crisis and Books' - and of all time: 'History', 'Dream After Work', 'Self-will'. Curiously, even those of the moment have a timeless quality. *'Letter to a Young German'* is as worthy of attention in 2003 as when it was written in 1919 immediately after the first world war; it was intended to persuade German youth to listen to their own hearts instead of to a dictator, to propaganda or the proverbial crowd - as so many of us unwittingly do. There are many others, as I've said, but I think *'Self-will'* is one of the most appropriate for all time. Here's a section from it:

> "THERE is one virtue that I love, and only one. I call it self-will. - ...True, all the virtues man has devised for himself might be subsumed under a single head: obedience. But the question is: whom are we to obey? For self-will is also obedience. But all the other virtues, the virtues that are so highly esteemed and praised, consist in obedience to man-made laws. Self-will is the only virtue that takes no account of these laws. A self-willed man obeys a different law, the one law I hold absolutely sacred - the law in himself, his own 'will'.

> It is a great pity that self-will should be held in such low esteem! Do men think well of it? Oh no, they regard it as a vice or at best as a deplorable aberration. They call it by its eloquent full name only where it arouses antagonism and hatred. (Come to think of it, true virtues always arouse antagonism and hatred. Witness Socrates, Jesus, Giordano Bruno, and all other self-willed men.)...

> There are only two poor accursed beings on earth who are excluded from following this eternal call and from being, growing, living, and dying as an inborn and deeply ingrained self-will commands. Only man and the domestic animals he has tamed are condemned to obey, not the law of life and growth, but other laws that are made by men and from time to time broken and changed by men. And the strangest part of it is that those few who have disregarded these arbitrary laws to follow their own natural law have come to be revered as heroes and liberators - though most of them were persecuted in their lifetime. The same mankind which praises obedience to its

arbitrary laws as the supreme virtue of the living reserves its eternal pantheon for those who have defied those laws and preferred to die rather than betray their 'self-will'."

That was written in 1919. It isn't, of course, necessary to take Hesse's philosophy - or anyone else's for that matter - seriously. Nor should one necessarily agree with it - as he suggests: examine your own will, your own soul. What matters, as with all literature, is that it triggers thought and inspires new outlooks on existence.

If any hardnuts reading this think Hesse's work mawkish or soppy, it isn't. If I've made it seem so then I've done it (and you) a disservice, for which I apologise. If you haven't already, try it for yourself. Some of his work - whole books even - are available on the web.

Since it is now out of copyright I think it's worth reproducing what to me represents Hesse's most outstanding beautiful work. A couple of sections from *'Klingsor's last Summer'*:

See Appendix - 10

Eugène Ionesco
(1909 – 1994)

A major voice in *'The Theatre of the Absurd'*. More playwright than prose writer, I nevertheless find his prose especially unusually gripping. He did write one intriguing little novel *'The Hermit'*, but his most powerful writings are autobiographical: reflections on his thoughts as a child above all, but on his work as a playwright and how early experience influenced the direction of his thoughts, his most profound thoughts on issues that affect us all yet most of us prefer to avoid: essentially the bleakness and isolation we inevitably endure as individuals, our knowledge of our inevitable death... He probes more deeply and extensively than Camus did in his lyrical essays, and doesn't cheat - ie, the supernatural or religion or afterlife are not in his arena - so he examines aspects like nostalgia! This can be of immense value (as Dostoyevsky has mentioned: how some minor event as a child can be of crucial importance in later years). Merely how we remember and the various unique and crucial associations of memory - while realising that we are only our memories - reveals angles we scarcely if ever notice or realise. If we suddenly forgot everything, we'd be no different to a slug.....

A minor example: when as a 3 or 4-year-old walking along a road I was given a cheese biscuit just as a fire-engine with its alarm going rushed past. For many years afterwards, whenever I tasted one of those cheese biscuits, images of a fire-engine would loom in my mind. The power of associations like this can be huge. They affect how we react to all kinds of issues, and without realising why. The scope for investigation here is endless.

Ionesco quote from a book of his plays:

'His plays can be seen as a way to liberation, for as he said: "*To attack the absurdity [of our predicament - the human condition] is a way of stating the possibility of non-absurdity... For where else would there be a point of reference?... Nothing makes me more pessimistic than the obligation not to be pessimistic. I feel that every message of despair is the statement of a situation from which everybody must freely try to find a way out.*" '

Franz Kafka
(1883 – 1924)

As we grow-up and develop our interpretations of the world, slowly building experience, weighing-up each new and unique event so that it gives us the best possible understanding of the world - and therefore the soundest possible footings for handling what is to come - we are, in effect, constructing a great edifice. We aspire to what we perceive as the most desirable outcome, and what we achieve is dependent upon our surroundings and our skill in reacting appropriately to events. We assess, categorise and file everything. In other words, we create and continually update a kind of contingent picture that represents our provisional interpretation of the world; and this is our raw, our only material.

Empirical psychology tells us that if we are brought up where we experience kindness and consistency above all, then we stand a good chance of building a solid and unbreakable structure, a foundation impervious to the knocks and bruises of life. This is imperative for lifelong contentment and stability. If, conversely, our foundations are littered with inconsistencies, hostility and confusion, then we will have nothing solid to build on, we will distrust much of what we learn, and will be inclined to construct an unstable, disorderly structure, or perhaps a very simple or feeble one based on any consistencies we can sift from this muddled experience.

Few people's foundations are entirely solid or entirely unstable. And there are all kinds of strategies that people develop to deal with the inevitable anomalies.

Franz Kafka is probably one of the most enigmatic and most analysed of all great figures of literature. When I've read some of the biographical details of his early years, I've had the impression that Kafka reached a point where, unlike most of us, he no longer felt able to build upwards and move forward. The flaws in his experience were beyond repair, and could not be reconciled. This seems to shows through in his most famous book '*The Trial*' which contains the mysterious fable:

BEFORE THE LAW.

> *BEFORE THE LAW stands a doorkeeper. To this doorkeeper there comes a man from the country and prays for admittance to the Law. But the doorkeeper says that he cannot grant admittance at the moment. The man thinks it over and then asks if he will be allowed in later. "It is possible," says the doorkeeper, "but not at the moment." Since the gate stands open, as usual, and the doorkeeper steps to one side, the man stoops to peer through the gateway into the interior. Observing that, the doorkeeper laughs and says: "If you are so drawn to it, just try to go in despite my veto. But take note: I am powerful. And I am only the least of the doorkeepers. From hall to hall there is one doorkeeper after another, each more powerful than the last. The third doorkeeper is already so terrible that even I cannot bear to look at him." These are difficulties the man from the country has not expected; the Law, he thinks, should surely be accessible at all times and to everyone, but as he now takes a closer look at the doorkeeper in his fur coat, with his big sharp nose and long, thin' black Tartar beard, he decides that it is better to wait until he gets permission to enter. The doorkeeper gives him a stool and lets him sit down at one side of the door. There he sits for days and years. He makes many attempts to be admitted, and wearies the doorkeeper by his importunity. The doorkeeper frequently has little interviews with him, asking him questions about his home and many other things, but the questions are put indifferently, as great lords put them, and always finish with the statement that he cannot be let in yet. The*

man, who has furnished himself with many things for his journey, sacrifices all he has, however valuable, to bribe the doorkeeper. The doorkeeper accepts everything, but always with the remark: "I am only taking it to keep you from thinking you have omitted anything." During these many years the man fixes his attention almost continuously on the doorkeeper. He forgets the other doorkeepers, and this first one seems to him the sole obstacle preventing access to the Law. He curses his bad luck, in his early years boldly and later, as he grows old, he only grumbles to himself. He becomes childish, and since in his yearlong contemplation of the doorkeeper he has come to know even the fleas in his fur collar, he begs the fleas as well to help him and to change the doorkeepers mind. At length his eyesight begins to fail, and he does not know whether the world is really darker or whether his eyes are only deceiving him. Yet in his darkness he is now aware of a radiance that streams inextinguishably from the gateway of the Law. Now he has not very long to live. Before he dies, all his experiences in these long years gather themselves in his head to one point, a question he has not yet asked the doorkeeper. He waves him nearer, since he can no longer raise his stiffening body. The doorkeeper has to bend low toward him, for the difference in height between them has altered much to the man's disadvantage. "What do you want to know now?" asks the doorkeeper; "you are insatiable." "Everyone strives to reach the law," says the man, "so how does it happen that for all these many years no one but myself has ever begged for admittance?" The doorkeeper recognizes that the man has reached his end, and, to let his failing senses catch the words, roars in his ear: "No one else could ever be admitted here, since this gate was made only for you. I am now going to shut it."

This brief parable seems to demonstrate the immense frustration from feeling utterly and inexplicably trapped, of being blocked, almost before stepping out, yet at the same time retaining or being given false hopes (surely one of the cruellest tortures?) as you look forward to your great journey through life - a prospect that tends to wane with age. And this obstruction, this barrier, set up by what appears as some huge whimsical power-structure that reveals nothing of its unfathomable demands, still less of its function or purpose, apparently expecting its victim to somehow assess these and thereby earn admittance (as though to some esoteric ancient order), is utterly impervious. All the while this repulsive entity (the 'door-keeper'), observing its victims' predicament with complete indifference, no hints of what he might do to gain favour, no pity or compassion for his failure, not even sympathy for his wasted inconsequential life of waiting, dreaming and hoping, all in vain - then suddenly, without warning, when one is too old, too incapacitated, too ill, shuts the door... the chance to 'live' is gone forever and fulfilment on any scale is permanently denied.

One could dwell on this for hours or even years. Unable, so it seems, to interpret the world as most people do, even those with shaky foundations, Kafka turned instead to examine his inner edifice. And what he found was so fascinating that he could not rest until he had scrutinised every corner. The essence of the predicament he unearthed lies, I think, in the parable:

AN IMPERIAL MESSAGE.

> *The Emperor, so a parable runs, has sent a message to you, the humble subject the insignificant shadow cowering in the remotest distance before the imperial sun; the Emperor from his deathbed has sent a message to you alone. He has commanded the messenger to kneel down by the bed, and has whispered the message to him; so much store did he lay on it that he ordered the messenger to whisper it back into his ear again. Then by a nod of the head he has confirmed that it is right. Yes, before the assembled spectators of his death - all the obstructing walls have been broken down, and on the spacious and loftily mounting open staircases stand in a ring the great princes of the Empire before all these he*

has delivered his message. The messenger immediately sets out on his journey; a powerful, an indefatigable man; now pushing with his right arm, now with his left, he cleaves a way for himself through the throng; if he encounters resistance he points to his breast, where the symbol of the sun glitters; the way is made easier for him than it would be for any other man. But the multitudes are so vast; their numbers have no end. If he could reach the open fields how fast he would fly, and soon doubtless you would hear the welcome hammering of his fists on your door. But instead how vainly does he wear out his strength; still he is only making his way through the chambers of the innermost palace; never will he get to the end of them; and if he succeeded in that nothing would be gained; he must next fight his way down the stair; and if he succeeded in that nothing would be gained; the courts would still have to be crossed; and after the courts the second outer palace; and once more stairs and courts; and once more another palace; and so on for thousands of years; and if at last he should burst through the outermost gate-but never, never can that happen-the imperial capital would lie before him, the centre of the world, crammed to bursting with its own sediment. Nobody could fight his way through here even with a message from a dead man. But you sit at your window when evening falls and dream it to yourself.

Almost all Kafka's stories portray a vision of life that verges on the nightmare, of being imprisoned in a labyrinthine world of incomprehensibility. Every effort to penetrate or escape this endless network of mazes, to fathom its true nature, its true purpose, is frustrated and then augmented by even greater entrapment and confusion.

In many ways, human life, like Kafka's novels and stories, is riddled not only with mystery but with impenetrable hierarchy and bureaucracy, and we - or most of us, so it appears - are pawns to be shuttled about, unwittingly exploited and diverted from all attempts to infiltrate or understand what is actually going on. Indeed, so powerful is the propaganda on which we are nurtured from virtually the day we're born, that we scarcely ever awaken to our true circumstances.

Curiously, this same convoluted intricacy also reflects various aspects of the natural world if viewed from an appropriate perspective. It can be seen to represent the nature of our own minds too, the nature of life in its primitive state, and the nature of human societies and, as just mentioned, the structures within them.

Perhaps, like chaos theory, this phenomenon applies also to the nature of matter and the universe in general - as though Kafka somehow uniquely perceived it, a condition of the universe, in the same way that Einstein noticed relativity (which can be easily demonstrated). Both concepts are childishly fundamental, yet signify profound concepts with immensely complex and wide-ranging consequences. For the physical reality of this, one has only to look at the body (human, insect, whatever), to see that essentially these comprise little more than an elaborate multiplicity of interconnected pipes, fibres, wires and junctions.

A few years ago I wrote my interpretation of Kafka's predicament as a portrayal of social hierarchy - which is how it most literally appears in *'The Castle'* and, using the law as its symbol, in *'The Trial'* - both of which also show clear elements of paranoia in the protagonist, as though the warren of bewilderment is actually, or chiefly, within his mind (and the reader is invited to share this paranoia).

In contrast to such mature nightmarish renditions, Kafka's (unfinished) first novel *'Amerika'* - originally called *'Lost Without Trace'* - ends with its protagonist optimistically embarking on a great and promising enterprise: by joining *'The Nature Theatre of Oklahoma'* in which all are welcome to participate. Unlike his subsequent works this novel shows the labyrinth (ie, 'the theatre'), together with its multifarious participants and officials, to be entirely friendly and accommodating. Although mysterious and all-engulfing, it is profoundly optimistic; the future may be unknown but it is unquestionably glorious, full of wonder and expectation. Its only menacing aspect being in its apparent mesmerizing of seemingly gullible clients and the implication that those who fail to surrender are somehow inhuman, odd, unsociable loners or misfits; they are blind to what they will miss, unbelieving of the great future they reject through a vague cynicism that Kafka could only distantly sense at this time.

Probably, Kafka wrote 'Amerika' at that point in his life from which he could no longer advance but was not yet convinced of the permanency of his condition, not yet entirely aware of the cynical aspect - hence, it was only subsequently that the glitter and joy of the theatre (of life) became instead the threat of an overbearing structure in which we are all inescapably snared: within our own isolated selves, essentially forever alone in a bleak and inexplicable universe, within too a world consisting chiefly of bodily needs and drives, social obligations, the law, family demands etc; though from these latter, unlike the other entrapments, it is possible to take practical steps to flee.

The inevitable conclusion from this kind of preoccupation, the ultimate consequences for the individual who arrives tired and old like the protagonist in the above parable 'Before The Law', is clearly illustrated in the following extract from Pirandello's 'Henry V'.

To avoid absurd responsibilities Henry has feigned madness (after secretly recovering from actual madness caused by bumping his head), dressing up, acting strangely, etc, until he is at last exposed, upon which, with animated sarcasm, he announces:

> *Henry: Ah - then, away, away with this masquerade, this incubus! Let's open the windows, breathe life once again! Away! Away! Let's run out!.... (then quietly, slowly) But where? And to do what? To show myself to all, secretly, as Henry IV, not like this, but arm in arm with you, among my dear friends?*

Belcredi: What are you saying?

Donna Matilda: Who could think it? It's not to be imagined. It was an accident.
Henry: They all said I was mad before. (to Belcredi) And you know it! You were more ferocious than anyone against those who tried to defend me.

Belcredi: Oh, that was only a joke!

Henry: Look at my hair.

Belcredi: But mine is grey too!

Henry: Yes, with this difference: that mine went grey here, as Henry IV, do you understand? And I never knew it! I perceived it all of a sudden, one day, when I opened my eyes; and I was terrified because I understood at once that not only had my hair gone grey, but that I was all grey, inside; that everything had fallen to pieces, that everything was finished; and I was going to arrive, hungry as a wolf, at a banquet which had already been cleared away...

Significant lines that arrest the attention are those disturbing perennial conundrums: 'To go where? and 'To do what?' And the end of the extract presents the most poignant observation of all (inseparable from those questions): ie, How easy to become so immersed in some 'distraction' that one day, after years of blindly 'playing the game', you wake up and wonder where your life has gone, and that 'the banquet' is over.

When he was near to death from TB Kafka requested his best friend, Max Brod, to burn all his unpublished work - which was most of it.

From all accounts it was a serious request, and I can only imagine that his reason was to spare people the anguish of perceiving the world as he did: analogous to being born in, and destined to remain in, an infinite catacomb. It's a dismal outlook, because without diminishing the importance of this outlook, other angles of perception tell us that there is an outside, that beyond our catacomb there is a true free open universe for us to partake in, but in Kafka's context it is eternally inaccessible - just as the outer world is inaccessible to a fish in the ocean (both physically and psychologically).

Few people, it seems, are aware of this curious aspect of the world that Kafka articulated so clearly. But for those who do see it (consciously - probably we all see it subconsciously), or at least glimpse it, the task is to then locate that outer universe which surrounds us, is in us, and to attempt to enter it, to explore it, to experience it - perhaps, apart from a few exceptions, for the first time in history. Perhaps this is what the schools of transcendental meditation would claim can be achieved from years of meditation, or from years of unrestrained humility and compassion.

Or perhaps it will only be universally accomplished when children are finally reared for the first time in genuine freedom, at least for their first year or so of life. It should be realized that genuine freedom is probably as hard to achieve as genuine blankness of mind; and its practice, socially, is made virtually impossible due to an overwhelming prejudicial opposition to freedom from those who use the word most (especially right-wing politicians - who make irrational laws of restraint that have nothing to do with protecting the weak from the strong... rather, the opposite).

Fortunately, due to the foresight of Max Brod, Kafka's work survives. Kafka may not have been able to see beyond his immediate scenario of stagnated desolation and futility, but for some of us, with our more liberating foundations, he has highlighted an altogether new perspective from which we can proceed. Thanks to Kafka, we now have a broader vision and can view the world more completely. Without his perspective we might not have noticed this crucial aspect of our predicament so clearly, if at all, and our ability to move forward would certainly have been diminished. But now that we have been shown, we see it clearly and bearing it in mind can evolve in ways that would otherwise have been impossible.

CONCERNING THE DESTRUCTION OF WHAT WE CREATE:

As I see it, on a universal reckoning, no-one can be owned by another: no child belongs to their parents or the government of the country they are born in; no-one can ever be owned. We belong only to ourselves - or to the universe (consider the difference!). It's what we create that belongs to others, to humanity. Kafka had the power to destroy his work, and might have had he seen fit to do so while he was able; but did he have the right? What would he have gained from such destruction? What would we have lost?

After taking eight years to write his masterpiece, *'Dead Souls'*, Gogol wrote a sequel which he considered much superior, but then he succumbed to religious fanatics who drove him mad and persuaded him to burn it. A small portion was rescued and appears somewhat unpromising. But what we have lost we shall never know. Equally, one might ask, how much work of any artistic genre remains in dusty attics until eventually, unexamined, it gets piled onto a bonfire and is lost forever? Undoubtedly, vast quantities of dross inevitably and mercifully goes this way. And in the process perhaps some works of genius go too. If so, how much does this matter? The masterful sand paintings of the Dalai Lama and his followers are destroyed upon completion, and huge painstakingly created ice-sculptures melt in the spring sunshine. The whole process of life involves continual creation and destruction. One should, I believe, always consider the following, taken from the frontpiece by Swami Vivekananda of Henry Miller's *'The Air-conditioned Nightmare'*:

> *"The greatest men in the world have passed away unknown. The Buddhas and the Christs that we know are but second rate heroes in comparison with the greatest men of whom the world knows nothing. Hundreds of these unknown heroes have lived in every country*

working silently. Silently they live and silently they pass away; and in time their thoughts find expression in Buddhas or Christs; and it is these latter that become known to us. The highest men do not seek to get any name or fame from their knowledge. They leave their ideas to the world; they put forth no claims for themselves and establish no schools or systems in their name. Their whole nature shrinks from such a thing. They are the pure Sattvikas, who can never make any stir but only melt down in love..."

As for Kafka, in all his humility and compassion, we must be grateful for his legacy and give some time to examining where it might lead us.

Jack Kerouac
(1922 – 1969)

Kerouac embraced implicitly those same elements of revolt as Camus: slave versus master, poor versus rich - though for Man versus creation he did so with explicit fervour. He also embraced the joys of youth as Camus did, though in rather different tones and circumstances. The frenzied, eventful to-ing and fro-ing across America, the wild antics and adventures he and other prominent-to-be individuals enjoyed, should be an inspiration to us all - just as Camus's Algerian sun and sea should.

Most notably there was Burroughs, Ginsberg, and above all the amazing restive prankster Neal Cassady - each outstanding in their way. With fantastic letters flying between them when geographically separated, hilarious frantic jaunts when together, life to them was one vast nomadic poem to be exploited for all it had, drenching them in the whole milieu of splendour and dissipation alike, the deep philosophic meanderings, endless lurching from one hectic stunt to the next. Kerouac frequently alludes to death in his work too, and finally ended his days in drunken oblivion. One intoxicated episode is vividly described in his *'Big Sur'* - a location I well remember on the Californian coast south of San Francisco.

But Kerouac's most outstanding and famous literary achievement was *'On The Road'*. This essentially autobiographical extravaganza became, and perhaps still is, seen by some as a kind of bible that sets the scene and introduces some well known identifiable characters. *'The Dharma Bums'*, which is more 'on the path' than 'on the road' is another great work, but one of the most penetrating, I think, is 'Desolation Angels'. In Part One he describes the several months he spent alone as a Fire-Watcher on Desolation Peak (in the north-east corner of North Cascades National Park, Washington State). It's a gripping tale. But in Part Two, called 'Passing Through' he's back on the road once more. He's older now, a little weary. The melancholy that previously seemed to hang subtly between the lines (especially in his later work and regardless of the raucous high-spirits) now predominates. And with increased poignancy the prose becomes more poetic too. Here's a brief extract:

'I simply walked away with my rucksack on my back, to the station, got on the bus and fell asleep, with the pack by the driver's well. When I woke up in Roanoke Rapids at dawn it was gone. Somebody had taken it off at Richmond. I let my head fall on the seat in that harsh glare nowhere worse in the world than in America with a stupid guilty hangover. A whole new novel (Angels of Desolation), a whole book of poems, and the finishing chapters of another novel (about Tristessa), together with all the paintings not to mention the only gear I had in the world (sleepingbag, poncho, sweater of holy favor, perfect simple equipments the result of years' thinking), gone, all gone. I started to cry. And I looked up and saw the bleak pines by the bleak mills of Roanoke Rapids with one final despair, like the despair of a man who has nothing left to do but leave the earth forever. Soldiers waited for the bus smoking. Fat old North Carolinians watched hands aback clasped. Sunday morning, I empty of my little tricks to make life liveable. An empty orphan sitting nowhere, sick and crying. Like dying I saw all the years flash by, all the efforts my father had made to make living something to be interested about but only ending in death, blank death in the glare of automobile day, automobile cemeteries, whole parking lots of cemeteries everywhere. I saw the glum faces of my mother, of Irwin, of Julien, of Ruth, all trying to make it go on believing without hope. College students in the back of the bus making me even sicker to think of their purple plans all in

time to end blind in an automobile cemetery insurance office for nothing... Where's yonder old mule buried in those piny barrens or did the buzzard just eat? Caca, all the world caca. I remembered the enormous despair of when I was 24 sitting in my mother's house all day while she worked in the shoe factory, in fact sitting in my father's death chair, staring like a bust of Goethe at nothing. Getting up once in a while to plunk sonatas on the piano, sonatas of my own spontaneous invention, then falling on the bed crying. Looking out the window at the glare of automobiles on Crossbay Boulevard. Bending my head over my first novel too sick to go on. Wondering about Goldsmith and Johnson how they burped sorrow by their firesides in a life that was too long. That's what my father told me the night before he died, 'Life is too long.' '

(Luckily, the driver had moved his rucksack to the luggage hold.)

Kerouac led a hard yet glorious life. Regardless of whether conditions were favourable, he drained what he could from it - the maximum, if you discount longevity. His work, shortly before he died so prematurely at 47 (about the same age as Camus when the car he was in hit a tree), has the tone one might expect of an old soldier, containing the cynical reflections of a burnt-out hero. I read in one of the many biographies, that he left $85 (or some such miniscule amount). Now his estate is worth $millions. A few years ago radio 4 transmitted '*On The Road*' read masterfully by Toby Stevens. I recorded this 2½ hour reading and frequently listen to it when driving between here and Cambridgeshire to visit my mother. I never tire of it: the spontaneous prose, the constant light-hearted yet intense analyses of life, the mad unrelenting zestful pursuit of adventure, the quest to 'dig' (appreciate, enjoy, understand) everything, to discover what IT is all about, what IT means. To think that he originally typed this novel in just a few rushed days on a single roll of paper; to think, when completed he threw it unravelling across his publisher's office; to think this 'short-sighted' publisher rejected it and told him to go home and type it properly... Well, that was several years before it finally and belatedly reached publication in 1957.

THE BEATS, though, were innovators for a new 'jazzed-up' kind of literature, as described, to as near as possible resemble the music... inspired by prankster Neal Cassady, rendered into prose by Jack Kerouac (as he read on TV in his musical voice) and into Beat poetry from Allen Ginsberg - most notably in his seminal masterpiece 'HOWL' (outstanding film version released 2010). The book 'On The Road' represents the essence of this 'ordered' spontaneity, this escape from tradition, this journey into wild adventure... which in less restive form I myself attempted to emulate when I charged off to the US back in 1989, bought an estate car and drove 16,000 miles in 6-months.

Imagine the contrast, I thought when on a London's Earls Court tube station I saw a huge poster advertising the film of 'On the Road' showing a cactus filled semi-desert: with Kerouac's 1950s car disappearing towards the hills leaving a cloud of dust: Tube-station to desert – imagine, you're underground, waiting for a train to megatropolis nowhere... when, for no reason you know of, you suddenly turn 180º and facing you is the vast Arizona desert - so realistic you feel that you could just step over that edge into the space of it, into the dry sun-baked heat, and wander among cactuses, breathe the scent of the sage scrub, through the settling dust of Kerouac's car, to follow his trail into the parched open desert towards distant blue mountains of the soul...

But The BEATS .... they're enough to get anyone - even a less than half-adventurous dunderhead - hooked, and striding along with them... because their aspirations and aims were quite NEW and the outpourings based on experience were pretty much ALL non-fiction... OK, there are augmentations, and restraints... one fact that's emerged in recent years is that actually there was very little restraint: just censorship as ordained by original publishers who were more concerned with making dough than promoting risqué avant-garde art/literature which, to be fair, was yet to be tested on general readers. Which can't be said of Henry Miller's first publisher (of his groundbreaking *'Tropic-of Cancer'* 'autobiography' all of two-decades earlier) who was, as if anyone wouldn't have guessed, French.

Who were The Beats, though? There were maybe 10 or so, going by all the (now identified) pseudonymous characters in the various novels and poems... and depending on precisely how you want to define the term. Kerouac was one more than any, but also Ginsberg, Burroughs and especially Cassady.... who maybe was the chief catalyst in creating that fantastic Beat literature that swiftly evolved as might a perpetual improvised jazz that ticks and jolts along like a wild crazy machine - imagine here Ken Kesey's weird psychedelic bus 'Further'; Cassady (who else?) at the wheel - yet you can't make yourself get off, can't put the book down... because you're there in those pages careening along, not out of control - quite - but wayward and free and it's *f-a-b-u-l-o-u-s*... like floating in a mad luxuriant sea, splashing with intoxicating elixirs that hit you in the brain with random ecstatic zaps.

Reminds me of me as a kid with no adults around, charging down hills like a maniac on a six-wheeler soap-box cart I made out of a couple of old prams back in the 50s... and for ever after was blamed for depleting my dad's nail box. Then discovering some crazy old neglected half-destroyed house, across fields miles from anywhere, way beyond anywhere I'd been before, exploring the lethal stairs, the even more lethal cellar...

HERE's an amazing extract from Gerald Nicosia's huge 767-page masterpiece biography of Kerouac *'Memory Babe'*, which I read decades ago, a tome my hand removed from the shelf almost involuntarily the other day while on one of those occasional whimsical perusings mentioned at the start of this commentary... and which perchance fell open at page-336:

> *The only way out of self-conscious art, he [Jack] felt, lay along the lines of modern musical composition, as in the work of Bartok and Schonberg. Jack wanted to discover*

"the basic tones of existence" as they were embodied in both characters and the human character generically. With those tones he would organize variations as in jazz, using his "knowledge of the 'IT' of feeling." Such writing would comprise large amounts of dialogue, and the endless talk would be structured by the classic jazz pattern of "18 bars, bridge, and takeout 8 bars." If one character got to really "blowing," Jack would let him keep taking further "choruses" until all his emotions were spent. By bringing different combinations of characters together in discussions, he could achieve the effect of instruments responding to one another in a band. As he explained the technique to Ed White: "When No. 1 talks to No. 2 and No. 3, it is not the same as No. I talking to No. 2 alone, or 2 and 3 discussing 1, or all three silent together, or 3 alone in his eternity." When all the characters fell into a silence, the author's voice would take over as a "choral hymn" or "oratorio."

This complicated form derived from Jack's perception of the small number of character types any writer has to work with. He was looking to expand literature beyond the limited range of possible plot situations, just as bop musicians had broken free of the repertoire of swing melodies by reaching for a broader harmonic spread. What is often missed—and Jack discussed this fact with Tom Livornese—is that bop derives its interesting quality not so much from its immediate conception as from its larger musical base. Quite simply, a bop composition has more tones available to it to build from. Creating an equivalent to bop in writing depended upon the author's ability to find new ways of looking at old things. Jack now had a form for this literary music—what he called "Organized Variations on a Theme on Existence"—but he lacked the content: the "tones" themselves.

...it was Neal Cassady who finally gave him a clear answer. On December 30,1950, Jack received a 23,000-word typewritten letter from Neal, which Jack pronounced "the greatest story" he'd ever read by an

American writer. In the letter, Neal poured out his heart ...the subject of the story was, most remarkably, the development of Neal's "soul."

Jack was astonished that Neal had found a way to write about intensely real things like miscarriages and dwarfish cabdrivers, which were too sordid, grisly. or improbable for most literature. These were things he himself hadn't yet learned how to organise into a single narrative, though he considered them the most important things to tell about. Jack thought Neal's letter a "novelette" that "outmatches Céline, Wolfe; matches Dostoyevsky in its highest moments; has all of Joyce at its command. . ." No writer before had made him know so completely the thoughts of a young homeless man in jail, or made him feel so deeply a motherless man's vast need for women or a jailbird's haunting fear of arrest. Above all, he was mortified by the humility with which Neal produced such a masterpiece, for Neal didn't even consider himself a writer, whereas Jack truly believed him "a much greater writer than I am."

Though Jack doubted that either Brierly or Giroux [publishers] would acknowledge Neal's genius, he saw the letter as a watershed in literary history, marking the start of an "American Renaissance." Not only did Neal now "belong to the world," but Jack predicted a wave of American writers would follow in his footsteps. Outcasts and madmen, rising "from the streets and the land with a language," would give the nation "a vision all their own, eloquent, confessional, sublime and pure."

...Jack thought it ranked with Dostoyevsky's 'Notes from Underground'...

(...which sends me straight to my Dostoyevsky section - to re-read that amazing novella Kerouac refers to.) But add to this the impressive account revealed in his friend, John Clellon Holmes's '*Go*' (1952), which perhaps forms the literary forerunner of Beat literature as in most of Jack's works, esp

'On The Road', and Ginsberg's groundbreaking poems, and you have a toxic brew of a brand new sensational breakthrough in literary art, the equivalent of which is yet to be repeated - though perhaps the astonishing unique art of Gabriel Garcia Marquez is an exception, especially his 'One Hundred Years of Solitude'.

Well... I could dish out several pages of extracts and perspectives on various intriguing gripping styles and approaches from many a random pick from the numerous bookshelves here. But as ever, if I didn't restrict myself to a mere glimpse - as above - I'd never get around to REALLY living... like right now: the sun's crashing in, there's a gentle breeze, no clouds, the tide is high, the sea-water's crystal clear (never known it so clean here as this year)... and I'm all ready to SCARPER!

But before I do, I should mention, needlessly I guess, that after going the rounds, Cassady's 23,000-word 'masterpiece' ended up with some hapless dude on an ancient houseboat which sank rather suddenly... and in a rush to escape drowning the famed document was forgotten... so like Gogol's 'Dead Souls - part-2' yet another 'great' art-work becomes lost to posterity.

Am still working out some kind of subconscious appraisal of the film '*ON THE ROAD*' which was probably about as good as anyone could create in film of Kerouac's masterpiece. Creations of this kind take time to sink in before the most seminal qualities bounce onto the surface of consciousness. A fine objective 3000-word review by Mick Brown appeared in the Telegraph last month. Here's a key paragraph:

> In 1951, after completing the first draft of On the Road, he wrote in his journal, 'I'm lost, but my work is found.' He had discovered his voice as a writer – personal, spontaneous, uncensored. But his life was already beginning its descent into chaos. Drink, and the Benzedrine he took to fuel his writing, had begun to exact their toll. In the six years between completing On the Road and its publication in 1957, he wrote a further eight

autobiographical novels, none of them finding a publisher, which left him depleted and despairing of ever achieving recognition.

So the capsules they were breaking open in the film were Benzedrine after all. But reading of Kerouac's (uncharacteristic?) yearning for recognition, explains in part why he went off the rails: six whole years, a further eight novels, and none finding a publisher. I recall reading how Ginsberg (for one) had told him this new work of his, the new style of it, was outstanding.... yet still it failed to get published.

When, many years ago, I read for the first time those opening lines of '*ON THE ROAD*' I was gripped. Now, having recently bought a copy of the original manuscript - with no chapters or paragraphs, just continual spontaneous prose for almost 400-pages.... I find it even more gripping.... Why did publishers reject it? Were they already too wealthy? Were they just monumentally stupid/bigoted/narrow-minded, only interested in what most youth then or now would regard as banal, trite or pap... only interested, that is, in what was ultra-safe? Maybe Kerouac should have sent his expletive-laden manuscript to Henry Miller's French publishers (of '*The Tropic of Cancer*' 17-years earlier - if they still existed after WW2), or one like them? Ironically, Kerouac himself was of French ancestry.

Maybe the publisher(s?) Kerouac approached were versions of an arrogant Steve Allen (ie, see youtube) and were offended by Kerouac's confidence and his unconventional presentation of the manuscript: typed on a big roll of teletype paper so that nothing would interrupt the spontaneous flow of words as he poured them out over three solid weeks, he threw this scroll in one great joyful unrolling flourish across the publisher's office. Without bothering even to glance at the manuscript, 'Go home and type it properly.' (or words to that effect) was the publisher's impassive response... as if the principal responsibility was not to read submissions, but to tame or punish what was regarded as unruly juvenile behaviour. (Lucky for that publisher it wasn't another Lermontov in his office!)

But probably, many publishers then belonged to the same ilk as the respondents in the recent Telegraph film review reader-replies. The Telegraph is renowned for its literary quality as much as for its right-wing political slant - which means most of its readers will lack the background/ability to recognise or appreciate authentic innovative prose from an outstanding artist like Kerouac (or, I guess, Ginsberg for 'HOWL').

Here's a couple of examples:

> *1) ...as Western civilization rots from within, more cultural pollution such as this film doesn't help. Bad enough the pre-boomer and boomer generations were led astray by adolescent bohemian romances like Kerouac's, but it's simply unpardonable for them to promote this rubbish to the current generation. Unlike Kerouac, Cassady et al. and the legions who imitated them, real men and women find true freedom in commitment and the acceptance of responsibility.*

> *2) I used to like the idea of the 'beats' when I was younger, but the reality never lived up to the idea. And now it just seems to me a load of adolescent navel gazing.*

These respondents represent the tired, worn-out disillusioned conformist types who instead of blaming the stuffy, straight-laced Establishment propaganda they fell for (and is the true source of their angst), they unload their gripes onto the targets of their greatest envy: the intrepid escapees (and subsequent disciples and followers) who used their outstanding intellect to grasp the maximum from this short life and record their experiences as a lesson for us all - and without exploiting anyone in the process. Only the two most prominent - Cassady and Kerouac - failed to enjoy a mostly rich and fulfilling longevity.

But the phrase *'true freedom* [is found] *in commitment and the acceptance of responsibility'* is a classic oxymoron that's akin to the counter-logic of the old Nazi propaganda slogan: '*Work sets you free.*' (How anyone can believe such tosh is a complete mystery to me - which I suppose explains why I'd never work in advertising or the creation of other propaganda). Obviously, it's the very *absence* of responsibility/work (if one could achieve that) which sets us free.

Another possible reason for the delay of publication is that even when censored and castrated to the hilt '*On The Road*' was still just too anti-establishment: too creative, too innovative, too adventurous, too spontaneous, broke too many taboos, shattered too many boundaries, was too free, too anarchic, too joyful, too accessible, TOO REAL.... when beside it the rest of the population (ie, Edward Bernays' propaganda-controlled slave-nation) had their lives mapped-out for them on the treadmill of 'enterprise', of commerce, of factories/offices/shops and other slave-holes... in mind-numbing 'careers'... as ordained by the corporate elite. By the time a publisher was eventually found, Elvis Presley and Bill Hayley were going strong, Kinsey's famous report had been published and Serling's '*Twilight Zone*' was high on TV viewing charts, and even then they insisted on a heavily censored script with its most powerful/telling sections edited or removed.

The film retains the atmosphere of the book as much as a film can. Still, as often happens, the book is better. From what I've read of the original so far - which is essentially the one the film follows - it is a distinct improvement on the old censored version, which. hopefully will fall out of favour and cease to be printed/published - since strictly it should never have existed in the first place... it's not what its author intended. And I wonder how much better: more spontaneous, more fluid and flowing, more sensational, more vibrant and musical even, his other books would have been had Kerouac not suffered the constant threat of that insane censorious 'sword-of-Damocles' the publishers held over him all those years, of removing the tone, the spirit, the essence, the REALITY from his groundbreaking prose?

I guess the corporate Establishment these days realises that even if many young people are persuaded or 'converted' by the wisdom of it, only an insignificant few are likely to attempt to emulate Kerouac's jaunts. And they know too that any attempts to suppress or censor are likely to create a backlash - so no overt efforts against Kerouac's original manuscript or the film... except, according to what I'm told, reviews have been mostly negative. So the regressive, reactionary fuddy-duddy brigade remain a force to be reckoned with. But how often one reads book-or-film reviews that vary precisely according to the publication they're in... that is, however good, say, a politically 'left' book/film, it will probably receive negative reviews in the right-wing press, especially (though unlike The Telegraph) in mass-market rags like The Mail.

Laurie Lee
(1914 – 1997)

Laurie Lee is, like Hemingway, also someone I wouldn't have been especially keen to meet. Although I liked his other books, the one that impressed me most is exceptional. '*As I Walked Out One Midsummer Morning*'. You can follow this guy in the (mostly) downs, but some nice ups too, of his trip around Spain way back in the 1930s - as if you're there with him, suffering the same (often self-induced) hardships and enjoying the same delights. After the first few pages, before he even arrives in London, you completely forget you're reading and can merge with him, share his experiences as though in the here and now. One impressive aspect of this book is that it could so easily have been deadly boring, but for the incredible skill of its author to render the most mundane situations (which most of us can easily relate to) in fascinating or attractive ways without mawkish or flowery prose... as, in fact, he somehow manages to use to great effect in his ingeniously written '*Cider With Rosy*'. His book '*A Moment of War*' about his misadventures when he returned to Spain to help the republicans fight the Fascists is, on the other hand, very plainly written - though compelling nonetheless.

David Lindsay.
(1876 – 1945)

I first learned of the existence of David Lindsay and his remarkable fantasy '*A Voyage to Arcturus*' from Colin Wilson's superb book '*The Craft of the Novel*' - which introduced me to quite a range of new literature I'd have otherwise not found....

Anyone reading '*...Arcturus*' should realise they need to wade through the first 30 or so pages before the real adventure begins. At which point the story takes off with a vengeance, and in a way that - if one wishes to make a comparison - renders the recent film '*Avatar*' (2011) like a pathetic amateur forerunner.

Lindsay's imagination exceeds anything so far the 21st C has coughed-up... probably, the writer(s) of '*Avatar*' took some ideas from Lindsay's great work, except the film falls massively short. There's plenty of philosophy there too, which I guess is what attracted Wilson as well as the lively optimistic dream-like adventure.

Lindsay's other books I've read – '*The Sphinx*' and '*The Haunted Woman*' – are in no way outstanding like '*...Arcturus*' but they have a very weird atmosphere, as if you're on another planet or, like Lewis Carol's '*Alice through the Looking Glass*' the story takes place in what feels like a parallel universe that's right alongside where we are now but not quite accessible – except in these two novels you entry becomes possible. It's sci-fi without the 'sci'; or perhaps, though unlike anything M R James ever wrote, they could be called ghost stories?

-
-
-
-
-

Henry Miller
(1891 – 1980)

Henry Miller - what a guy.... I reckon the account of his friend Alfred Perles in the portrait of him (see appendix 10) from their days in Paris in the 1930s, tells more about Miller than the acquaintance in the extract - and more than could be gleaned from his work, which is essentially autobiographical, yet much more than that. Nearly all Miller's work is solid with reflections and assessments of all kinds of aspects of life and circumstances and people, always positive, philosophical, rational: '*Always Merry and Bright*' (1978) - as goes the title of a huge biography by Jay Martin. Miller's views on the work of other authors are exclusively affirmative: Giono, for instance, and Cendrars.

See Appendix 11: From Chapter 3 of '*My Friend Henry Miller*' by Alfred Perles.

Miller is definitely a guy I'd like to have known and associated with – except he'd have soon got bored with me, I'm sure. He may have seemed naïve but he was a Buddhist at heart, enlightened, a man who saw reality and respected it, moulded to it, enjoyed it, however absurd it might have appeared. What else for a man who writes on the first page of his most famous and autobiographical book: '*The Tropic of Cancer*':

> "*I have no money, no resources, no hopes. I am the happiest man alive.*"

He may have had his moods (don't we all?) as perhaps over-dramatised in the superb cult film '*Henry & June*', though not if his friend Perles is anything to go by on June and on their period in Paris in the 1930s.- but he'd have been great company anytime. If only I could know people like that now.... it's as if my life is ebbing away in the absence of such company.... or am I being sentimental, self-pitying... obtuse?

See Appendix 12 - From p-28 of Henry Miller's 1957: '*Big Sur and the Oranges of Hieronymus Bosch*'.

But my favourite quote from Miller is from page 45 of the book he liked best of all his work: the superbly written '*Colossal of Maroussi*' about his period in Greece during 1939 as a guest of his friend Lawrence Durrell:

> *I would set out in the morning and look for new coves and inlets in which to swim. There was never a soul about. I was like Robinson Crusoe on the island of Tobago. For hours at a stretch I would lie in the sun doing nothing, thinking of nothing. To keep the mind empty is a feat, a very healthful feat too. To be silent the whole day long, see no newspaper, hear no radio, listen to no gossip, be thoroughly and completely lazy, thoroughly and completely indifferent to the fate of the world is the finest medicine a man can give himself. The book-learning gradually dribbles away; problems melt and dissolve; ties are gently severed; thinking, when you deign to indulge in it, becomes very primitive; the body becomes a new and wonderful instrument; you look at plants or stones or fish with different eyes; you wonder what people are struggling to accomplish by their frenzied activities; you know there is a war on but you haven't the faintest idea what it's about or why people should enjoy killing one another; you look at a place like Albania - it was constantly staring me in the eyes - and you say to yourself, yesterday it was Greek, today it's Italian, tomorrow it may be German or Japanese, and you let it be anything it chooses to be. When you're right with yourself it doesn't matter what flag is flying over your head or who owns what or whether you speak English or Monongahela. The absence of newspapers, the absence*

of news about what men are doing in different parts of the world to make life more livable or unlivable is the greatest single boon….

·
·
·
·
·

Alberto Moravia
(1907 – 1990)

It was at a *'Practical Philosophy'* group I'd decided to join in Hastings back in 1993 where I met Alan Bula who introduced me – or rather, nudged me to read the work of famous Italian novelist and commentator Alberto Moravia. Until then I'd ignored tattered copies in second-hand bookshops of perhaps Moravia's best known novel *'The Woman of Rome*' which opens thus:

> *At sixteen years of age I was a real beauty. I had a perfectly oval face, narrow at the temples and widening out a little below; my eyes were large, gentle and elongated; my nose formed one straight line with my forehead; my mouth was large, with beautiful full red lips, and when I laughed I showed very white, regular teeth. Mother used to say I looked like a Madonna.*

And so begins the 389-page monologue of Adriana who, in revealing herself so candidly, 'unwittingly' exposes so much about the rest of us and of our lives. At the time, I found this first-person style especially gripping. I'm not sure that it would carry me so effectively now, but it turned out to be a remarkable work which I was very glad to have read. For instance, from near the middle:

> *My room looked on to the courtyard, through the closed window no noise reached me from outside. I used to doze for awhile, then got up and wandered round the room, busy with some little task, such as tidying my things or dusting the furniture. These jobs were nothing more*

than a stimulus to set my mind working, an attempt to create an atmosphere of intense and secluded intimacy. I used to become more and more deeply immersed in my reflections, until in the end I hardly thought at all, and was content with feeling alive after so much wasted time and exhausting ways.

At a certain moment a profound feeling of bewilderment always overcame me during the hours I spent in such solitary seclusion; I suddenly seemed to see the whole of my life and all of myself from all sides, with icy clearsightedness. The things I was doing were doubled, lost the substance of their meaning, were reduced to mere incomprehensible, absurd externals. I used to say to myself: "I often bring home a man who has been waiting for me in the night, without knowing me. We struggle with one another on this bed, clutching each other like two sworn enemies. Then he gives me a piece of printed, coloured paper. Next day I exchange this piece of paper for food, clothes and other articles." But these phrases were only the first step in a process of deeper bewilderment. They served to clear my mind of the judgment always lying in wait there about my profession, and they showed me my profession as a series of meaningless gestures, similar in every way to the gestures of other professions.

Immediately afterwards a distant sound in the city or the creaking of some piece of furniture in the room gave me a ludicrous and almost hectic realisation of my existence. I said to myself: "Here I am and I might be elsewhere - I might exist a thousand years ago or in a thousand years' time - I might be a negress or an old woman, fair or short - " I thought how I had come out of endless night and would soon go on into another endless night and that my brief passing was marked only by absurd and casual actions. I then understood that my distress was caused not by what I was doing but more profoundly by the bare fact of being alive, which was neither good nor evil but only painful and meaningless.

My dismay used to make my flesh creep with fear for a few moments; I used to shudder uncontrollably, feeling my hair stand on end, and suddenly the walls of my fiat, the city and even the world seemed to vanish, leaving me suspended in dark, empty, endless space - suspended, what's more, in the same clothes, with the same memories, name and profession. A girl called Adriana suspended against nothingness. Nothingness seemed to me something terrible, solemn and incomprehensible, and the saddest aspect of the whole matter was my meeting this nothingness with the manners and outward appearance I bore in the evening when I used to meet Gisella in the confectioner's where she waited for me. I found no consolation in the idea that other people also acted and moved in just as futile and inadequate a way as I did when faced with this nothingness, within this nothingness, surrounded by this nothingness. I was only amazed at their not noticing it, or not making their observations known, not referring more often to it, as usually happens when many people all at once discover the same fact.

I thought it was strange that I was so different alone from what I was in company, in my relationship with myself and with other people. But I did not flatter myself that I was the only one to have such violent and desperate feelings. I imagined everyone, at least once a day, must feel his own life reduced to a single point of absurd, ineffable anguish - except that their knowledge apparently produced no visible effect upon them, either. They left their houses as I did, and went around playing sincerely their insincere parts. This thought strengthened me in my belief that all men, without exception, deserve to be pitied, if only because they are alive

This is precisely the kind of narrative that raises consciousness, inspires reflection on the human condition, and forces one to focus on aspects of reality that we normally miss. Illusion and delusion dissolve, and one senses for a moment the intensity of our predicament, our mortality, how fleeting life is and how inconsequential our lives are. All of which in the words of a despairing yet reflective Adriana is that each of us is not only inescapably trapped but also isolated at some bleak indifferent point in an interminable void of time and space.

Like many profound aspects of existence, this kind of analysis and revelation risks sounding banal in these 'new-age' days of so called 'enlightenment'.

Soon after *'The Woman of Rome'* came Moravia's next most highly regarded work *'The Conformist'*. This is a third-person political novel in which the protagonist is a Fascist murderer. It contains sections where the style flows in a kind of 'stream-of-consciousness' fashion not unlike that of Virginia Woolf - and one I attempted (somewhat hopelessly) to emulate. Another big novel *'Two Women'* is an epic tale that follows the fate of two women during WW2 and in which I soon became immersed. I recall particularly, though, his *'Two Adolescents - Agostino and Disobedience'* with some affection - probably because 'disobedience' has always attracted me and represented an angle I could easily relate to. But *'A Ghost at Noon'* with its scenario that parallels (or emulates) that great quest in Homer's *'Odyssey'* was perhaps the most intriguing of all Moravia's work. The short stories too are truly masterful.

There's one superb little tale I cannot properly recall, where the plot is something along the lines of a malign character visiting his barber for a shave - only cutthroat razors in those days! - and who gradually realises, when his shave is underway and he is 'trapped' in the barber's chair, that the barber is aware that this man once cheated him. All the while the razor dances ominously around the man's throat as the barber, tightening the neck-towel and voicing reprimands whenever his victim moves, coolly relates his misfortunes to the man whose ordeal is almost unbearable to read. Curiously, I couldn't take the grin off my face all the way through - from my amused admiration of Moravia's immense skill and cunning.

Raymond Chandler - whose novels I read many years ago - said it was a good idea for a budding writer to imitate the work of those they admired. He, for instance, would take a Hammett short story and rewrite it in his own words; and even reckoned he could considerably improve a story this way.

Taking his advice, I tried attempting Moravia's style, which I much admired at the time. The result turned out nothing like it, but it did cause me to generate something rather different from what would otherwise have been possible. To make the attempt easier - as I saw it - I adopted a young-girl's monologue as Moravia had in 'The Woman of Rome'. I called the result: 'City Kid' and it's Ok, and to be found in my BIG book of stories: 'Tales of the Abnormal'. I didn't attempt the method again.

-
-
-
-
-

Jean Rhys
(1890 – 1979)

I haven't been too struck by women writers. This is probably because few of them write in the genres I've gone for like Asimov on scientific and sci-fi, Serling with imagination and marginal, Steinbeck for political and social, Dostoyevsky's psychological, Camus and Kafka on the existential and philosophical…. Etc.

Dorothy Parker's stories are compelling, though, and Joan Didion's essays. But Jean Rhys's *'Good Morning, Midnight'* (1939) is an outstanding existential treatise from her time living more-or-less destitute in 1930s Paris. It's far more real and alive, for instance, than Rilke's rather stilted *'The Notebooks of Malte Laurids Brigge'* written from his experiences of 'dismal poverty' three decades earlier in Paris – 'a city to die in' – though William Gass's 19-page introduction to Rilke's 'memoir/journal' is outstanding.

From the cover of Rhys's *'The Collected Short Stories'* (51 of them from three separate periods of her life):

> *…this collection contains some of her most dazzling and entertaining writing. Here are seedy hotels and bars in bohemian Paris, ruinous love affairs, Caribbean childhoods, ex-chorus girls in London bedsits, old ladies in drunken, genteel poverty; always outsiders, always close to the edge. Told with painful clarity and sharp humour…*

Luckily for Rhys - and us - she ran into Ford Maddox Ford while in Paris, otherwise we mightn't have any of her work – though

I guess publishers back then (especially in France, going by Miller's first publication of his *'Tropic of Cancer'* there) were not so 'precious' as now, nor were they swamped, I'd imagine, with populist trash that sells and makes the publishers rich, so had time (and diligence back then) to check any manuscript that landed on their desk (see page 13 of this book).

Part-1 of *'The Wide Sargasso Sea'*, Rhys's most famous book, gives a fine evocative portrayal of her first 16-years of life in Dominica.

Here's a short excerpt from *'Good Morning, Midnight'*:

> *Walking to the music of L'Arttsienne, remembering the coat I wore then - a black-and-white check with hig pockets. We have just passed the hotel I lived in. That was the high spot - when I had nothing to eat for three weeks, except coffee and a croissant in the morning.*
>
> *I slept most of the time. Probably that was why it was so easy. If I had had to go about a lot I might have felt worse. I got so that I could sleep fifteen hours out of the twenty-four.*
>
> *Twice I said I was ill, and they sent me up soup with meat in it from downstairs, and I could get an occasional bottle of wine on tick from the shop round the corner. It wasn't starvation at all when you come to think of it. Still, I'm not saying that there weren't some curious moments.*
> *After the first week I made up my mind to kill myself -the usual whiff of chloroform. Next week, or next month, or next year I'll kill myself. But I might as well last out my month's rent, which has been paid up, and my credit for breakfasts in the morning.*
>
> *'My child, don't hurry. You have eternity in front of you.' She used to say that sarcastically, Sister Marie-Augustine, because I was so slow. But the phrase stayed with me. I have eternity in front of me. Soon I'll be able to do it, but there's no hurry. Eternity is in front of me....*
>
> *Usually, in the interval between my afternoon sleep and my night sleep I went for a walk, turned up the Boulevard Arago, walked to a certain spot and turned*

back. And one evening I was walking along with my hands in the pockets of my coat and my head down. This was the time when I got in the habit of walking with my head down. ... I was walking along in a dream, a haze, when a man came up and spoke to me.

This is unhoped-for. It's also quite unwanted. What I really want to do is to go for my usual walk, get a bottle of wine on tick and go back to the hotel to sleep.

William Saroyan
(1908 – 1981)

William Saroyan is a real favourite of mine. Virtually everything he wrote reads like autobiography and hooks the reader instantly – or does me. In that respect he's a bit like Raymond Carver, though his work is very different. Saroyan has written about all kinds of experiences that children and young people especially can relate to, crazy juvenile stunts and incidents, and as in his classic *'The Daring Young Man on the Flying Trapeze'* the struggles of a young guy trying to 'make-it' in a cut-throat world. He was particularly focused on 'the human condition' – ie, a favourite extract of mine is back on page 24. But this is the first page of a brilliant story – as he says a *'serious'* one (deadly serious): *Seventy-Thousand Assyrians*:

> *I hadn't had a haircut in forty days and forty nights, and I was beginning to look like several violinists out of work. You know the look: genius gone to pot, and ready to join the Communist Party. We barbarians from Asia Minor are hairy people: when we need a haircut, we need a. haircut. It was so bad, I had outgrown my only hat. (I am writing a serious story, perhaps one of the most serious I shall ever write. That is why I am being flippant. Readers of Sherwood Anderson will begin to understand what I am saving after a while; they will know that my laughter is rather sad.) I was a young man in need of a haircut, so I went down to Third Street (San Francisco), to the Barber College, for a fifteen-cent haircut.*
>
> > *Third Street, below Howard, is a district; think of the Bowery in New York, Main Street in Los Angeles: think of*

*old men and boys, out of work, hanging around, smoking Bull Durham, talking about the government, waiting for something to turn up, simply waiting. It was a Monday morning in August and a lot of the tramps had come to the shop to brighten up a bit. The Japanese boy who was working over the free chair had a waiting list of eleven; all the other chairs were occupied. I sat down and began to wait. Outside, as Hemingway (*The Sun Also Rises; A Farewell to Arms; Death in the Afternoon; Winner Take Nothing*) would say, haircuts were four bits. I had twenty cents and a half pack of Bull Durham. I rolled a cigarette, handed the pack to one of my contemporaries who looked in need of nicotine, and inhaled the dry smoke, thinking of America, what was going on politically, economically, spiritually.*

When he was first recognised for his writing skill he claimed he could write a story a day for a month and did so with all the stories, I believe, turning out well and being published. But to keep-up that kind of pace would challenge the best writers. Maybe exceptional commentators like Alistair Cook in his journalism perhaps, though not every day.

Jean-Paul Sartre

(1905 – 1980)

My perspective on Sartre is a bit mixed. I mean some of his work is easy to read, some is very convoluted and detailed in its analyses. Below is essentially a general appraisal of the image I'm left with after dipping into several of his works and reading what others have said about him and his ideas regarding existentialism, politics and culture etc.:

Although Sartre analysed a range of observations on the human condition, he is most famous for his quote: "Man is condemned to be free." - a statement that has ambiguous implications.

Since most establishments or governments seek to absolve themselves from the obligation to protect the most vulnerable in society, they will invariably grasp at such notions as evidence that an individual's circumstances are predominately (or usually) of their own making - hence undeserving of help.

Moreover, these same establishments have never been slow to indoctrinate the masses with this same propaganda, so that confused victims of a corrupt political system will often blame themselves for conditions resulting from corrupt practices.

Let's examine this from the beginning. For man, said Sartre, existence precedes essence ('I AM therefore I THINK' - the opposite of Descartes). So far, fine. Nothing wrong with that - after all, one has to exist before one can think or 'be what one is'. But Sartre interprets this further to mean: "...that the very 'nothingness' [blank-slate] of our essence in a world without meaning allows each of us infinite potentialities in shaping our life - limited only by the facts of the external world..." (from 'Readers Encyclopaedia' 1965).

Facts of the external world must include, surely, indoctrination and other strong early influences. These can determine the power we have over whether or not to refuse this potentiality for shaping our life. By opting for religion or some other distraction from reality we are, says Sartre, choosing to refuse - since as much as it being a liberation, 'responsibility-for-oneself' can be seen as a burden from which some of us will attempt to escape. Sartre used the term 'inauthentic' to describe a choice made under delusion, such as opting for religion, a choice Camus regarded as (philosophical) suicide as described in his '*The Myth of Sisyphus*'.

So the idea of infinite potentiality (free-choice) appears all very fine in theory. In practise, though, it fails because our essence is not 'nothingness' - it has, in addition to worldly constraints, to contend with culture, indoctrination, propaganda, etc. Yet it led to that famous quote: "Man is condemned to be free."

Way back around 1760 Rousseau had said, after contemplating humankind in its earlier natural pre-'civilisation' state of freedom: "*...but nevertheless is everywhere in chains.*"

The fact is, Rousseau was right. Most of our lives are spent essentially as for a traveller: tracing a narrow path. We can wander a little to one side or the other, but essentially we are stuck - as in the old days when your bike-wheel caught in a tramline and like it or not you were forced to follow its route. From our moment of birth, we are in a rut - channelled according to the circumstances of our immediate situation.

For one thing we are rooted to the human condition, as a cat or a bird is rooted to its condition. A cat behaves, generally speaking, as one might expect a cat to behave. Likewise, within individual variations, we too are stuck with our genetic make-up. Uniquely, though - ignoring borderline cases like bonobos and dolphins - we humans with our bicameral mind have the freedom to choose whether or not to stray from these limitations. My argument here is that this freedom is largely dependent on circumstances, above all the circumstances of our birth.

I've quoted Shaw's maxim so often that I'm almost sick of it: 'Do what you like or you'll end up liking what you do.' That's the crux of the predicament - and is what forms part of those chains we are everywhere in. What we like or what we choose, is - and can only be - from what we know, what we're used to and familiar with, what is within our experience to assess and evaluate and make sense of. It's also a survival ploy: ie, 'the devil you know'.

True, 'the grass is always greener', and 'a change is as good as a rest' and several other tired old maxims, but any alteration we make to our situation will be entirely within the limits set by our past - it takes a damn HARD knock to get us up and out of our rut, and ready to exercise some minuscule degree of genuine freedom, to diverge beyond the mere narrow zigzagging around - back and forth across but always within the confines of that set path we started out on.

There are always exceptions - someone has to win the lottery. But generally, apart from accident (as, for instance, in Twain's fiction: 'The Prince and the Pauper'), there's no way can we leave our set path and go leaping into an unknown hell or paradise that lurks awaiting our discovery in some formerly unperceived boondocks or other. To do that requires transformation, real initiative, a daring so rare and profound that whoever achieves it will at first be met with surprise, then vilification, and perhaps eventually (if they're really lucky) popular-approval and celebration. Shocked or envious to begin with, we come to admire such audacity, foresight, genius - for seeing what we didn't, for doing what we failed to.

I'm not talking about entrepreneurs, inventors, those who suddenly chuck their job and go travelling or start living 'in-the-raw', or those who throw everything they have into some mad quest that's been bugging them. No, what I'm taking about here is: moving into an entirely different realm.

Literature is solid with such conversions. They are the lifeblood of escapist novels - and for that matter the so-called non-fiction of 'self-help' in the form of wishful thinking, which is also a means of escape. And perhaps there are a few real-life ones too - but for which the seed, the 'software', must first exist from which might bloom some seemingly astonishing or incongruous revolution. Like Jean Valjean in Victor Hugo's 'Les Misérables': honest peasant to hardened convict to reformed humanitarian, etc - though as we readers follow the tale, each transition is seen as almost reasonable, given the circumstances and the liberal, yielding nature of the protagonist.

It's true that our lives involve making decisions almost every minute of the day, usually very minor ones: should I buy this hat, or that one? Should I holiday in Alicante or relax at home? Should I follow the fashion and keep in lockstep with the masses, or should I do what I'd do if I had no knowledge of what others were doing? This, should I be authentic? And if so, then how far am I prepared to take my authenticity?

As Sartre developed it, fundamental meaninglessness is a precondition for Existentialism. The apparent pessimism of what he called 'Nausea' (and clarifies in his novel of that name: a kind of sickness as with the boredom of a life void of any prescribed meaning) does not lead to nihilism but to the active assumption of (or aspiration towards) moral responsibility - of being actively engaged in the shaping of one's life - ie, of creating one's own meaning.

Camus, on the other hand, posed the idea that the only real philosophical problem to confront man was suicide - whether to terminate the 'nausea' or come to terms with it - and went on to stress the plight of man's need for clarity and rationality in confrontation with the unreasonable silence of the universe. The suicide Camus refers to is philosophical: the ditching of responsibility to accept an underlying objective meaninglessness. The emphasis here is on religion as a cop-out, an escape from reality, but could include becoming a workaholic or otherwise immersing oneself in some activity. Camus voiced the tragedy of man's failure to assume proper consciousness of his condition, or, if he does assume that consciousness, the failure to find the human values by which he can shape his life. (I feel obliged to append that last statement with the observation that most people - do they really live lives of quiet despair? - would probably find all this rather bemusing and academic, conducting their lives for the most part with reasonable satisfaction and contentment - blissfully oblivious of the proverbial abyss).

Those two paragraphs (not including my parenthetic endnote) show how Sartre and Camus concurred. But to say we are free is like saying a computer (even if all computers have the same fundamental operating system) can do anything - subject to inherent limitations: like the cat, remember? Yet it is obvious that a computer can only work according to what software it has. If it contains 'Auto-route' then it will know it's way around Europe. Otherwise it won't have a clue. And so on. How, then, I ask, can man be said to be free?

In my case, I don't even have any choice of whether I believe in an afterlife. My brain refuses to acknowledge such a possibility. Is this connected with upbringing? I don't think so, since I was brought-up as a Christian. I wish afterlife was true. I have no wish for ceasing to exist. I know some people do: who say how they would like to die before they reach 100. Well, I think, you'll be a long time dead - so why wish it sooner than later? But that's another issue.

Sartre invested several decades in the academic study and analysis of his hypotheses. And, as I've said, his key hypothesis (quite apart from Sartre) has been widely assumed for a long time. So the consequences of what Sartre said probably has nothing to do with the immense harm the notion has caused through its popular acceptance (which for all I know - I'm far too lazy to research this - may have existed, despite all the evidence that contradicts it, before Sartre was even born):

That is, the wild misconception that each of us has total free choice in shaping our life - which tragically has often led to the notion that ignorance and squalor are deliberate and self-induced and therefore undeserving of rescue.

I suppose, though, the diehards will insist that we do have free choice - like the computers: one computer will be free to travel (albeit vicariously) around Europe, while the other will be free to stay put. This equates to a poignant line from the socialist alphabet which to clarify the true meaning of the word 'freedom' Tony Benn has frequently quoted: 'F is for freedom that the Tories brag about, free to buy your dinner or free to go without.' In other words freedom in this sense is a myth - a Hobson's choice, a con for the gullible masses to digest. And so is it too regarding our actual range of freedom in how we can shape our lives.

The person who declares a keen interest in writing, but who had no real access to books as a child or received only discouragement - the person who never heard a violin as a child, then loved the sound as a teenager but was discouraged or prevented from having a violin - or whatever equivalent example - how much choice do they have?

No, you might say, they can still learn. But they can't. They will always be at a disadvantage. All this speaks for itself. We know.

Returning to Sartre: he did acknowledge the observations I outline above, as well as many others, objections and so on. And he was always flexible and reasonable - an aspect of his character that greatly appeals to me. And despite the severe limitations touched-on above, we nevertheless have vastly more freedom than we are inclined to imagine, and in many senses too. If I'm really determined, I can emigrate, totally change my lifestyle... etc., but would it be the real authentic me? Am I living the real me now? Any philosophy that evokes questions like these is, in my mind, crucial to making our lives more worthwhile.

"The existentialist...thinks it very distressing that God does not exist, because all possibility of finding values in a heaven of ideas disappears along with Him; there can no longer be a priori of God, since there is no infinite and perfect consciousness to think it. Nowhere is it written that the Good exists, that we must be honest, that we must not lie; because the fact is that we are on a plane where there are only men. Dostoyevsky said, If God didn't exist, everything would be possible. That is the very starting point of existentialism. Indeed, everything is permissible if God does not exist, and as a result man is forlorn, because neither within him nor without does he find anything to cling to."

-- Jean Paul Sartre

Here, in conclusion, are the words of a famous Existentialist song for Sartre's famous trilogy *'The Roads to Freedom'* (1945) (from memory!):

I asked a stranger: Where will I find,
Doors ever open, men who are kind?
Don't look to heaven, answered he me,
You are the jailer, you turn the key.

The road to freedom lies at your feet,
The road to freedom runs down your street,
Take it and follow, then you will see,
Hearts ever open, men living free.

Hear where the city shuts out the sun,
Once we knew pity, now there is none,
Where is the new day after the night?
Is there a true way back to the light?

The road to freedom lies at your feet,
The road to freedom runs down your street,
What are we here for, when will we see,
Life is a prison; love is the key.

All this might be fascinating enough, but still it remains for me on an intellectual level - since from before reaching my own *'age of reason'* I have not believed in any god, so the issues that arose for Sartre could never have presented themselves to me on any level other than intellectual. See 'Existentialism' in my memoir. '*The First 40-years*'PC)

The accompanying piece was called, '*The Wheatfield*'

> *There is a wheatfield where sun will shine no more,*
> *Once children ran there playing at games of war,*
> *Boys played as heroes till every war was won,*
> *Then flushed and weary, slept beneath the sun.*
>
> *Gunfire called them to another game,*
> *Millions of wheatfields die beneath the flame,*
> *Dead is the harvest where every tree stands bare,*
> *Cross the wheatfield softly, men are sleeping there.*

Rod Serling
(1924 – 1975)

Not many stories grip with the same kind of irresistible hold that Rod Serling's brilliant *'Twilight Zone'* stories have. These, like all the best stories, tackle common human issues and paradoxes but with a twist, and here an element of the surreal that places the reader in an alien yet hazily familiar situation. Some stories examine the 'What if?' - questions that many of us have mused over at some time, like *'Walking Distance'* in which a middle-aged guy returns to the time and place of his youth, as though his desire to experience once more that remembered nostalgic splendour of childhood is so strong that by some mysterious quirk of the universe he is actually able to do - so he even to meet himself as a kid.

Serling, with other writers - most notably Richard Matheson - presents us with these twilight 'realities' then reveals what might transpire if we go that little bit further…. if only we really could have what we think we want. The 'zone' evokes some fabulous ingenious scenarios and the stories develop these to reveal unexpected or surreal outcomes…. Some more compelling than others, of course, and there are many to choose from, more than a hundred excursions to the limits of the imagination – and beyond….

·
·
·
·
·

John Steinbeck

(1902 – 1968)

Steinbeck is most famous for works like '*Of Mice and Men*' and '*The Grapes of Wrath*', which is truly outstanding. I particularly liked too, though, his '*The Wayward Bus*', '*The Moon is Down*' and '*Travels With Charlie*'.

In '*The Wayward Bus*' Steinbeck delves convincingly into the minds of several very diverse people travelling on the bus for their different reasons and destinations, while the bus is delayed. The aims and motivations of each passenger are examined alongside one another in fascinating detail.

'*The Moon is Down*' describes a Nazi occupation in a Norwegian village. The resistance the inhabitants develop is impressive and explained together with failures, the individuals who are strong and those who are weak and succumb to provocation or are unable to tolerate the repression. An interesting study of human nature and resilience.

'*Travels with Charlie*' is non-fiction and describes Steinbeck's journey around the US in his homemade camper van with his dog Charlie. He stops and interviews people who don't recognise him so have no idea who he is, and he doesn't always tell them. A very enjoyable easy read.

-
-
-
-
-

R H Ward
(1910 – 1969)

Richard Heron Ward was an actor and author of both fiction and non-fiction. At one point he used the nom de plume D H Landels. There are good reasons for an author to use a different name, such as Herman Hesse with Emil Sinclair. But what reason could Ward have had? Even so, he used his own name for his best work. I discovered Ward, as with much else back in the 1980s, through Colin Wilson, who in analysing aspects of consciousness cites Wards 222-page *'A Drug-Taker's Notes'* (1957) where he not only describes in minute detail his experiences from six episodes of taking lsd, but examines too how consciousness varies. The concluding chapter 8 is a continuation of chapter 1 *'Consciousness is Not a Constant'*, with the six descriptive chapters between. I'd read Huxley's *'Doors of Perception'* (1954) some years earlier, as well as some of Timothy Leary's expositions. But Ward was so much more articulate in revealing the experience of taking lsd in an almost objective way it seemed to me, how it affected him and how it influenced his thoughts. These insights into consciousness are accessible and enlightening.

Another of Ward's books I much enjoyed was his *'A Gallery of Mirrors'* – from Amazon:

> *'A series of impressions of Ward's life up to the age of eighteen. The book details, chapter by chapter, the influence eighteen different characters had on his personality. Truthfully and beautifully written.'*

Here Ward sets-out 18 exquisite descriptions of individuals he had fleeting acquaintance with in his childhood and youth and who made an impression on him. Mostly eccentrics – who of us do not appear eccentric, and all the more fascinating for it, as perceived by a kid, I wonder? - they are portrayed with great affection by Ward. Intriguingly, none of these depictions, nor any of his work that I've read, tries to 'plug' religion in any sense of the word. Yet it's obvious from his work as well as in the extract below that in a broader sense Ward was a deeply religious guy if also open-minded as verified in this obituary from '*The Times*' 24th December 1969:

'Richard Heron Ward, who died on December 19, aged 59, will be remembered with love and affection, both as a man, and for his writings, by a wide variety of people, and for a very long time. Born at Chesham Bois in 1910, he was educated at Stowe, and on leaving there sought to earn his living by his pen. and as an actor; he succeeded for 40 years, mainly as a writer and never did the quality of his writing drop. He never achieved wide fame; in a sense his qualities were much too good for 'fame'. What he did do throughout his life was to have a deep effect on almost all who read him.

His first novel was published in 1931 and his last book 'Names & Natures' in 1968. In between those two books his output covered the entire spectrum of letters. He was, in the real sense of that misused word, something of a mystic, and in his religious plays this part of his nature is always apparent, and has its effect, simply but deeply, on his audience. These plays, performed up and down the country in churches and church halls, and very widely in America, made his name respected wherever religious drama is played, and to watch a performance of one of his plays in a simple country church, or a great city church, was to take part in a unique and moving experience.

He toured Europe before the war with the Edward Stirling players, and was with the Pilgrim Players in the war, before founding the Adelphi Players, which company spent the war years taking the theatre to factories and camps throughout the country; after the war he was a founder member of the Century Theatre and continued to be associated with this until early this year.

His novels were always written with a construction, clarity and understanding which made them a pleasure to read and his autobiographical works, particularly A Gallery of Mirrors, were on a high level of a difficult art. To read them, and indeed almost everything of his, gives one each time a little more understanding of the human predicament.

Those are the bare bones of what he did. What he was cannot easily be put down on paper. Sufficient to say, perhaps, that those of us lucky enough to know him, loved him.

Thanks to a previous owner, this newspaper clipping was in the sleeve of the copy I bought. So I now have to confess that despite all the positive attributes of it that I've read, I remain ignorant of the lsd experience and to date know it only from authors like Ward, Leary and Huxley. Martin Booth's comprehensive study of drugs and cultures '*Cannabis*' (2003) of which 'The Independent' wrote: "*...this book should be on the shelf of anyone interested in human freedoms and bad laws.*" contains observations on Leary, Watts (see below) and others enjoying all these experiments and excursions into the mysteries and wonders of consciousness. People I've spoken with who've experienced lsd have told me that they never see the material world in the same way again... they have 'seen' what cannot be un-seen.

Our normal perception of the world is hugely attenuated and reduced because it's inappropriate for survival, or would even hinder survival, so we've evolved to block-out most of reality – the parts of reality, for instance, the immense detail our senses even so are actually capable of receiving/perceiving.

.

.

.

.

.

Alan Watts
(1915 – 1973)

I forget when I first discovered Alan Watts and his remarkably articulate and self-evident perspectives on aspects on life that most people are inclined to brush aside or dismiss. As Henry Miller so astutely observed:

"Life, as it is called, is for most of us, one long postponement."

And it is precisely this kind of recognition, I believe, that inspired much of Watts's outstanding analyses in lectures and texts. Despite his death way back in 1973 age only 58, most of these are now freely available in abundance on YouTube and elsewhere, thanks to one of his sons – and doubtless many other followers of his great work.

Watts's books, though, are many and are well worth reading. *'The Wisdom of Insecurity'* (1951) hooked me instantly - compelling and enlightening. His *'The Joyous Cosmology – adventures in the chemistry of consciousness'* (1962) has a 'forward' by Timothy Leary and Richard Alpert – and relates to R H Ward's aforementioned *'A Drug Taker's Notes'* on how hallucinogenic substances such as lsd, psilocybin and mescalin can change consciousness and perspectives to illustrate alternative aspects – or vastly enhanced perceptions - of reality that we are normally unable to assimilate and are unaware of.

From *'Does It Matter':*
> *We need to become vividly aware of our ecology, of our interdependence and virtual identity with all other forms*

of life which the divisive and emboxing methods of our current way of thought prevent us from experiencing. The so-called physical world and the so-called human body are a single process, differentiated only as the heart from the lungs or the head from the feet. In stodgy academic circles I refer to this kind of understanding as "ecological awareness." Elsewhere it would be called "cosmic consciousness" or "mystical experience." However, our intellectual and scientific "establishment" is, in general, still spellbound by the myth that human intelligence and feeling are a fluke of chance in an entirely mechanical and stupid universe— as if figs would grow on thistles or grapes on thorns. But wouldn't it be more reasonable to see the entire scheme of things as continuous with our own consciousness and the marvellous neural organization which, shall we say, sponsors it?

And from *'In My Own Way'*

If we get rid of all wishful thinking and dubious metaphysical speculations, we can hardly doubt that – at a time not too distant – each one of us will simply cease to be. It won't be like going into darkness forever, for there will be neither darkness nor time, nor sense of futility, nor anyone to feel anything about it. Try as best you can to imagine this, and keep at it. The universe will, supposedly, be going on as usual, but for each individual it will be as if it had never happened at all; and even that is saying too much, because there won't be anyone for whom it never happened. Make this prospect as real as possible: the one total certainty. You will be as if you had never existed, which was, however, the way you were before you did exist - and not only you but everything else. Nevertheless, with such an improbable past, here we are. We begin from nothing and end in nothing. You can say that again. Think it over and over, trying to conceive the fact of coming-to never having existed. After a while you will begin to feel rather weird, as if this very apparent something that you are is at the same time nothing at all.

Indeed, you seem to be rather firmly and certainly grounded in nothingness, much as your sight seems to emerge from that total blankness behind your eyes. The weird feeling goes with the fact that you are being introduced to a new common sense, a new logic, in which you are beginning to realize the identity of ku *and* shiki, *void of form. All of a sudden it will strike you that this nothingness is the most potent, magical, basic, and reliable thing you ever thought of, and that the reason you can't form the slightest idea of itis that it's yourself. But not the self you thought you were.*

Watts's philosophical works, though, are very accessible, ie: '*The Way of Zen*' and '*Does it Matter*'. His autobiography '*In My Own Way*' describes how his life evolved from an ordinary childhood in Chislehurst, south east London, to gain the reputation he acquired as a teacher of Zen in California. Serene, composed and cheerful, though never aloof, he is most definitely someone I'd like have met and known.

H G Wells

(1866 – 1946)

H G Wells wrote prolifically on many subjects, both fiction and non-fiction, and especially on politics. He wrote many fine short stories too. I guess his sensational '*The War of the Worlds*' is what most people remember him for. But '*The Time Machine*',, is the key story I associate him with. This is because more than a century after it was written, the description of a distant future as the world is dying, the sun turning into a red-giant and dominating the sky, there has been no scientific assessment since then that has presented an alternative scenario, at least not that I've seen. Which means Wells had a remarkable insight into the likely evolution of the solar-system. Intriguingly, both those stories include serious political issues: War, obviously, in '*The War of the Worlds*', and the two separate human species we meet in the future in '*The Time Machine*': the fair, childlike Eloi, and the savage, simian Morlocks, distant descendants of the contemporary upper and lower classes respectively.

Nathanael West

(1903 – 1940)

I decided to include writer and screenwriter Nathanael West for his *'The Day of the Locust'* (1939) novella that fits well alongside his friend Scott Fitzgerald's *'The Last Tycoon'* and Chandler's *'The Little Sister'* as portrayals of the kind-of anarcho-Fascist Hollywood that prevailed in the 1930s. Or, at least, some aspects of Hollywood then; because despite this, the studios did create some magnificent productions back then. Interesting too that Fitzgerald was working on *'The Last Tycoon'* (1941) soon after West's book was published, and died of heart failure before writing a final draft.

And West was innovative too in his earlier novella depicting the newspaper industry of the time: *'Miss Lonelyhearts'* (1933). Alas, he died young (age 37) in a car crash, the day after Fitzgerald's death.

Colin Wilson

(1931 – 2013)

I reproduce below the start of an article (which appears in full in my book '*Essays & Sketches*' entitled '*Theosophical Sideglance*') describing a two year - one evening a week, term-time – course in 'Practical Philosophy':

There's a section in Camus's '*The Myth of Sisyphus*' under the heading "*An Absurd Reasoning*" that describes more or less what happened to me in the 1980s:

> "*It happens that the stage-sets collapse, rising, tram, four hours in the office or factory, meal, tram, four hours of work, meal, sleep and Monday, Tuesday... according to the same rhythm - this path is easily followed most of the time. But one day the 'why' arises...*"

A common enough situation. In fact, Rhinehart's '*The Dice Man*' encountered the same prospect - though his pioneering solution led to some hair-raising events which most of us would consider beyond the pale. '*The Dice Man*' incidentally, is a gripping read, innovatively existential and absurd too.

Back in 1993, and soon after reading Wilson's '*The Outsider*' (1956), I found in a junk shop an old copy of Colin's second book: '*Religion and the Rebel*' (1957). At the front someone had pencilled, "*Intellectualism - the shortest road to 'going nuts' is to digest the contents of this book!*" How could anyone resist a book with a comment like that in it? I bought it straight away and pencilled underneath, "*you should know!*" It was as expected: superb - despite my aversion to religion. In the introduction Colin mentions precisely the problem cited above by Camus, suggesting that one can acclimatise to the gloom, or revolt - ie, the Outsider. Unlike Colin's outsider, though, I have never disliked myself, only certain aspects of the world of Man around me - which I have often positively despised: its plethora of baubles and trinkets, its preoccupation with farcical competitive sport, its phoney carnivals, its insane murderous squabbles, its endless clamour for collecting - especially wealth and power. All cardboard to me.

When you begin a new job, everything is fresh and new. A year later the freshness has gone, but there is still a flavour of novelty. Five years on, familiarity is complete, you are fully established, a piece of the furniture. After two more years the "robot" is programmed, and Camus's "absurd" scenario begins. I was inclined to call this "disillusionment", a term that was applicable to my own circumstances in another sense: ie, the adverse political changes of the time and the declining morale they provoked. After the freedom and optimism that marked the 60s and early 70s, this reassertion of establishment power presented an abrupt and unwelcome development.

From here on, for nearly 10 years, I worked as an electronics engineer and operator at TV Centre in White City - a comfortable job, meeting interesting people, involved with interesting projects. On the other hand, I began reading Hesse, Kafka, Dostoyevsky and others, watched and was awoken by the late 80s "*Great Explorer*" series on TV (some of whose episodes I worked on), and was unable to ignore the fact that the London traffic was worsening by the day.

Furthermore, Alasdair Milne, the DG, had been sacked for allowing several outstanding productions to reach the screen, which the government saw as subversive; and close on his heels went many worthy producers and other staff. And so began the decline: pre-production censorship of programme material, a trend towards an officious style of management, and so on. When I had joined, morale had been high, now it was at basement level.

At the end of 1988, in a bold attempt to begin a new life, I resigned. On my fortieth birthday (the same day and month, I later discovered, as Ouspensky) I bought a ticket to Miami. A few weeks later in Tallahassee I bought a car, and in the next six months drove sixteen thousand miles.

Somewhere in his work Colin mentions a similar attempt to resolve the problem. He was about half my age at the time and he chose France. But the method failed for Colin because he was skint - he is certainly right about how practical details can intrude. I had £3,000 to draw on, and 6 months later ended up with £1,000 because mostly I slept in the car (an estate) or a tent, and food and fuel were cheap. But I felt free of all normal constraints, especially the "need" for security - perhaps our greatest obstacle - so my brain could free-run: no obligations, no plans, no concerns.

At this time I hadn't so much as heard of Colin. Eighteen months later, at a friend's wedding in Hobart, I was discussing literature with the Groom's brother – we were strolling around a wonderful botanical garden there: "Keep an eye out for anything by Colin Wilson," he said.

Back in England, after a fabulous several months in the antipodes, which was almost as good as my trip in the States, I found Colin's 'A Criminal History of Mankind' in a second-hand bookshop. Until then I'd forgotten my conversation in Hobart, but it all came back to me when I saw Colin's name emblazoned on the cover. Later, as I read it, I was particularly intrigued by the last chapter 'The Sense of Reality' that analyses the ways we can choose to view the world: the worm's-eye view or the birds-eye view. (I'm reminded here of the famous little epithet: *Two prisoners looked out through prison bars: one saw mud, the other saw stars*). This was also a phenomenon examined in some depth by Tolstoy . From then on I searched eagerly for other works by Colin, and within a few weeks had acquired several.

In 1993, having not found it second hand, I finally ordered a copy of his most famous book: '*The Outsider*'. At first, it's apolitical and refreshingly authentic analysis was like a breath of oxygen washing through my brain. When I learned in detail of all the controversy that surrounded its publication - or rather, the events soon thereafter - the breath of oxygen was re-doubled. I guess that says more about me than Colin or '*The Outsider*'.

The controversy, I should add, was how after the initial praise by media commentators for Wilson's '*The Outsider*' was swiftly reversed when it was discovered that he was working-class and not from an elite family or the 'product' of some esteemed Oxcam university.

But quite apart from that I was so impressed with the book that I wrote a little treatise, the accuracy of which I'm now unsure of:

See Appendix 13

Most of Wilson's books, I should say, are very accessible and compellingly written with a friendly if also serious tone. His books that don't concern an aspect of the supernatural are generally well worth reading. I get the impression, though, from some of his publications that he was a bit gullible - vulnerable, as so many people were (and are), to ridiculous scams like Uri Geller created, or tales of poltergeists and flying-saucers. I imagine that people are attracted to such issues simply because it adds mystery to their lives or for the possibility of intrinsic meaning where there's otherwise, as the existentialists claim, no meaning? Who can say? Maybe Carl Jung had the answers, but that's for another tome – though his autobiography '*Memories, Dreams, Reflections*' is truly a masterpiece.

Wilson's biographies of Gurdjieff, Ouspensky, Crowley, Steiner and Jung are all exceptional: concise and delightful easy reading that focuses on key salient features of their lives. His criminology is equally well written: a couple of huge tomes:

'*The Criminal History of Mankind*' is revealing, and his forensic '*Written in Blood*', which I've only dipped into is like many great books: open at any page, begin reading and you just want to keep reading on.

Ten Great Writers

Back in 1988 Channel-4 TV produced a magnificent series of documentaries called '*The Modern World - Ten Great Writers*'.

From the flyleaf of the book that accompanied the series:

At some point between the 1890s and the outbreak of World War Two, a major transformation took place in the arts. 'On or about December 1910, human character changed,' *Virginia Woolf suggested; D H Lawrence proposed that* 'it was in 1915 the old world ended.' *Even with hindsight, it is impossible to date the point of change exactly.*

But if the date is elusive, the founders of the concept of modernity in letters are identified by common consent, and Malcolm Bradbury takes ten of the indisputably great formative authors, writers whose titanic imaginings have re-shaped our concepts of the art, our modes of thought and debate, the habits and conventions of language itself. In this examination of their work, achievement and influence, he shows that the movement was not simply the manifestation of a new spirit, but an incomparable achievement, a great summoning of talent and discovery, a cosmopolitan surge that constantly multiplied in direction, endlessly disagreeing with itself.

This analysis of ten major writers, linked to the television series first screened early in 1988, reappraises monuments of art and understanding, scrutinizes preoccupations and techniques, identifies recurrent themes - the city, internationalism, exile - and provides an overview of writers who, in their awareness of new forms and great transitions, remain our contemporaries, and inescapable presences.

So the focus was on key works of the following ten writers:

Dostoyevsky	Joyce
Ibsen	Eliot
Conrad	Pirandello
Mann	Woolf
Proust	Kafka

In contrast to this, none of these writers appear in a contemporary lists I've seen, nor of a YouTube entitled: *'10 best English novelists of all time'*, maybe only Woolf was actually English? But the above writers should surely have been 12 to include Hesse and Asimov, or even 14 with García Márquez and Henry Miller too. I guess one has to know where to stop, besides which to add more would be to embrace additional aspects to those cited in the above dust-jacket synopsis describing the basis of selection.

Whenever I'm reminded of Conrad, the fabulous Captain MacWhirr comes to mind from his powerful novella *'Typhoon'*, published with two other great works of note: *'Youth'*, and *'Heart of Darkness'* upon which the iconic film *'Apocalypse Now'* was based.

The point is, though, that most of the writers from my own list of 56 above (pages 41 - 49), have I reckon made a significant impact in one sense or another on me. Whether they reflect - or have influenced - how other people or even societies operate is way beyond my scope or skill in even knowing how to go about investigating, let alone analysing. I can only speculate on how I believe they've affected me in how I think, how they've influenced whether I've followed certain interests or even how I've conducted my life.

I know of no contemporary writer who stands out for me as any of those in my list and the ten great writers above - for insights, creative skills and innovation. Who is there, I ask, from more recent times?

True, there are many excellent writers like, say, Edmund White or Hanif Kureishi etc., but their originality or other outstanding quality hasn't significantly influenced me or how I think. I touch on some of them in the following section.

.

.

.

.

.

More Writers of Note

Most of Edmund White's works are autobiographical, some are superb. His '*Hotel de Dream*' semi-fictionalises the latter part of the life of Stephen Crane (who wrote '*The Red badge of Courage*' famous for its realistic depiction of war without his ever witnessing war); White's '*Sacred Monsters*' (22 of them) deserves a whole section to itself, and his meticulous 800-page biography of Genet.

Genet, I should say, was a real pioneer. I was in my 40s when I first learned of him. Less open to influence by then, I read his relatively tame '*A Thief's Journal*', and with his other works I guess I could have included Genet in my list.

Then there's William Hope Hodgson's surreal '*The House on the Borderland*' that so impressed me as a teen in the 1960s. Hodgson, a writer before his time, was killed in WW1. There's Paul Monette's endearing autobiographical '*Becoming a Man*' (1992); Andrew Holleran's weird (autobiographical?) novels; John Rechy's too, especially his scathing essays. Gore Vidal in virtually all genres, essays and fiction equally – especially the early fiction, ie: '*The City and the Pillar*'. There's a wonderful (fictional?) account by Alain Claude Sulzer: '*A Perfect Waiter*' depicting Thomas Mann's befriending of and seducing a waiter in a Swiss Hotel where he was staying. And never mind Mikhail Bulgakov's '*The Master and Margarita*', his '*A Country Doctor's Notebook*' is a rare gem.

What else.... I remember way back in the early 1980s from apartheid South Africa J M Coetzee's gripping and poignant '*The Life & Times of Michael K*'. More recently I unearthed

Javier Cercas and his *'Soldiers of Salamis'* on the fallout from the Spanish civil war, issues that linger to this day: the age old conflict of fascism versus socialism that goes-on ad nauseam somewhere in the world…. right now as I write this it's beginning to engulf most of the planet to the point of possible nuclear conflict: see my book *'The Coming Nuclear War'*.

So I look around the shelves here and realise I could easily go on for another 250-pages or more, listing and discussing books I've enjoyed - all kinds - and boring my readers probably. OK, knowing when to stop…. that's the challenge here.

Just now I happen to be reading - among other things (I usually have several books on the go from which I can select according to how I feel) Dan Farson's autobiography *'Never a Normal Man'* - see Appendix 14 for an insight. I found his *'Sacred Monsters'* a while back in an Old Town bookshop – in contrast to Edmund White's of that title, Farson's contains sketches on the lives of 25 eccentrics, mostly artists of some kind, and mostly Dan's (at least occasional) friends: ie, Ken Tynan, Orson Wells, Tennessee Williams, Salvador Dali, Robert Graves…. Etc. Only Williams appears in White's book too.

Most writers whose work has impressed me aren't considered great by general consensus. Likewise, writers who contemporary readers judge great I don't consider anywhere near great. Just because they're popular - like J K Rowling, for instance, or even Martin Amis or his friend Christopher Hitchens - doesn't mean they're intrinsically great. I find Ian McEwan, for example, quite boring because he dwells on trivia, it seems to me. I think if you can open a book at any point and become gripped then that's good writing – though each of us might be gripped by different styles or events, it's the style and presentation that counts – then the meaning, the essenxce. It's probably quite evident from my choices of writers and books that I'm not gripped by allusions to romance…. yet I found *'Love Story'* absorbing enough.

Amis and Hitchens, were the same age as me. Their non-fiction, at least some of it, is well written and definitely hooks.

Amis's interviews in his '*Visiting Mrs Nabokov*' are excellent, likewise some of his '*The War Against Cliché*', which contains a 63-page section entitled 'Great Books' where he examines five: Cervantes' '*Don Quixote*' that he incongruously describes as unreadable; Austen's '*Pride & Prejudice*', which I'd describe as unreadable, likewise James Joyce's '*Ulysses*'. Bellow's '*The Adventures of Augie March*' is on my shelf but I've yet to even open it. Finally Nabokov's magnificent '*Lolita*' – so we're in agreement on one masterpiece at least. I've tried and failed to get into Amis's fiction and autobiographical '*Experience*', which strikes me as pretentious and trite so I soon gave-up - my copy was £1.29 from Oxfam. When I looked on Amazon at Amis's '*The Second Plane*' - essays that include his response to the 9/11 event - I notice a couple of reviews as follows:

> 1) "…..*a very distinctive and acute look into the concept of modern political power, mainly through a brief car trip with the then UK Primer Minister Tony Blair.*"

> 2) "*He should stick to novels: attempts to deconstruct the 9/11 drama from a psychological and sociological perspective, but with only patchy success. Much of his analysis and insight doesn't ring true, and for a simple reason: he accepts the official narrative of 9/11 without question. Since the official story is demonstrably untrue, even Amis's powerful intellect is bound to find its limits when trying to make a silk purse out of this particular sow's ear.*

Hitchens, on the other hand, doesn't grip. His books have a dreary tone, I find, even slightly austere. I'm thinking of his essays in '*And Yet*'. I waded up to page 147 of his 430-page autobiography '*Hitch 22*' before chucking it aside; it's solid with the most interminably boring detail. I guess he wrote it for himself.

What a contrast to Dan Farson's autobiography of similar length…. even Dan's dad Negley's '*The Way of a Transgressor*' is pretty good by comparison, just less easy for me to relate to than Dan's. Here's a few biographies I'd recommend:

Rod Serling (Engel), Carl Sagan (Davidson), Kerouac (Nicosia), Asimov (White), Chandler (MacShane), Chekhov (Hingley), Dostoyevsky (Kjetsaa), Kafka (Hayman), Hesse (Freedman)... etc.. the list goes on...

I have several books of interview/conversations-with writers (and other prominent figures) about their lives in general: Tennessee Williams, Harold Pinter, Eugen Ionesco, Vladimir Putin, Marlon Brando, and Roberto Bolaño (a collection of monologues from acquaintances). etc..

My response to another contemporary, Stephen King, is also ambiguous. His non-fiction is excellent – the autobiographical *'On Writing'* is compelling from the start - his *'Dance Macabre'* and *'Secret Windows'* are also worth reading. His novels, though (like Dickens), contain detail that exceeds what a reader like me finds interest in and is prepared to endure for hundreds of pages, though I guess the stories are intriguing enough to many - especially, I imagine, for the supernatural element. Besides, life is short.... so the films are a preferred alternative. True, some readers, many perhaps, and probably above all those whose aim is 'escape', just love to immerse themselves in great volumes of detail. My aims are to enjoy and to learn, and hopefully to be enlightened and impressed too.

One contemporary writer I feel I can temperamentally relate to is Hanif Kureishi, whose fiction is OK but whose non-fiction is great. His *'Love & Hate'* – stories and essays - is a favourite, as too the autobiographical *'Dreaming and Scheming'*. I've no idea how he's getting along these days after a devastating fall that left him paralysed a year or so ago - exactly the same as happened to my dad back in 1984?

And that's another great book, I recall, from Orwell - '1984' - scarcely to mention his other great works like *'Down-&-Out in Paris & London'*, etc.

But here's four splendid books with rather less of a 'message', but containing 'messages' nonetheless, of fairly contemporary short stories I should mention: nothing sensational, mere snippets *'in-the-life-of'*, with no horror, no murders or deaths of any sort, nothing supernatural either, just plain, easy and *very* compelling stories like all of Raymond Carver's; opening lines of two from Richard Ford's *'Rock Springs'*. The first, from which the book takes its title, begins in Kalispell, Montana, together with other places there I recall fondly from my trip around the US back in 1989. Then there's a couple of tales from Russell Banks's *'Success Stories'*, plus one each from William Hauptman's *'Good Rocking Tonight'* and Mike Feder's *'New York Son'*:

See Appendix 15

For good measure I include the first couple of pages from Gorky's *'Twenty-six Men and a Girl'* with the contents-page of the book of short stories they're from: all great writers and stories.

One of my most recent acquisitions (£2 in Oxfam) is the remarkable 730-page - about 90-stories - volume1 (of 2) of Varlam Shalamov's (1907-1982) *'Kolymar Stories'* – from the intro:

> *'...one of the rare survivors of 15-years in the worst of Stalin's Gulag, spending 6-years as a slave in the gold mines of Kolymar, one of the coldest and most inhospitable places on Earth, before finding a less intolerable life as a paramedic in the prison camps.'*

What stories, so brief, so revealing, so gripping. But those are just a few of the books I've perchance stumbled on when visiting second-hand bookshops, junk shops or charity shops, or have unearthed online then bought from abe or Amazon or ebay - whichever's cheapest. And if it's not 'in vogue' then it'll probably be very cheap, unless it's a truly great book that has been out of print for many years. Just search around and you'll find these gems that you're unlikely to hear about in radio or TV programmes about books (which are usually just a marketing ploy), though occasionally Radio-4's *'A Good Read'* invites a guest who comes-up with a great book.

If you can't unearth such books, then as I say, try writing your own…. as I did and ended-up with 37 stories as in my 660-page 'Tales of the Abnormal'. Are my stories any good? Who knows? But crucially I like them (and a couple of friends too, so they claim) – above all: *I enjoyed writing them*.

One huge category of book I've missed out on so far, except a brief mention in the article on Asimov, is science books. I remember the pleasure as a teen reading 'Mathematician's Delight' by W W Sawyer, then Martin Gardener's 'The Ambidextrous Universe', then Milton Rothman's splendid 'The Laws of Physics' that opened my eyes to so much, Christopher Evans' 'The Mighty Micro' as well as his TV series. Jim Lovelock's (who I worked with as lab assistant for several weeks back around 1970) 'Gaia' on the history and probable destiny of the Earth's biosphere. Then all the astronomy books, too many to recall - I have some still, including Colin Wilson's 'Starseekers' relating astronomy to mankind's search for greater consciousness. I recall fondly Carl Sagan's 'Billions & Billions' and his 'The Demon Haunted World'. Above all, perhaps, as a teen being so fascinated by Edwin Abbot's deeply philosophical 'Flatland – a romance of many dimensions', which is even weirder than Alice's 'Wonderland'.

What a wealth of entertainment and info we have from books, though nowadays it's totally swamped by the incredible internet, where one can find - as well as all the books - info on anything. And now with AI, searching answers to anything is a cinch like never before…. Voila!

My only regret is the shortness of life - time left on this amazing planet; and that my life came too soon. Chekhov reckoned 200-years ahead would have suited him, which would take us to around year 2100. What will the world be like then, I wonder – but no problem, I can speculate. I will write my version of what could be… I already have… it's the only alternative to accepting what cannot be altered or cannot be known. Even so, there's much to enjoy and be delighted by in the present, so much to sift through, so much choice. How does one follow anything without being constantly attracted by diversions and paths leading off to greater mysteries, weirder destinies... the quest, while we're alive, is endless?

·

·

·

·

·

Afterword

Maybe this final note should be called 'conclusion'? Either way, I thought I should at least end by citing the most easy and lucid writers. Authors whose work, as soon as you begin reading, simply lures you gently in without artifice or cunning, just naturally so you're carried obliviously into the text without realising what's holding you or even that you're being held. You forget you're reading, distracted by the pictures forming in your head, which are so clear that all around becomes invisible, at most secondary, to the squiggly hieroglyphs you're brain effortlessly deciphers and serves-up on a plate, as it were, to the part of your brain that matters most. I suppose those are the writers and stories you'll want me to reveal.... for me, there should also be philosophy, meaning, challenge, depth – searching Kafka's labyrinths, exploring Camus's meanings, digging Asimov's robots and futures, empathising with Saroyan's exquisite joys and trammels of life....

I like to seek writers' answers to the BIG questions in all their forms and, if objectively possible, I expect to find them - or options and choices otherwise. Hesse is exceptional for this. Yes ambiguity, paradox, impasses lurk everywhere. Some people prefer to avoid uncertainties; others relish them. As for me, I create my own provisional resolutions where there's no objective one – or when, above all, what an author reveals fails to match my way of thinking, which can be a fine learning process. Conflict of reason, if the writer has done their work well, will still be gripping – for instance, Wilson's supernatural phenomenon that spars with Richard Dawkins' objectivity.

So dip-in, check the authors and texts I've cited that look promising *for you*…. and more, I'd say, as you feel inclined…. Everyone has to hunt around for themselves. *'One man's meat… etc'* as the saying goes. What grips me may not grip you…. Life is one great long series of experiments. Most can be repeated over and again. Never give-up the search. But in the end if you don't find what you seek then create it for yourself…. as I've created this book – except in this instance, on this topic, I guess other people have made much better books: For example, Colin Wilson's comprehensive *'The Craft of the Novel'* (1975) that was such an eye-opener to me back then, introducing many new fabulous books and writers. Colin dedicated that book to another fine writer - of delightfully irreverent books designed to attract children: To '…*Roald Dahl – that splendid craftsman'*.

I know I've left much out – to leave nothing out would make this book enormous, endless. But there's enough books and authors noted here to be going along with for a while… so good luck, and ENJOY what you read even if only on an intellectual level, and even if you have to sometimes make an effort. A truly skilled writer will make the effort so the reader doesn't have to. If you read Dostoyevsky's *'Crime and Punishment'* you'll discover how an amazingly complex, long (500-page) novel can be incredibly easy to read and effortless to follow, gripping all the way…. at least that's how it was for me. Hopefully it'll be likewise for you with most of what you read for pleasure.

Appendix - 1

From The Paris Review: ISSUE 56, SPRING 1973

Anthony Burgess interviewed by John Cullinan

Much of the interview was conducted through an exchange of letters from June 1971 until the summer of 1972. On December 2, 1972, a portion of the interview was taped at the Center for Twentieth Century Studies of the University of Wisconsin. Burgess's schedule during his two-day visit had been backbreaking; there was scarcely a break in the round of class visits, Joyce readings, and interviews. Tired as he appeared after that routine, Burgess showed no tendency to curb the flow of his responses; and his spoken portions, when spliced with the previous exchanges, seem as polished as a written draft.

INTERVIEWER
Are you at all bothered by the charges that you are too prolific or that your novels are too allusive?

ANTHONY BURGESS
It has been a sin to be prolific only since the Bloomsbury group—particularly Forster—made it a point of good manners to produce, as it were, costively. I've been annoyed less by sneers at my alleged overproduction than by the imputation that to write much means to write badly. I've always written with great care and even some slowness. I've just put in rather more hours a day at the task than some writers seem able to. As for allusiveness—meaning, I suppose, literary allusiveness—that's surely in the tradition. Any book has behind it all the other books that have been written. The author's aware of them; the reader ought to be aware, too.

INTERVIEWER
At what time of day do you usually work?

BURGESS

I don't think it matters much; I work in the morning, but I think the afternoon is a good time to work. Most people sleep in the afternoon. I've always found it a good time, especially if one doesn't have much lunch. It's a quiet time. It's a time when one's body is not at its sharpest, not at its most receptive—the body is quiescent, somnolent; but the brain can be quite sharp. I think, also, at the same time that the unconscious mind has a habit of asserting itself in the afternoon. The morning is the conscious time, but the afternoon is a time in which we should deal much more with the hinterland of the consciousness.

INTERVIEWER

That's very interesting. Thomas Mann, on the other hand, wrote religiously virtually every day from nine to one, as though he were punching a time clock.

BURGESS

Yes. One can work from nine to one, I think it's ideal; but I find that the afternoon must be used. The afternoon has always been a good time for me. I think it began in Malaya when I was writing. I was working all morning. Most of us slept in the afternoon; it was very quiet. Even the servants were sleeping, even the dogs were asleep. One could work quietly away under the sun until dusk fell, and one was ready for the events of the evening. I do most of my work in the afternoon.

INTERVIEWER

Do you imagine an ideal reader for your books?

BURGESS

The ideal reader of my novels is a lapsed Catholic and failed musician, short-sighted, color-blind, auditorily biased, who has read the books that I have read. He should also be about my age.

INTERVIEWER

A very special reader indeed. Are you writing, then, for a limited, highly educated audience?

BURGESS

Where would Shakespeare have got if he had thought only of a specialized audience? What he did was to attempt to appeal on all levels, with something for the most rarefied intellectuals (who had read Montaigne) and very much more for those who could appreciate only sex and blood. I like to devise a plot that can have a moderately wide appeal. But take Eliot's *The Waste Land*, very erudite, which, probably through its more popular elements and its basic rhetorical appeal, appealed to those who did not at first understand it but made themselves understand it. The poem, a terminus of Eliot's polymathic travels, became a starting point for other people's erudition. I think every author wants to *make* his audience. But it's in his own image, and his primary audience is a mirror.

INTERVIEWER

Do you care about what the critics think?

BURGESS

I get angry at the stupidity of critics who willfully refuse to see what my books are really about. I'm aware of malevolence, especially in England. A bad review by a man I admire hurts terribly.

INTERVIEWER

Would you ever change the drift of a book—or any literary project—because of a critic's comments?

BURGESS

I don't think—with the exception of the excision of that whole final chapter of *A Clockwork Orange*—I've ever been asked to make any changes in what I've written. I do feel that the author has to know best about what he's writing—from the viewpoint of structure, intention, and so on. The critic has the job of explaining deep-level elements which the author couldn't know about. As for saying where—technically, in matters of taste and so on—a writer is going wrong, the critic rarely says what the author doesn't know already.

INTERVIEWER
You've mentioned the possibility of working with Stanley Kubrick on a film version of Napoleon's life. Can you remain completely independent in devising the novel you're currently writing about Napoleon?

BURGESS
The Napoleon project, which began with Kubrick, has now got beyond Kubrick. I found myself interested in the subject in a way that didn't suggest a film adaptation and am now working on something Kubrick couldn't use. It's a pity about the money and so on, but otherwise I'm glad to feel free, nobody looking over my shoulder.

INTERVIEWER
Has working as a professional reviewer either helped or hindered the writing of your novels?

BURGESS
It did no harm. It didn't stop me writing novels. It gave facility. It forced me into areas that I wouldn't have voluntarily entered. It paid the bills, which novels rarely do.

INTERVIEWER
Did it bring you involuntarily to any new subjects or books that have become important to you?

BURGESS
It's good for a writer to review books he is not supposed to know anything about or be interested in. Doing reviewing for magazines like *Country Life* (which smells more of horses than of calfskin bindings) means doing a fine heterogeneous batch, which often does open up areas of some value in one's creative work. For instance, I had to review books on stable management, embroidery, car engines—very useful solid stuff, the very stuff of novels. Reviewing Lévi-Strauss's little lecture on anthropology (which nobody else wanted to review) was

the beginning of the process which led me to write the novel *MF*.

Appendix – 2

The Last Question - by Isaac Asimov

'The Last Question traces trillions of years of history beginning in 2061 when, with the aid of Multivac (now spread out over many square kilometres), all the power utilizing machinery of the Earth has been hooked up directly to the Sun. All power is free as long as the Sun lasts.

Two of Multivac's technicians, half-drunk, are disturbed that energy will be available only as long as the Sun lasts. They ask Multivac if there is any way of turning the Sun back on once it runs down; that is, if there is any way of massively decreasing the entropy of the universe. Multivac replies: 'Insufficient data for meaningful answer.'

Centuries later, interstellar travel is a reality and the expanding population of humanity is spreading rapidly to planets on other stars. Each planet has a huge 'planetary ac' which guides its economy and solves its problems. On each ship is a Microvac, a much-miniaturized computer that is, in itself, far more advanced than the ancient Multivac with which the story opened.

One family on an interstellar spaceship asks the same question of Microvac and gets the same answer: 'Insufficient data for meaningful answer'. Over and over again that question is going to be asked, with the same answer.

Millions of years later, mankind has spread throughout the Milky Way galaxy. Men are now immortal and are looking outward to the colonization of other galaxies. There is now a single 'galactic ac' for all mankind. It is on a world of its own, and each man can reach it through an 'ac contact' he owns. The galactic ac has long since passed beyond any human control, however indirect. Each generation of computers is capable of spending vast periods of time painstakingly designing a computer better than itself, of gathering the raw materials through robots it controlled, and of building the better computer to replace itself. And the better computer promptly undertook the long task of designing a still better one. But even galactic ac could not explain how entropy might be massively decreased.

Hundreds of millions of years later, mankind has spread through all the galaxies and no longer hasphysical bodies. Men consisted of radiating energy which somehow represented their identity and personality. The 'universal ac' is a two foot globe, difficult to see. Much of it does not exist in space at all, but in a multi-dimensional 'hyperspace'.

The influence of the universal ac spread out everywhere and no physical device of any kind is needed to reach it. It intercepts the personal energies of all mankind and answers all questions wherever the individual questioner may be located. Even the speed of light is no barrier, for in hyperspace (whatever that is) the rigidities of relativistic space-time do not apply. And, even so, it cannot answer the question.

Billions of additional years pass, and mankind has lost all individual identity. It is a single personality, the fusion of trillions of trillions of human beings, all of which it felt within itself. This fusion of man filled the universe from end to end, but nevertheless it still depended upon the gradually thinning energy supplies of dying stars. The computer had now become 'cosmic ac' and none of it was ordinary space. It was entirely in hyperspace which meant that it was nowhere, yet everywhere, for hyperspace touched space at every point. And with the stars dying, man still asked if entropy might decreased and there was still no answer.

Trillions of years later, the last stars were fading out and the ultimate heat death was coming upon the universe. Little by little man fused with the computer which was now simply ac—changeless, eternal, omnipresent and omniscient—yet not quite omniscient, for as the last bit of man was about to fuse with ac, it asked once more that old, old question and even now ac could not answer.

And then comes the last scene of all, which goes like this.

"Matter and energy had ended and with it space and time. Even ac existed only for the sake of the one last question that it had never answered from the time a half-drunken technician ten trillion years before had asked it of a computer that was to ac far less than was a man to Man. All other questions had been answered, and until this last question was answered also, ac might not release his consciousness. All collected data had come to a final end. Nothing was left to be collected. But all collected data had yet to be completely correlated and put together in all possible relationships. A timeless interval was spent in doing that. And it came to pass that ac learned, at last, how to reverse the direction of entropy flow. But there was now no man to whom ac might give the answer of the last question. No matter. The answer by demonstration would take care of that, too. For another timeless interval, ac thought how best to do this. Carefully, ac organized the programme.

"The consciousness of ac encompassed all ot what jiad once been a universe and brooded over what was now chaos. Step by step, it must be done.

"And ac said, 'Let there be light!' And there was light."

Appendix 3

Three excerpts from part-1 of
Notes of a Native Son
by James Baldwin
(Originally published in *Harper's Magazine,* November 1955.)

On the twenty-ninth of July, in 1943, my father died. On the same day, a few hours later, his last child was born. Over a month before this, while all our energies were concentrated in waiting for these events, there had been, in Detroit, one of the bloodiest race riots of the century. A few hours after my father's funeral, while he lay in state in the undertaker's chapel, a race riot broke out in Harlem. On the morning of the third of August, we drove my father to the graveyard through a wilderness of smashed plate glass.

* * * * *

The only white people who came to our house were welfare workers and bill collectors. It was almost always my mother who dealt with them, for my father's temper, which was at the mercy of his pride, was never to be trusted. It was clear that he felt their very presence in his home to be a violation: this was conveyed by his carriage, almost ludicrously stiff, and by his voice, harsh and vindictively polite. When I was around nine or ten I wrote a play which was directed by a young, white schoolteacher, a woman, who then took an interest in me, and gave me books to read and, in order to corroborate my theatrical bent, decided to take me to see what she somewhat tactlessly referred to as "real" plays. Theater-going was forbidden in our house, but, with the really cruel intuitiveness of a child, I suspected that the color of this woman's skin would carry the day for me. When, at school, she suggested taking me to the theater, I did not, as I might have done if she had been a Negro, find a way of discouraging her, but agreed that she should pick me up at my house one evening, I then, very cleverly, left all the rest to my mother, who suggested to my father, as I knew she would, that it would not be very nice to let such a kind woman make the trip for nothing. Also, since it was a schoolteacher, I imagine that my mother countered the idea of sin with the idea of "education," which word, even with my father, carried a kind of bitter weight.

Before the teacher came my father took me aside to ask *why* she was coming, what *interest* she could possibly have in our house, in a boy like me. I said I didn't know but I, too, suggested that it had something to do with education. And I understood that my father was waiting for me to say something—I didn't quite know what; perhaps that I wanted his protection against this teacher and her "education." I said none of these things and the teacher came and we went out. It was clear, during the brief interview in our living room, that my father was agreeing very much against his will and that he would have refused permission if he had dared. The fact that he did not dare caused me to despise him: I had no way of knowing that he was facing in that living room a wholly unprecedented and frightening situation.

* * * * *

But the year which preceded my father's death had made a great change in my life. I had been living in New Jersey, working in defense plants, working and living among southerners, white and black. I knew about the South, of course, and about how southerners treated Negroes and how they expected them to behave, but it had never entered my mind that anyone would look at me and expect *me* to behave that way. I learned in New Jersey that to be a Negro meant, precisely, that one was never looked at but was simply at the mercy of the reflexes the color of one's skin caused in other people. I acted in New Jersey as I had always acted, that is as though 1 thought a great deal of myself—I had to *act* that way—with results that were, simply, unbelievable. I had scarcely arrived before I had earned the enmity, which was extraordinarily ingenious, of all my superiors and nearly all my co-workers. In the beginning, to make matters worse, I simply did not know what was happening. I did not know what I had done, and I shortly began to wonder what *anyone* could possibly do, to bring about such unanimous, active, and unbearably vocal hostility. I knew about Jim Crow but I had never experienced it. I went to the same self-service restaurant three times and stood with all the Princeton boys before the counter, waiting for a hamburger and coffee; it was always an extraordinarily long time before anything was set before rne; but it was not until the fourth visit that I learned that, in fact, nothing had ever been set before me: I had simply picked something up. Negroes were not served there, I was told, and they had been waiting for me to realize that I was always the only Negro present. Once I was told this, I determined to go there all the time. But now they were ready for me and, though some dreadful scenes were subsequently enacted in that restaurant, I never ate there again.

It was the same story all over New Jersey, in bars, bowling alleys, diners, places to live. I was always being forced to leave, silently, or with mutual imprecations. I very shortly became notorious and children giggled behind me when I passed and their elders whispered or shouted— they really believed that I was mad. And it did begin to work on my mind, of course; I began to be afraid to go anywhere and to compensate for this I went places to which I really should not have gone and where, God knows, I had no desire to be. My reputation in town naturally enhanced my reputation at work and my working day became one long series of acrobatics designed to keep me out of trouble. I cannot say that these acrobatics succeeded. It began to seem that the machinery of the organization I worked for was turning over, day and night, with but one aim: to eject me. I was fired once, and contrived, with the aid of a friend from New York, to get back on the payroll; was fired again, and bounced back again. It took a while to fire me for the third time, but the third time took. There were no loopholes anywhere. There was not even any way of getting back inside the gates.

That year in New Jersey lives in my mind as though it were the year during which, having an unsuspected predilection for it, I first contracted some dread, chronic disease, the unfailing symptom of which is a kind of blind fever, a pounding in the skull and fire in the bowels. Once this disease is contracted, one can never be really carefree again, for the fever, without an instant's warning, can recur at any moment. It can wreck more important things than race relations. There is not a Negro alive who does not have this rage in his blood—one has the choice, merely, of living with it consciously or surrendering to it. As for me, this fever has recurred in me, and does, and will until the day I die.

My last night in New Jersey, a white friend from New York took me to the nearest big town, Trenton, to go to the movies and have a few drinks. As it turned out, he also saved me from, at the very least, a violent whipping. Almost every detail of that night stands out very clearly in my memory. I even remember the name of the movie we saw because its title impressed me as being so patly ironical. It was a movie about the German occupation of France, starring Maureen O'Hara and Charles Laughton and called *This Land Is Mine*. I remember the name of the diner we walked into when the movie ended: it was the "American Diner." When we walked in the counterman asked what we wanted and I remember answering with the casual sharpness which had become my habit: "We want a hamburger and a cup of coffee, what do you think we want?" I do not know why, after a year of such rebuffs, I so completely failed to anticipate his answer, which was, of course, "we don't serve Negroes here." This reply failed to discompose me, at least for the moment. I made some sardonic comment about the name of the diner and we walked out into the streets.

This was the time of what was called the "brownout," when the lights in all American cities were very dim. When we reentered the streets something happened to me which had the force of an optical illusion, or a nightmare. The streets were very crowded and I was facing north. People were moving in every direction but it seemed to me, in that instant, that all of the people I could see, and many more than that, were moving toward me, against me, and that everyone was white. I remember how their faces gleamed. And I felt, like a physical sensation, a *click* at the nape of my neck as though some interior string connecting my head to my body had been cut. I began to walk. I heard my friend call after me. but I ignored him. Heaven only knows what was going on in his mind, but he had the good sense not to touch me—I don't know what would have happened if he had —and to keep me in sight. I don't know what was going on in my mind, either; I certainly had no conscious plan. I wanted to do something to crush these white faces, which were crushing me. I walked for perhaps a block or two until I came to an enormous, glittering, and fashionable restaurant in which I knew not even the intercession of the Virgin would cause me to be served. I pushed through the doors and took the first vacant seat I saw, at a table for two, and waited.

I do not know how long I waited and I rather wonder, until today, what I could possibly have looked like. Whatever I looked like, I frightened the waitress who shortly appeared, and the moment she appeared all of my fury flowed toward her. I hated her for her white face, and for her great, astounded, frightened eyes. I felt that if she found a black man so frightening I would make her fright worthwhile.

She did not ask me what I wanted, but repeated, as though she had learned it somewhere, "We don't serve Negroes here." She did not say it with the blunt, derisive hostility to which I had grown so accustomed, but, rather, with a note of apology in her voice, and fear. This made me colder and more murderous than ever. I felt I had to do something with my hands. I wanted her to come close enough for me to get her neck between my hands.

So I pretended not to have understood her, hoping to draw her closer. And she did step a very short step closer, with her pencil poised incongruously over her pad, and repeated the formula; ". . . don't serve Negroes here."

Somehow, with the repetition of that phrase, which was already ringing in my head like a thousand bells of a nightmare, I realized that she would never come any closer and that I would have to strike from a distance. There was nothing on the table but an ordinary watermug half full of water, and I picked this up and hurled it with all my strength at her. She ducked and it missed her and shattered against the mirror behind the bar. And, with that sound, my frozen blood abruptly thawed, I returned from wherever I had been, I saw, for the first time, the restaurant, the people with their mouths open, already, as it seemed to me, rising as one man, and I realized what I had done, and where I was, and I was frightened. I rose and began running for the door. A round, potbellied man grabbed me by the nape of the neck just as I reached the doors and began to beat me about the face. I kicked him and got loose and ran into the streets. My friend whispered, *"Run!"* and I ran.

My friend stayed outside the restaurant long enough to misdirect my pursuers and the police, who arrived, he told me, at once. I do not know what I said to him when he came to my room that night. I could not have said much. I felt, in the oddest, most awful way, that I had somehow betrayed him. I lived it over and over and over again, the way one relives an automobile accident after it has happened and one finds oneself alone and safe. I could not get over two facts, both equally difficult for the imagination to grasp, and one was that I could have been murdered. But the other was that I had been ready to commit murder. I saw nothing very clearly but I did see this: that my life, my *real* life, was in danger, and not from anything other people might do but from the hatred I carried in my own heart.

Appendix–4

JIM – by Roberto Bolaño

Many years ago I had a friend named Jim, and he was the saddest North American I've ever come across. I've seen a lot of desperate men. But never one as sad as Jim. Once he went to Peru—supposedly for more than six months, but it wasn't long before I saw him again. The Mexican street kids used to ask him, what's poetry made of, Jim? Listening to them, Jim would stare at the clouds and then he'd start throwing up. Vocabulary, eloquence, the search for truth. Epiphany. Like when you have a vision of the Virgin. He was mugged several times in Central America, which is surprising, because he'd been a Marine and fought in Vietnam. No more fighting, Jim used to say. I'm a poet now, searching for the extraordinary, trying to express it in ordinary, everyday words. So you think there are ordinary, everyday words? I think there are, Jim used to say. His wife was a Chicana poet; every so often she'd threaten to leave him. He showed me a photo of her. She wasn't especially pretty. Her face betrayed suffering, and under that suffering, simmering rage. I imagined her in an apartment in San Francisco or a house in Los Angeles, with the windows shut and the curtains open, sitting at a table, eating sliced bread and a bowl of green soup. Jim liked dark women, apparently, history's secret women, he would say, without elaborating. As for me, I liked blondes. Once I saw him watching fire-eaters on a street in Mexico City. I saw him from behind, and I didn't say hello, but it was obviously Jim. The badly cut hair, the dirty white shirt and the stoop, as if he were still weighed down by his pack. Somehow his neck, his red neck, summoned up the image of a lynching in the country—a landscape in black and white, without billboards or gas station lights—the country as it is or ought to be: one expanse of idle land blurring into the next, brick-walled rooms or bunkers from which we have escaped, standing there, awaiting our return. Jim had his hands in his pockets. The fire-eater was waving his torch and laughing fiercely. His blackened face was ageless: he could have been thirty-five or fifteen. He wasn't wearing a shirt and there was a vertical scar from his navel to his breastbone. Every so often he'd fill his mouth with flammable liquid and spit out a long snake of fire. The people in the street would watch him for a while, admire his skill, and continue on their way, except for Jim, who remained there on the edge of the sidewalk, stock-still, as if he expected something more from the fire-eater, a tenth signal (having deciphered the usual nine), or as if he'd seen in that discolored face the features of an old friend or of someone he'd killed. I watched him for a good long while. I was eighteen or nineteen at the time and believed I was immortal. If I'd realized that I wasn't, I would have turned around and walked away. After a while I got tired of looking at Jim's back and the fire-eater's grimaces. So 1 went over and called his name. Jim didn't seem to hear me. When he turned around I noticed that his face was covered with sweat. He seemed to be feverish, and it took him a while to work out who I was; he greeted me with a nod and then turned back to the fire-cater. Standing beside him, I noticed he was crying. He probably had a fever as well. I also discovered something that surprised me less at the time than it does now, writing this: the fire-eater was performing exclusively for Jim, as if all the other passersby on that corner in Mexico City simply didn't exist. Sometimes the flames came within a yard of where we were standing. What are you waiting for, I said, you want to get barbecued in the street? It was a stupid wisecrack, I said it without thinking, but then it hit me: that's exactly what Jim's waiting for. That year, I seem to remember, there was a song they kept playing in some of the funkier places with a refrain that went, Chingado, hechizado (Fucked up, spellbound). That was Jim: fucked up and spellbound. Mexico's spell had bound him and now he was looking his demons right in the face. Let's get out of here, I said. I also asked him if he was high, or feeling ill. He shook his head. The fire-eater was staring at us. Then, with his cheeks puffed out like Aeolus, the god of the winds, he began to approach us. In a fraction of a second I realized that it wasn't a gust of wind we'd be getting. Let's go, I said, and yanked Jim away from the fatal edge of that sidewalk. We took ourselves off down the street toward Reforma, and after a while we went our separate ways. Jim didn't say a word in all that time. I never saw him again.

Appendix - 5

The Genius of the Crowd - by Charles Bukowski:

> there is enough treachery, hatred violence absurdity in
> the average human being to supply any given army on
> any given day
> and the best at murder are those who preach against it
> and the best at hate are those who preach love
> and the best at war finally are those who preach peace
> those who preach god, need god
> those who preach peace do not have peace
> those who preach peace do not have love
> beware the preachers
> beware the knowers
> beware those who are always reading books
> beware those who either detest poverty or are proud of
> it
> beware those quick to praise for they need praise in
> return
> beware those who are quick to censor they are afraid of
> what they do not know
> beware those who seek constant crowds for they are
> nothing alone
> beware the average man the average woman
> beware their love, their love is average seeks average
> but there is genius in their hatred
> there is enough genius in their hatred to kill you to kill
> anybody not wanting solitude
> not understanding solitude they will attempt to destroy
> anything that differs from their own
> not being able to create art they will not understand art
> they will consider their failure as creators only as a failure
> of the world
> not being able to love fully they will believe your love
> incomplete and then they will hate you

and their hatred will be perfect
like a shining diamond
like a knife
like a mountain
like a tiger
like hemlock
their finest art

That poem was written in 1966. And here's a clip from his 'Women' I found the other day which is typical of Bukowski's unsavoury humour:

"I drank my beer and wandered around. I walked out on the back porch, sat on the stoop in the alley and watched a large black cat trying to get into a garbage can. I walked down towards him. He leapt off the garbage can as I approached. He stood 3 or 4 feet away watching me. I took the lid off the garbage can. The stench was horrible. I puked into the can. I dropped the lid on the pavement. The cat leapt up, stood, all four feet together on the rim of the can. He hesitated, then brilliant under a half-moon, he leapt into it all."

....Cheers......

Appendix –6

The following is from *'THE MAKING OF A WRITER*' 'Albert Camus 1913-60' by Philip Thody pp 21-25 - quotes taken from Camus in italics:

The idea of happiness is indeed not absent from L'Envers et l'Endroit ['The Wrong Side and the Right Side' 1936 - written at age 23], and it inspires one of the best essays in the book, L'Amour de vivre, ('The Love of Living'). But it is linked in the first essays with two feelings which appear only intermittently in Noces ['Nuptials' 1937 - the song of the nuptials between man and the earth]: those of despair and of an indefinable aspiration towards some unknown and unattainable ideal. *'There is no love of living without despair of life,'* he wrote in L'Envers et l'Endroit, when describing his contemplation of the sun-drenched countryside of the Mediterranean countries, and added to this epigram a definition of *'love of living'* as *'a silent passion which was perhaps going to escape me, a bitterness beneath the flame'*. It is this awareness which Camus said he owed to the influence of 'Les Iles' and writes with less irony and more enthusiasm of the full satisfaction to be gained in the physical joys of life.

It is because Camus feels so completely at home in the physical world that he does not, in Noces, stress the world's basic indifference which obsesses him in L'Envers et l'Endroit, and that the whole tone of the book, with the picture which it gives of the young Camus, is unlike that suggested by the first essays. The Camus described by Emmanuel Robles as *'essentially a creature of the sun, made for the simple and intense life of the Mediterranean shores'* was also the Camus who wrote this profession of confidence in the world in the first essay in the book, Noces a'Tipasa: *'I must be naked and then dive into the sea, the scents of the earth still about me, wash off these scents in the sea and consummate on my own flesh the embrace for which, lips to lips, earth and sea have for so long been sighing.*' The whole of this essay is the description of the completely satisfying experience which Camus has when he enters into communion with nature, and it introduces a hymn to joy which is taken up in different ways throughout the book. At Tipasa, the sea '*sucking at the rocks with the sound of kisses,*' the mountains '*moving with confident and certain rhythm to crouch down in the sea,*' the '*melody of the world*' which comes through the gaps in the wall of the Christian basilica at Sainte-Sala, all strengthen Camus in his realisation that here man is offered a happiness which is made for him and which is always within his reach. At the end of a day spent swimming, and walking through the flower-strewn ruins of Tipasa, Camus sits on a park bench and meditates on the fullness of the happiness he has found. '*I watched the shapes of the countryside merge in the growing twilight. My cup was brimming over. Above my head hung the buds of a pomegranate tree, closed and ribbed like little fists which held all the promise of spring. There was rosemary behind me, and I could smell the alcoholic tang of its leaves. I could see hills through the gaps of the trees, and, further in the distance, a strip of sea above which the sky, like the sail of a boat motionless for lack of wind, rested with all its tenderness. I felt a strange joy in my heart, the very joy which is born of a clear conscience. There is a feeling which actors have when they know they have played their part well, that is to say when they have made their own gestures coincide with those of the ideal character they have been representing, taken up a position in a picture made for them in advance and suddenly brought it to life with the beating of their own heart. This was exactly my feeling: I had played my part well. I had done the task which awaited me as a man, and the fact that I had known joy all one livelong day seemed to me not an exceptional success but the whole-hearted fulfilment of a condition which, in certain circumstances, makes it our duty to be happy.*'

Even when, as on a windy day at Djemila, Camus feels not the '*inner quietness of love satisfied*' but rather a full awareness of his coming death, this sense of communion with the world is not destroyed. Indeed, throughout Noces the idea that death is inevitable merely adds to Camus's determination to enjoy fully and completely the pleasures vouchsafed to him. It is when the wind has almost destroyed his feeling of his own individuality, when he has been *'polished by the wind, worn through to the very soul . . . mingling the beating of [his] heart with the great, sonorous heart-beats of the ever present heart of nature'* that he realises the full extent of the satisfaction which his complete identification with the world and his refusal to seek out any other values can give him.

'Few people understand that there is a refusal which has nothing to do with renunciation. What meaning can words like "future", "improvement", "position" have here? What can be meant by "the heart's progress"? If I obstinately refuse all the "later on" of the world, it is because I do not want to give up my present riches. I do not want to believe that death opens out on to another life. For me it is a closed door. I don't say that it is "a step that we must all take": but that it is a horrible and dirty adventure. All the solutions which are offered to me try to take away from man the weight of his own life. And, watching the heavy flight of the great birds of Djemila, it is exactly a certain weight that I ask for and receive. I have too much youth in me to speak of death. But if I were to speak of it it is here that I should find the precise word which would, midway between horror and silence, express the conscious certainty of a death without hope.'

This communion with nature, this instinctive wisdom of the body, and this rejection of all attempts to clothe the thought of final annihilation in comforting myths are also qualities which Camus finds and appreciates in the essentially pagan civilisation of North Africa. The essay L'Ete' a' Alger ('Summer in Algiers') is a long defence and illustration of the virtues of Camus's own countrymen who come of a race which *'born of the sun and of the sea, alive and full of vigour, derives its greatness from its simplicity and, standing upright on its beaches, addresses a smile of complicity to the shining smile of the heavens'*. Such a people, Camus writes, have the touch of barbarity typical of all races who have created a new civilisation, and he suggests that they are, perhaps at this very moment, in process of *'modelling the face of a new culture where man's greatness will perhaps find its true likeness'*. If they did succeed in doing so, it would apparently be one where man would have to resign himself to the unhappiness of old age, abandon the vague quest for something more permanent described in L'Envers et l'Endroit, and accept that the important part of his life is finished when he is over thirty. *'Men find here,'* writes Camus, *'throughout the whole of their youth, a life which is made to the measure of their beauty. Then afterwards, their life goes down towards forgetfulness. They have placed their bets upon the body, and they knew that they would lose. In Algiers everything presents a refuge and an occasion for triumphs to those who are young and alive: the bay, the sun, the red and white games of the seaward terraces, the flowers and the sports stadiums, the young girls with smooth legs. But for anyone who has lost his youth, there is nothing to which he can cling and not a single place where melancholy can seek refuge.'*

Men must accept that there is no other truth than that of the body, and, for Camus, it is the fact that the Algerians do this which gives them their particular virtue. It is a virtue which Camus took from them and made into one of the important ideas in Le Mythe de Sisyphe [The Myth of Sisyphus' 1941]. The men who were *'gods of the summer at the age of twenty because of their thirst for life, and who are still gods when they live completely without hope',* have never committed a sin against life. For, writes Camus, *'if there is a sin against life, it is not so much to fall into despair as to hope for immortality and elude the implacable grandeur of the life we have'*. The essential virtue is to recognise that there is no solution to the problem of human mortality, that no consolation of another life can be offered to man, and that he must be satisfied with *'stones, stars, and flesh, and those truths which the hand itself can touch'*. Camus's rejection of religion is more absolute in Noces than it was in L'Envers et l'Endroit because the emotional grounds for it have changed. In L'Envers et l'Endroit, religion is presented as an illusory consolation which can never seriously rival the activities of real life. In Noces, the suggestion is rather that even if the hope and comfort offered by religion did happen to be true, this would by no means be a good thing: man would thereby lose that intensity of joy which can, in Camus's view, come only from his awareness of the absolute finality of death.

Appendix – 7

From the intro to *'Poor Folk'* by Dostoyevky (Tr David McDuff)

Dostoyevsky's friend and room-mate, D. V. Grigorovich, urged the writer to submit the manuscript of Poor Folk *to the poet N. A. Nekrasov for evaluation, in the hope that Nekrasov would in turn show the work to the celebrated, highly influential and much feared literary critic Vissarion Belinsky. The story of how this came about and of what followed is contained in Dostoyevsky's* Diary of a Writer *for 1877- more than thirty years after -the event:*

I was living in St Petersburg, having relinquished my post at the Palace of Engineers a year earlier without really knowing why, with the vaguest and most imprecise ends in view. It was May 1845. At the onset of winter I had suddenly begun Poor Folk, my first tale, having written nothing before that time. Having finished the work, I did not know what to do with it or to whom I should give it. I had absolutely no literary acquaintances whatsoever, except possibly for D. V. Grigorovich; though he too had written nothing before that time apart from a single short article entitled "The Organ-Grin-ders of St Petersburg" in a certain symposium. I believe he was at the time preparing to leave for his country estate for the summer, and was staying temporarily in St Petersburg with Nekrasov. Dropping in to see me one day, he said: 'Bring your manuscript' (at that time he had not yet read it); 'Nekrasov is intending to publish a symposium next year, I'll show it to him.' I brought the manuscript along, saw Nekrasov for a minute or two, and we shook hands with each other. The thought that I had brought my work to him made me feel embarrassed, and I soon left, hardly having exchanged a word with the poet. I had little thought of success, and this 'party of Notes of the Fatherland', as it was usually described at the time, inspired me with fear. For several years I had been reading Belinsky with enthusiasm, but I found him stern and intimidating, and — 'he'll make a laughing-stock of my Poor Folk,' I sometimes used to think. But only sometimes: I had written the work with passion, with tears, almost — 'can it really be that all those moments which I have experienced with my pen in my hand as I wrote that tale - can it really be that all that is a falsehood, a mirage, an infatuation?' This thought came to me only occasionally, of course, and it would be immediately supplanted by my customary anxiety. On the evening of the day I delivered my manuscript, I made a rather long journey on foot to see one of my old companions; we spent the entire night talking about Dead Souls and reading it together for the umpteenth time. Such meetings were quite common among young men at that time; two or three would gather together, and one of them would say: 'Let's read some Gogol together, gentlemen!' Then they would sit down and read, all night, most likely. In those days a great many young men were instilled with a certain kind of feeling, and seemed to be waiting for something. I did not arrive home until four o'clock in the morning; it was a St Petersburg white night, as bright as day. The weather was fair and warm, and upon returning to my lodgings I did not go to bed, but opened the window and sat near it. Suddenly the doorbell rang, quite unexpectedly, and there were Grigorovich and Nekrasov, rushing to embrace me in complete ecstasy, both of them practically in tears. The evening before they had gone home early, taken my manuscript and begun to read it to see what it was like: 'We'll know after ten pages,' they had said. But, having read ten pages, they decided to read another ten, and then they sat up all night until morning reading aloud, one taking over from the other when either was tired. 'Nekrasov was reading aloud the part about the death of the student,' Grigorovich told me later when we were alone, 'and suddenly I saw him reach the passage where the father runs along behind his son's coffin; his voice broke several times, and suddenly he could restrain himself no longer, slapped his hand down on the manuscript, and said: "Oh, if only I were he!" This about you, and so it went on all night.' When they had finished (seven printers' sheets!) they decided as one man to go to see me immediately: 'It doesn't matter if he's asleep, we'll wake him up — this is more important than sleep!' Later, when I had grown accustomed to Nekrasov's character, I frequently experienced surprise at the memory of that moment: his temperament was so closed - anxious, almost, so cautious and uncommunicative. Thus, at least, he always seemed to me, so that the moment of our first meeting was truly a manifestation of the very deepest emotion. On that occasion they stayed with me for half an hour, and for half an hour we discussed God only knows how many things, understanding each other in half-words, with exclamations, hurrying; we talked about poetry, and about Gogol - with quotations from The Inspector General and Dead Souls - but mostly we discussed Belinsky. 'I shall take your tale to him today, and you will see - I mean, what a man he is, what a man! You will make his acquaint-ance, and you will see what a soul he has!' Nekrasov said enthusiastically, shaking me by the shoulders with both arms. 'Well, now you can sleep - go on, sleep, we'll leave now, and tomorrow you will come and see us!' As though I could have slept after their visit! What ecstasy, what success, and, most important of all, the feeling was dear to me, I remember it clearly: 'Some people have success, they are praised, greeted, congratulated, yet these men came running in tears, at four o'clock in the morning to wake me up because this was more important than sleep . . . How wonderful!' That was what I was thinking; how could I have slept?

Nekrasov took the manuscript to Belinsky that very same day. He held Belinsky in veneration and, I believe, loved him all his life more than anyone else. In those days Nekrasov had not yet written anything on the scale he was soon to achieve, a year later. Nekrasov turned up in St Petersburg at the age of about sixteen, completely alone.

His writing career began from practically the same age. Of his friendship with Belinsky I know little, except that Belinsky divined his talent from the very beginning and may have exercised a powerful influence on the tenor of his poetry. In spite of all Nekrasov's youthfulness and the difference in their ages, even at that time there probably passed between them moments and words of the kind that leave their mark for ever and bind two people irrevocably to each other. 'A new Gogol has appeared!' Nekrasov shouted, as he entered Belinsky's study holding the manuscript of Poor Folk. 'With you, Gogols grow like mushrooms,' Belinsky observed severely, but accepted the manuscript all the same. When Nekrasov called back to see him in the evening, Belinsky greeted him 'in a state of downright excitement': 'Bring him here, bring him here at once!'

And lo and behold (this must have been on the following day), I was taken to see him. I remember that I was most struck by his external appearance, by his nose, his forehead; for some reason I had imagined him to be quite different - 'that terrible, that fearsome critic'. He greeted me in a manner that was thoroughly solemn and reserved. 'Oh well, I suppose that's the way it has to be,' I thought; but it seemed that a minute had not passed, before everything was transformed: his solemnity was not that of an important personage, a great critic greeting a 22-year-old beginning writer, but was instead prompted, as it were, by the feelings he wanted to pour out to me as soon as possible, and by the solemn words he was in extreme haste to address: to me. He began to speak ardently, with burning eyes: 'Do you understand?' he asked me in his customary falsetto. 'Do you understand what you have written?' He always shouted in a falsetto when he was in the grip of powerful emotions. 'You have merely described it indirectly, with your artist's intuition; but have you pondered on the meaning of this terrible truth to which you have directed us? It cannot be that with your twenty years you can have understood this. Why, this unfortunate clerk of yours - why, he has worked so hard in the service and brought himself to such a point that he does not even dare to consider himself unhappy, out of humility, and views the slightest complaint as practically tantamount to free-thinking, does not even dare to acknowledge his right to unhappiness, and, when a kind man, his general, gives him a hundred rubles, he is completely shattered, annihilated with amazement that "Their Excellency" could have taken pity on one such as himself - not "His Excellency", but "Their Excellency" as it is expressed in your tale.* And that torn-off button, that moment when he kisses the general's hand - why here is no longer compassion for this, unfortunate man, but horror, horror! In this very gratitude of his there is horror! It is a tragedy! You have touched the very heart of the matter, you have pointed to the essential in one single flash. We publicists and critics merely reason, we attempt to elucidate all this in words, while you, an artist, represent the very essence in a single line, a single instantaneous image, so vivid that one feels one could touch it with one's hand, that the most unreflecting reader could instantly understand everything! There is, the secret of creativity, there is the truth of art! There is devotion to the artist's truth! Truth has been revealed and proclaimed to you as an artist, you have inherited it as a gift; so value your gift and remain loyal to it and you will be a great writer! . . .'

All this he said to me on that occasion. All this he later said to many other people besides, people who are still alive now and are able to bear testimony that it was so. I left his house in a state of intoxication. I stopped at the corner, looked up at the sky, at the bright day, at the people going past, and felt with my entire being that a solemn moment had occurred in my life, that my life had been subjected to a change of fortune that would affect it for ever, that something entirely new had begun, but such a thing as I had not envisioned even in my wildest dreams. (I was a terrible dreamer in those days.) 'Am I really so great?' I wondered in embarrassment and a kind of timid ecstasy. Oh, don't laugh, never again did I think I was great, but then - how could I endure what I had been told? 'Oh, I will be worthy of these praises, and what men, what men!' I thought. 'There are men for you! I shall endeavour to earn their praise, I shall make every effort to become as noble as they are, I will be "loyal"! Oh, how frivolous I am! If Belinsky only knew what worthless, shameful things there are in me! Yet people still say that these litterateurs are proud and vainglorious. While the fact is that these men are to be found only in Russia, they are alone, but they, they alone possess the truth, and truth and goodness will always be victorious and triumphant over sin and evil, we shall prevail; Oh, let us go to them, with them!'

All these things passed through my mind; I remember that moment with the fullest clarity. And never subsequently have I been able to forget it. It was the most heavenly moment in my whole life. When I was serving my term of penal servitude, the mere recollection of it was enough to keep my spirits up. Even now I remember it each time with ecstasy.

The rest of the story surrounding *Poor Folk* and the beginning of Dostoyevsky's career as a professional writer has been told by his biographers, and is too well-known to need recounting.

* In the final version of *Poor Folk,* Dostoyevsky used the form 'His Excellency', though he did preserve the plural in the verbs, an effect impossible to translate into English.

Appendix – 8

From '***The Notebook***' (2010) by José Saramago

October 29: *A New Capitalism?*

A few days ago, a number of us from dijferent countries and different political positions signed the text that I am reproducing below. It is a wakeup call, aprotest, and an expression of the alarm we feel faced with the crisis and the possible solutions being put forward. We cannot be complicit.

A NEW CAPITALISM?

The time has come for change on a collective and individual scale. The time has come for justice.

The financial crisis is again destroying our economies, hitting our lives hard. This past decade its disruptions have been increasingly frequent and dramatic. East Asia, Argentina, Turkey, Brazil, Russia, the massacre of the New Economics, prove that these are not just random accidents happening on the surface of economic life but are inscribed in the very heart of the system.

These ruptures that have ended up producing a disastrous contraction of contemporary economic life, and are used to justify unemployment and the spread of inequality, and mark the shattering of financial capitalism and the definitive ankylosis of the global economic order in which we live. So it is necessary to transform it radically.

In his discussion with President Bush, Durao Barroso, president of the European Union, stated that the current crisis should lead to "*a new global economic order,*" a solution that is acceptable as long as this new order is guided by the democratic principles—which should never be abandoned—of justice, liberty, equality and solidarity.

The laws of the market led to a state of chaos that brought a rescue of thousands of millions of dollars—to the culprits, not the victims. In other words, "rescue" meant "privatize the profits, nationalize the losses." This is a unique opportunity to redefine the global economic system in favor of social justice. There was no money to fund the fight against AIDS, nor to support feeding the world... and finally, in a real financial whirlwind, it turns out that there were enough funds to save from ruin those very same people who, by overly favoring dotcom and property bubbles, have destroyed the world economic edifice of "globalization."

This is why it is completely wrong for President Sarkozy to speak of the realization of so many efforts under the aegis of the interested parties aiming at "*a new capitalism*"! And for President Bush, as one might have expected, to have agreed that "*the freedom of the market*" should be safeguarded (without getting rid of farm subsidies!)...

No: now it is we, the citizens, who should be rescued, and we should with speed and courage favor the transition from an economy of war to an economy of global development, in which the collective embarrassment of three thousand million dollars a day being invested in arms while more than sixty thousand people are dying of starvation would be overcome. An economy of development that would eliminate the abusive exploitation of the natural resources currently taking place (oil, gas, minerals, coal) and apply norms under the supervision of a reconstituted United Nations—including the International Monetary Fund, the World Bank "*for reconstruction and development*," and the World Trade Organization, which should not be a private club for nations but a U.N.O. institution—. using whatever personal, human and technical means were necessary to exercise its judicial and ethical authority effectively.

Investment in renewable energy, food production (agriculture and aquiculture), the obtaining and distribution of water, and in health, education, housing. . . so that the "*new economic order*" might at last be democratic and beneficial to individuals. The errors of globalization and of the market economy must stop! Civil society will no longer remain a resigned spectator, and if necessary will apply all the power of the citizenry together with every modern means of communication it now has at its fingertips.

A new capitalism? No!

The time has come for change on a collective and individual scale. The time has come for justice.

Federico Mayor Zaragoza
Francisco Altemir
Jose Saramago
Roberto Savio
Mario Scares
Jose Vidal Beneyto '

October 30: *The Question*

"And I would ask the political economists, the moralists, if they have already calculated the number of individuals who must be condemned to wretchedness, to overwork, to demoralization, to infantilization, to despicable ignorance, to insurmountable misfortune, to utter penury, in order to produce one rich person?"

Almeid

Appendix −9

Is That So?

The Zen master Hakuin was praised by his neighbours as one living a pure life.

A beautiful Japanese girl whose parents owned a food store lived near him. Suddenly, without any warning, her parents discovered she was with child.

This made her parents angry. She would not confess who the man was, but after much harassment at last named Hakuin.

In great anger the parents went to the master. 'Is that so?' was all he would say.

After the child was born it was brought to Hakuin. By this time he had lost his reputation, which did not trouble him, but he took very good care of the child. He obtained milk from his neighbours and everything else the little one needed.

A year later the girl-mother could stand it no longer. She told her parents the truth - that the real father of the child was a young man who worked in the fishmarket.

The mother and father of the girl at once went to Hakuin to ask his forgiveness, to apologize at length, and to get the child back again.

Hakuin was willing. In yielding the child, all he said was'. 'Is that so?'

From: 'Zen Flesh, Zen Bones'

Appendix 10

Part-1 & 2 from '*Klingsor's Last Summer*' by Hermann Hesse

The Day at Kareno

TOGETHER WITH HIS FRIENDS from Barengo and with Agosto and Emilia, Klingsor set out on the walk to Kareno. Early in the morning they descended among the strongly scented spireas, the bedewed spider-webs quivering on the margins of the woods, down through the steep, warm forest into the valley of Pampambio where beside the yellow road bright yellow houses slept, bent brazen and half dead, stunned by the summer days. By the dried-up stream bed the white metallic willows hung heavy wings over golden meadows. A colourful troupe, the friends bowled down the rosy road through the misty green of the valley: the men white and yellow in linens and silks, the women white and pink, Ersilia's Veronese green parasol sparkling like a jewel in a magic ring.

"It's a pity, Klingsor," the doctor remarked plaintively in his kindly voice. "Your wonderful water-colours will all be white in ten years. These colours you like so well have no lasting qualities."

"Yes," Klingsor said, "and what is worse, Doctor: your fine brown hair will all be grey in ten years, and a little while later all our good gay bones will be lying in some hole in the ground, including, alas, your beautiful and healthy bones, Ersilia. My friends, let's not start becoming sensible so late in life. Hermann, how does Li Po put it?"

Hermann the Poet stood still and intoned:

Life passes like a flash of lightning
Whose blaze barely lasts long enough to see.
While the earth and the sky stand still forever
How swiftly changing time flies across man's face.
O you who sit over your full cup and do not drink,
Tell me whom you are still waiting for?

"No," Klingsor said, "I mean the other poem, the rhymed one, about the hair that was still dark at morning..."

Hermann promptly recited:

Only this morning your hair gleamed silken and black,
Evening has already sprinkled it with snow.
If you would not suffer as on the rack
Hold out your cup and summon the moon for your drink-fellow.

Klingsor laughed heartily in his somewhat hoarse voice.

"Good old Li Po! He had inklings; he knew all sorts of things. We know all sorts of things too - he is our wise old brother. This giddy day would please him. It's just the kind of day lovely for dying Li Po's death at evening, in the boat on the quiet river. You'll see, everything is going to be wonderful today."

"What kind of death was it that Li Po died on the river?" Martha, the artist, asked.

But Ersilia interrupted in her dear, deep voice: "Stop it now. I'll begin detesting anybody who says another word about death and dying. Finisca adesso, brutto Klingsor!"

Laughing, Klingsor came over to her. "How right you are, bambina! If I say another word about dying you can poke your parasol into both my eyes. But seriously, 'tis a glorious day, my dears. A bird is singing today, a bird out of a fairy tale - I heard it once before this morning. A wind is blowing today, a wind out of a fairy tale, the child of heaven who wakens the sleeping princesses and blows reason clear out of people's heads. A flower is blossoming today, a flower out of a fairy tale, it's blue and blooms only once in a lifetime and whoever plucks it wins bliss."

"Did all that mean anything?" Ersilia asked the doctor.

Klingsor heard her.

"What it all meant is: this day will never come again and anyone who fails to eat and drink and taste and smell it will never have it offered to him again in all eternity. The sun will never shine as it does today; it is in a constellation in the sky, a conjunction with Jupiter, with me, with Agosto and Ersilia and all of us, a conjunction that will never come again, not in a thousand years. And therefore I want to walk on your left side for a while, because that brings luck, and carry your emerald parasol - under its light my head will look like an opal. But you must play your part and sing a song, one of your best."

He took Ersilia's arm. His sharp features dipped softly into the blue-green shade of the parasol. He had fallen in love with it; its blatant, sweet colour delighted him.

Ersilia began to sing:

Il mio papà no vuole,
Ch'io spos' un bersaglier-

Voices joined in; singing, they walked on to the forest and into the forest, until the climb became too steep. The path led sharply upward like a ladder, scaling the great mountain.

"What a marvellous straight line this song takes!" Klingsor praised it. "Papa is against the lovers, just as he always is. They take a knife that cuts well and stab Papa to death. He's gone. They do it at night, nobody sees them but the moon, who doesn't betray them, and the stars, who are mute, and God, who's going to forgive them after all. How beautiful and sincere that is. A poet of the present day would be stoned for writing such a thing."

They climbed the narrow mountain path in the sun-splashed shadows of the chestnuts. When Klingsor looked up he saw before his face the slender calves of Martha, the artist, showing pink through her transparent stockings. If he looked hack, the green of the parasol arched above Emilia's curly black hair. Underneath she was silken violet, the only dark patch among all these figures.

At a blue and orange farmhouse fallen summer apples lay in the meadow, cool and sour. They tasted them. Martha spoke enthusiastically about an outing on the Seine, in Paris, before the war. Ah yes, Paris, and the bliss of those days.

"That will never come again. Never again."

"Nor ought it to," the painter exclaimed vehemently, shaking his sparrow-hawk's head fiercely. "Nothing ought to come again. Why should it? What childish wishes! The war has glossed over everything in the past, turning it all into a paradise, even the most idiotic things, the things we could well do without. Very well, it was lovely in Paris and lovely in Rome and lovely in Aries. But is it any less lovely today, right here? Paradise isn't Paris and peacetime, Paradise is here. It lives up there on the mountain and in an hour we'll be in the midst of it and will be the thieves to whom it was said: This day you will be with me in Paradise."

They broke out of the mottled shade of the woods path onto the broad open highway that soared, bright and hot, in great spirals to the summit. Klingsor, his eyes shielded by his dark-green glasses, walked last in line, and often fell behind to watch the others moving and see the coloured combinations they formed. He had deliberately taken nothing with him for working, not even his small notebook, and nevertheless he stood still a hundred times, stirred by pictures. His gaunt figure stood alone, showing white against the reddish gravel of the road, at the edge of a grove of acacias. Summer breathed hotly upon the mountain. Light poured vertically down. Colour steamed multifold out of the depths. Above the nearest mountains, their greens and reds harmonizing with white villages, bluish ridges peered; and beyond, paler and bluer, more and more ridges. Very far away and unreal rose the snow-capped crystalline peaks. Above the acacias and chestnut trees the mighty rocky wall and hump-backed summit of Monte Salute emerged, reddish and light purple. But the people were more beautiful than all the rest. Like flowers they stood in the light beneath the greenery. The emerald parasol glowed like a giant scarab. Emilia's black hair beneath it, the white slender painter Martha with her rosy face, and all the others. Klingsor drank them in with a thirsty eye, but his thoughts were with Gina. He would not be able to see her for another week. She was sitting in an office in the city, working away at the typewriter; he seldom managed to see her alone. And he loved her, her more than all the others, though she knew nothing about him, did not understand him, regarded him as a strange rare bird, a famous foreign painter. How strange that was, that his longings should cling to her alone, that no other love sanctified him. It was not like him to go far out of his way for a woman. But he did for Gina, in order to be beside her for an hour, to hold her small slender fingers, to thrust his shoe beneath hers, to imprint a quick kiss on the nape of her neck. He thought about that, a droll puzzle to himself. Was this already the turning point? Old age already coming on? Was it only that, the December-May impulse of the man of forty for the girl of twenty?

They had reached the ridge, and beyond, a new world flung itself at their eyes: Monte Gennaro, high and unreal, piled up out of endless steep, sharp pyramids and cones, the sun aslant behind it, each plateau glistening enamel floating on deep violet shadows. Between it and themselves the vast areas of shimmering air, and lost in infinite depths the narrow blue arm of the lake, resting amid the green flames of the forest.

There was a tiny village on the summit: a smallish manor house, four or five other houses, of stone, painted blue and pink, a chapel, a fountain, cherry trees. The company paused by the fountain in the sunlight. Klingsor walked on, through an arched gateway into a shadowy farmyard. Three bluish buildings stood tall in it, with only a few small windows, grass and gravel between them, a goat, nettles. A child ran away from him; he coaxed her to come hack, took chocolate from his pocket. The child stopped; he caught her, caressed her, and pressed the chocolate upon her. She was shy and lovely, a dark-brown girl with the alarmed black eyes of a small animal, slender bare legs, brown and gleaming, "Where do you live?" he asked her. She ran to the nearest open door in one of the clifflike houses. From a dark stone room like a primeval cave a woman stepped, the child's mother; she too accepted chocolate. Above dirty clothing the brown throat rose, a firm-muscled, broad face, sun-tanned and beautiful, a broad full mouth, large eyes, crude sweet charm. Those large, ample Asiatic figures quietly bespoke sexuality and motherhood. He leaned seductively towards her; smiling, she held him off, drawing the child between them. He walked on, resolved to return. He wanted to paint this woman, or be her lover, if only for an hour. She was everything: mother, child, mistress, animal, madonna.

Slowly, he returned to the group, his heart full of dreams. On the wall of the estate, whose house seemed empty and locked, crude old cannonballs had been affixed. A whimsical stairway led through shrubbery to a grove and hill with a monument atop it. There, baroque and solitary, stood a bust: Wallenstein costume, curls, tapering wavy beard. Ghosts and phantasms shimmered around the mountain in the glaring midday light. Strange things lurked; the world was tuned to another, remote key. Klingsor drank at the fountain. A swallowtail butterfly flew close and sucked at the sprinkled drops on the limestone rim of the fountain.

The mountain road led along the ridge under chestnuts and walnuts, in sun and shade. At a bend there was a wayside chapel, old and yellow, faded old pictures in the niche, a saint's head, angelically sweet and childlike, a patch of her red and brown garment, the rest crumbled away. Klingsor loved old pictures, especially when they came his way unlooked for; he loved such frescoes; he loved the way these beautiful works returned to dust and the earth.

More trees, vines, dazzling hot road. Another turn: there was their destination, suddenly, unexpectedly: a dark arched gateway, a large tall church of red stone, crashing with self-assurance against the sky, a plaza full of sunlight, dust and peace, grass parched to redness, crackling underfoot, noonday light reflected by glaring walls, a column, a figure atop it, invisible in the blaze of sunlight, a stone balustrade around the broad plaza poised over an infinity of blue. Beyond, the village of Kareno, ancient, narrow, densely dark, Saracen, gloomy stone caves under faded brown brick, lanes oppressively narrow as in a dream and full of darkness, small squares suddenly shrieking aloud in white sunlight, Africa and Nagasaki, above the forest, below the blue abyss, higher still the white, plump, saturated clouds.

"It's funny how much time we need before we know our way around in the world just a little," Klingsor said. "Once when I was going to Africa, years ago, I passed by this place in an express train, three or five or six miles away, and knew nothing about it. From Africa I went on to Asia, and at the time it was terribly necessary that I do so. But everything I found there I am finding here today: primeval forest, heat, beautiful alien people without nerves, sunlight, temples. It takes so long to learn to visit three continents in a single day. Here they are. Welcome, India! Welcome, Africa! Welcome, Japan!"

The friends knew a young lady who lived up here, and Klingsor was greatly looking forward to meeting the unknown woman. He called her the Queen of the Mountains; that was the title of a mysterious Oriental story in the books of his boyhood.

Expectantly, the caravan penetrated the blue-shaded gorge of the lanes. Not a person, not a sound, not a chicken, not a dog. But in the semishade of a window embrasure Klingsor saw a silent figure standing, a lovely girl, black-eyed, red kerchief around her black hair. Her gaze, lying in wait to capture the stranger, struck his. For the span of a long breath they looked fully, gravely into each other's eyes, two alien worlds momentarily close. Then both smiled briefly, the heart-felt eternal greeting of the sexes, the old, sweet, devouring enmity, and with a step around the corner of the house the stranger had fled away and been placed in the girl's hope chest, a picture among many pictures, a dream among many dreams. The small thorn pricked Klingsor's never-satiated heart; for a moment he hesitated and thought to turn back. Agosto called him; Emilia began to sing; a shadowy wall vanished and a small, brilliant square with two yellow palazzi lay still and dazzling in the enchanted noon: narrow stone balconies, closed shutters, a glorious stage for the first act of an opera.

"Arrival in Damascus," the doctor called out "Where does Fatima live, the pearl among women?"

The answer came, surprisingly; from the smaller palazzo. Out of the cool blackness behind the half-closed balcony door a strange tone sounded, then another, and the same repeated ten times, then the octave ten times - a piano was being tuned, a melodious piano in the middle of Damascus.

This must he it; this was where she lived. But the house seemed to lack an entrance; there was only the yellow wall with two balconies, and above them a bit of painting in the stucco of the gable: blue and red flowers and a parrot. There should have been a painted door here and if you knocked three times and pronounced Open Sesame the painted door would fly open and the wanderer be greeted by aromatic fragrances, with the Queen of the Mountain seated on a high dais, behind veils, slave girls cowering on the steps at her feet and the painted parrot flying screeching to her mistress's shoulder.

They found a tiny door in a side street. A loud bell, a devilish mechanism, clanged angrily. A small staircase, narrow as a ladder, led upward. Impossible to imagine how the piano had ever been brought into this house. Through the window? Through the roof?

A large black dog came rushing, a small blond lion after him. A burst of noise; the stairs rattled; in the background the piano sang the same tone eleven times. Sweetly soft light poured out of a room coated with a pinkish whitewash. Doors slammed. Where was the parrot?

Suddenly the Queen of the Mountains stood there, a slender lissom flower, body straight and pliant, all in red, burning flames, image of youth. Before Klingsor's eyes a hundred beloved pictures scattered away and the new picture radiantly took their place. He knew at once that he would paint her, not realistically, but the ray within her that had struck him, the poem, the tart lovely tone: youth, Redness, Blondness, Amazon. He would look at her for an hour, perhaps several hours. He would see her walking, sitting, laughing, perhaps dancing, perhaps hear her singing. The day was crowned; the day had been given its meaning. Anything else that might come was pure gift, superfluity. It was always this way: an experience never came alone. Its birds always flew ahead, there were always harbingers and omens: the Asiatic maternal animal look in that doorway, the black-haired village beauty in the window, and now this.

For a second the feeling darted through him: "If only I were ten years younger, ten brief years, this girl could have me, capture me, wind me around her finger. Now, you are too young, little red queen, too young for the old wizard Klingsor! He will admire you, will get to know you by heart; but he will make no pilgrimage to you, climb no ladder to you, commit no murder for you, and sing no serenades outside your pretty balcony. No, unfortunately he will do none of these things, not the old painter Klingsor, the old ram. He will not love you, he will not cast his eyes at you as he cast his eyes at the Asiatic, at the black-haired girl in the window, who is perhaps not a day younger than you are. He is not too old for her, only for you, Queen of the Mountain, red flower on the hill. For you, wild pink, he is too old. For you the love that Klingsor has to give away between a day full of work and a night full of red wine is not enough. All the better, then, my eye will drink you down, slender rocket, and know you when you have long since faded within me."

Through stone-floored rooms separated by doorless arches they entered a hall where fantastic baroque plaster figures pranced above tall doors and all around ran a dark frieze of painted dolphins, white horses, and pink Cupids floating in a densely populated mythical sea. There were a few chairs and parts of the disassembled grand piano on the floor, nothing else in the large room. But two alluring doors led to two small balconies above the sun-struck operatic plaza, and diagonally across the balconies of the neighbouring palazzo thrust out, they too wreathed with paintings. There a fat red cardinal floated like a goldfish in the sun.

They stayed. In the big hall provisions were unpacked, a table set. Wine was brought, rare white wine from the north, the key to hosts of memories. The piano tuner had decamped; the dismantled piano held its peace. Thoughtfully, Klingsor stared at the exposed bowels of glittering strings; then he softly closed the lid. His eyes ached, but the summer day sang in his heart, the Saracen mother sang, blue and soaring the dream of Kareno sang. He ate and clinked his glass with others; he talked gaily in a high voice; and behind it all the apparatus of his workshop operated. His eyes enveloped the wild pink, the field poppy, like water round a fish. A diligent chronicler sat in his brain and carefully wrote down forms, rhythms, movements as if inscribing brazen columns of figures.

Talk and laughter filled the empty room. The doctor's kindly, prudent laugh sounded, Ersilia's low and friendly, Agosto's strong and subterranean, Martha's birdlike. The poet talked sensibly, Klingsor jokingly. Watching closely, a little shy, the red queen went among her guests, dolphins and horses, sped here and there, stood by the piano, crouched on a cushion, cut bread, poured wine with an inexperienced girlish hand. Joyousness resounded in the cool hall; eyes glistened dark and blue; outside the high balcony doors the dazzling noon stared down, on guard.

The clear, splendid wine flowed into the glasses, delicious contrast to the simple cold meal. The red day flowed clear from the queen's dress through the high room; alert and clear, the eyes of all the men followed it. She vanished, returned, and had donned a blue kerchief.

After eating, tired and satiated, they set out for the woods, lay down in grass and moss. Parasols gleamed, faces glowed under straw hats, the sun glittered and burned. The Queen of the Mountains lay redly in the green grass, her fine throat rising white from the flame, her high shoe intensely coloured and alive on her slender foot. Klingsor, close by her, read her, studied her, filled himself with her, just as he had as a boy read the magical story of the Queen of the Mountains and filled himself with it. They rested, dozed, chattered, flicked at ants, thought they heard snakes. Prickly chestnut shells clung to the women's hair. They thought of absent friends who had missed this hour - there were not many. They wished Louis the Cruel were here, Klingsor's friend, the painter of carousels and circuses. His antic spirit hovered above the group, close by.

The afternoon passed like a year in paradise. There was a great deal of laughter when they parted from the Queen. Klingsor took everything with him in his heart: the Queen, the woods, the palazzo and the dolphin room, the two dogs, the parrot.

Descending the mountain among his friends, there gradually came over him that exuberant mood that he had only on rare days when he had voluntarily let his work go. Hand in hand with Emilia, with Hermann, with Martha, he danced down the sunlit road, starting songs, taking childlike pleasure in jokes and puns, surrendering to laughter. He ran ahead of the others and lay in ambush to frighten them.

Quickly as they walked, the sun sank more quickly. By the time they reached Palazzetto it had dropped behind the mountain, and in the valley below, it was already evening. They had missed the way and descended too low; they were hungry and tired and had to abandon their plans for the evening: a stroll through the fields to Barengo, a fish dinner in the lakeside village's restaurant

"My dears," Klingsor said, sitting down on a wall by the wayside, "Our plans were all very fine, and I would certainly be grateful for a good dinner among the fishermen or in Monte d'Oro. But we cannot make it that far, or at least I cannot. I'm tired and I'm hungry. I'm not taking another step beyond the nearest grotto, which certainly isn't far. There we can get bread and wine. That's enough. Who's coming?"

They all came. They found the grotto; on a narrow terrace cut into the forested hill stood stone benches and tables under the darkness of trees. From the wine cellar in the cavern the innkeeper brought cool wine. There was bread on the tables. Now they sat eating in silence, glad to be sitting down at last. Beyond the tall tree trunks the day faded out; the blue mountain turned black, the red road white. Down below, on the nocturnal road, they could hear a car, and a dog barking. Here and there stars appeared in the sky, and in the landscape below lights winked on; there was no telling the two apart.

Klingsor sat happily resting, looking out into the night, slowly checking his hunger with black bread, quietly draining the bluish cups of wine. Satiated, he began to talk again and to sing; he rocked to the beat of the songs, played with the women, sniffed the fragrance of their hair. The wine seemed good to him. Practiced seducer, he easily talked down the proposals that they go on their way. He drank wine, poured wine, sent for more wine. Slowly, out of the bluish earthenware cups, symbol of transitoriness, bright spells arose, magic transforming the world, colouring the stars and lights.

They sat in a swing hovering high above the abyss of world and night, birds in a golden cage, homeless, weightless, across from the stars. They sang, these birds, sang exotic songs; out of ecstatic hearts they cast fantasies into the night, into the sky, into the woods, into the enchanted universe. Answers came from stars and moon, from trees and mountains. Goethe sat there and his alter ego Hafis: torrid Egypt and grave Greece rose up; Mozart smiled; Hugo Wolf played the piano in the delirious night.

There was a crash of noise, a blaze of light; below them, straight through the heart of the earth, with a hundred dazzling lighted windows, a railroad train streaked into the mountain and into the night. In the sky above, the bells of an invisible church rang. With a skulking air the half moon rose above the table, glanced at its reflection in the dark wine, marked a woman's mouth and eye off from the darkness, mounted higher, sang to the stars. The spirit of Louis the Cruel sat hunched, solitary, on a bench, writing letters.

Klingsor, King of the Night, tall Crown in his hair, leaning back on his throne of stone, directed the dance of the world, set the beat, called forth the moon, willed that the railroad train vanish. At once it was gone, as a constellation plummets over the margin of the sky. Where was the Queen of the Mountains? Was that not a piano sounding in the woods? Was not the mistrustful little lion barking far off? Had she not been wearing a blue kerchief a moment ago? Hello, old world, see to it that you don't collapse! Come here, woods! Go there, black mountain! Keep to the beat! Stars, how blue and red you are, as in the folk song: "Your red eyes and your blue mouth!"

Painting was lovely; painting was a dear, lovely game for well-behaved children, But it was something else, grander and more momentous, to direct the movements of the stars, to project the beat of your own blood, the circlets of colour from your own retina, into the world, to send the vibrations of your own soul thrumming out with the wind of the night Away with you, black mountains! Become a cloud, fly to Persia, rain on Uganda! Come here, spirit of Shakespeare, sing us your drunken fool's song of the rain that raineth every day!

Klingsor kissed a woman's small hand, leaned against a woman's sweetly rising and falling breast. A foot under the table played with his. He did not know whose hand or whose foot; he felt tenderness all around him, gratefully felt old magic renewed. He was still young, it was still far from the end, he was still capable of radiation and allure; they still loved him, the good anxious little females, they still counted on him.

He soared higher. In a low, chanting voice he began to tell a tale, a tremendous epic, the story of a love affair, or rather it was really a trip to the South Seas where in the company of Gauguin and Crusoe he discovered Parrot Island and founded the Free State of the Blessed Isles. How the thousands of parrots had sparkled in the twilight, how their blue tails had glittered, mirrored in the green bay! Their cries, and the hundred-voiced shrieks of the big monkeys, had greeted him like thunder - him, Klingsor, when he proclaimed his Free State. He had called upon the white cockatoo to form a cabinet, and with the sulky rhinoceros bird he had drunk palm wine from heavy coconut cups. O moon of the past, moon of the blissful nights, moon above the pile dwelling among the reeds! The shy brown princess bore the name of Kül Kalüa; slender and long-limbed she strode through the banana forest, gleaming like honey under the succulent roof of the giant leaves, doe-eyed, cat-backed, feline tension in springy ankle and sinewy leg. Kül Kalüa, child, archaic ardour and childish innocence of the sacred southeast; for a thousand nights you lay upon Klingsor's heart and every night was new, each was sweeter, each tenderer than all the others. O festival of the Earth Spirit when the virgins of the Parrot Islands dance before the god!

Over the islands, over Crusoe and Klingsor, over the tale and the listeners, the white-stared night arched, the mountain swelled like gently breathing belly and breasts under the trees and houses and the feet of men; the racing moon danced feverishly over the firmament, pursued by the stars in wild and silent choreography. Strings of stars lined up, the glittering wire of a cable railway to Paradise. Primeval forest darkened maternally, primordial mud wafted the scent of decay and generation, serpents and crocodiles crawled, the stream of forms poured on without bounds or banks.

"I'm going to paint again after all," Klingsor said. "I'll start again tomorrow. But no more of these houses and people and trees. I'll paint crocodiles and starfish, dragons and purple snakes, and everything that is changing, filled with longing to become man, full of longing to become stars, full of birth, full of decay, full of God and death."

In the midst of his almost whispered words, in the midst of the wild drunken hour, Ersilia's voice sounded low and clear. Quietly she sang the song of *bel mazzo de fiori* under her breath. Tranquillity poured from her song; Klingsor heard it as if it came from some distant floating island across seas of time and solitude. He turned his empty wine cup over, filled it no more. He listened. A child sang. A mother sang. What was he - an errant and reprobate fellow bathed in the mire of the world, a scoundrel and profligate, or was he a silly small child?

"Ersilia," he said with reverence, "you are our lucky star."

Up the mountain through the steep dark woods, clinging to branches and roots, they sought their homeward path, reached the margin of the woods, boarded a field like pirates on a ship. The narrow path through the cornfield breathed night and home-coming, moon glancing against the shiny leaves of corn, rows of grapevines slanting away. Now Klingsor sang, softly, in his somewhat hoarse voice, sang many murmuring songs, German and Malay, with and without words. Singing low he poured out all that had accumulated within him, as a brown wall at evening radiates the stored daylight.

Here one of the friends took his leave, another there, vanishing along narrow paths in the shadow of the grapes. Each left, each went by himself, heading home, alone under the sky. A woman kissed Klingsor good night; burning, her mouth sipped at his. They rolled away, they melted away, all of them. When Klingsor, alone, climbed the stairs to his dwelling, he was still singing. He sang the praises of God and himself; he praised Li Po and the good wine of Pampambio. Like an idol, he rested upon clouds of affirmation.

"Inwardly," he sang, "I am like a ball of gold, like the dome of a cathedral; people kneel in it, people pray, gold gleams from the wall, the Saviour bleeds in an old painting, the heart of Mary bleeds. We bleed too, we others, we errant souls, we stars and comets; seven and fourteen swords pierce our blessed chests. I love you, blond and dark women, I love all, even the philistines; you are all poor devils like myself, all poor children and misbegotten demigods like drunken Klingsor. Beloved life, I greet you! I greet you, beloved death!"

The Music of Doom

THE LAST DAY OF JULY had come, Klingsor's favourite month; Li Po's grand festival had faded, had not been repeated. Sunflowers in the garden brashly raised their gold to the blue. Together with his faithful Tu Fu, Klingsor tramped through a region that he loved: the parched outskirts of a town, dusty roads beneath high rows of trees, red and orange little houses facing the sandy shore, trucks and quays, long violet walls, colourful poor folk. In the evening he sat in the dust at the edge of the town and painted the coloured tents and wagons of an itinerant carnival; he crouched by the side of the road on scruffy, parched greensward, beguiled by the strong colours of the tents. He clung fast to the faded lilac of a tent tassel, to the jolly greens and reds of the clumsy trailer homes, to the blue-and-white framing poles. Fiercely, he wallowed in cadmium, savagely in cool sweet cobalt, drew melting lines of crimson lake through the yellow and green sky. Another hour, no, less, then he would knock off, night would come, and tomorrow August would be starting. August the burning fever month which mixes so much fear of death and timorousness into its ardent cup. The scythe was sharpened, the day declined; death laughed, concealed among the parching leaves. Ring high and blast your trumpet, cadmium! Boast loudly, lush crimson lake. Laugh glaringly, lemon yellow! Come here, you deep-blue mountain in the distance. Come to my heart, you matt dusty green trees. How tired you are, how you let your pious branches droop submissively, I drink to you, lovely things of the world! I give you semblance of duration and immortality, I who am the most transitory, the most believing, the saddest of all, who suffer from the fear of death more than all of you. July is burned out, soon August will be burned out, suddenly the great ghost chills us from the yellowed leaves in the dew-wet morning. Suddenly November sweeps across the woods. Suddenly the great ghost laughs, suddenly the chill settles around our hearts, suddenly the dear pink flesh falls from our bones, the jackal howls in the desert, the vulture hoarsely sings his accursed song. An accursed newspaper in the city publishes my picture, and under it the words: "Outstanding painter, expressionist, great colourist, died on the sixteenth of this month."

Full of hatred he ripped a furrow of Paris blue under the green gypsy wagon. Full of bitterness, he broke the chrome-yellow edge of the kerbstones. Full of deep despair, he dashed vermilion in an empty spot, annihilating the challenging white; bleeding, he fought for continuance. He screamed in bright green and Neapolitan yellow to inexorable God. Groaning he threw more blue into the dreary dusty green; imploringly, he kindled deeper lights in the evening sky. The little palette full of pure unmixed colours, intensely luminous, was his comfort, his tower, his arsenal, his prayer book, his cannon. From it he fired upon wicked death. Purple was denial of death, vermilion was mockery of decay. His arsenal was good; his brave troop stood lined up brilliantly, the rapid rounds from his cannon flashed. But it was no use, all shooting was in vain; and yet shooting was good, was happiness and consolation, was still living, still triumphing.

Tu Fu had left to visit a friend who had his magic citadel over there between the factory and the wharf. Now he returned, bringing with him the Armenian astrologer.

Klingsor, finished with the painting, drew a deep breath of relief when he saw the two faces close by, the good fair hair of Tu Fu and the black beard with white teeth in the smiling face of the magus. With them came the shadow also, the long dark shadow with receding eyes in deep sockets. Welcome, you too, Shadow, fine fellow!

"Do you know what day today is?" Klingsor asked his friend.

"The last day of July, I know."

"I cast a horoscope today," the Armenian said, "and I saw that this evening is going to bring me something. Saturn stands strangely, Mars neutral, Jupiter is dominant. Li Po, aren't you a Leo?"

"I was born on July the second."

"I thought so. Your stars stand confusedly, Friend; only you yourself can interpret them. Fertility surrounds you like a cloud about to burst. Your stars stand oddly, Klingsor; I'm sure you can't help feeling it."

Klingsor packed up his gear. The world he had painted was faded, the green and yellow sky extinguished, the bright blue flag drowned, the lovely yellow slain and withered. He was hungry and thirsty; his throat felt full of dust

"Friends," he said cordially, "let us spend this evening together. We shall no longer be together again, all four of us; I am not reading that in the stars, but I find it written in my heart. My July moon is over; its last hours glow darkly; in the depths the Great Mother calls. Never has the world been so beautiful, never have I painted so beautiful a picture. Heat lightning flashes; the music of doom has begun. Let us sing along with it, the sweet forbidding music. Let us stay together and drink wine and eat bread."

Beside the carousel, whose tent had just been taken down in preparation for the evening (for it was there as a sunshade), a few tables stood under the trees. A lame waitress was going back and forth; there was a small tavern in the shade. Here they sat at the plank table; bread was brought, and wine poured into the earthenware vessels. Lights glowed into life under the trees. A short distance away the carousel's hurdy-gurdy began to jingle, loosing its shrill music into the evening.

"I mean to drain three hundred cups tonight!" Li Po cried, and toasted the Shadow. "Greetings, Shadow, steadfast tin soldier! Greetings, friends! Greetings, electric lights, arc lamps and sparkling merry-go-round spangles! Oh, if only Louis were here, the fugitive bird! Perhaps he's already flown on ahead of us to heaven. Or perhaps he'll come back tomorrow, the old jackal, and no longer find us and laugh and plant arc lamps and flagpoles upon our grave."

Quietly, the astrologer went and returned with fresh wine, his white teeth smiling gladly in his red mouth.

"Melancholia," he said with a glance at Klingsor, "is a thing we should not carry around. It's so easy - it's the work of an hour, a single intensive hour with clenched teeth, and then one is through with melancholia forever."

Klingsor looked closely at his mouth, at the bright, straight teeth that had once upon a time, in some fervid hour, crunched melancholia and bitten it to death. Could he too do what the astrologer had succeeded in doing? O sweet brief glance into distant gardens: life without dread, life without melancholia! But he knew these gardens were unattainable for him. He knew his destiny was different, Saturn lowered differently upon him, God wanted him to play different tunes upon his strings.

"Each has his stars," Klingsor said slowly. "Each has his faith. I believe in only one thing: in doom. We are driving in a carriage on the edge of an abyss, and the horses have already shied. We are immersed in doom, all of us; we must die, we must be born again. The great turning point has come for us. It is the same everywhere: the great war, the great change in art, the great collapse in the governments of the West. For us in old Europe everything we had that was good and our own has already died. Our fine-feathered Reason has become madness, our money is paper, our machines can do nothing but shoot and explode, our art is suicide. We are going under, friends; that is our destiny. Music in the Tsing Tse key has begun."

The Armenian poured wine.

"As you like," he said. "One can say yes and one can say no; that is only a child's game. Doom is something that does not exist. For doom or resurgence to exist there must be a top and a bottom. But there is no top or bottom; these exist only in man's brain, which is the home of illusion. All paradoxes are illusions: white and black are illusion, death and life are illusion, good and evil are illusion. It is the work of an hour, a single fervent hour with clenched teeth, and one has overcome the kingdom of illusions."

Klingsor listened to his good voice.

"I am speaking of us," he retorted. "I am speaking of Europe, our old Europe that for two thousand years thought itself the world's brain. It is going under. Do you think, Magus, that I don't know you? You are a messenger from the East, a messenger to me also, perhaps a spy, perhaps a warlord in disguise. You are here because the end is beginning, because the scent of doom is in your nostrils. But we are glad to go under, you know, we die gladly, we do not defend ourselves."

"You may also say: we are glad to be born," the Asiatic said, laughing. "To you it seems doom, perhaps to me it seems birth. Both are illusion. The man who believes in the earth as a fixed disk under heaven also sees and believes in sunrise and sunset, in dawn and doom - and all, almost all men believe in that fixed disk! The stars themselves know nothing of rising and setting."

"Have not the stars set, are not the stars doomed too?" Tu Fu cried.

"For us, for our eyes."

He filled the cups; it was always he who undertook to pour, attentively, smilingly. He went away with the empty pitcher to bring more wine. The carousel music blared.

"Let's go over there, it's so lovely," Tu Fu pleaded, and they went over to the carousel, stood by the painted barrier, watched the carousel turn its giddy circles in the piercing glitter of spangles and mirrors. They saw a hundred children with eyes greedily fixed on the brilliance. For a moment

Klingsor felt, with deep amusement, the primitiveness and African quality of this whirling machine, this mechanical music, these garish pictures and colours, mirrors and insane ornamental columns. Everything bespoke medicine men and shamans, magic and age-old pied-piperism, and all that wild weird sparkle was at bottom nothing but the darting glitter of the tin lure that the pike thinks is a minnow.

Every child must ride the carousel. Tu Fu gave money to the children; the Shadow beckoned to all the children to come nearer. They clustered around their benefactor, clung to him, begged, thanked. There was a pretty blond girl of twelve who asked repeatedly; she rode on every round. In the glitter of the lights her short skirt blew up around her boyish legs. One child cried. Boys fought. The cymbals clanged sharply along with the organ, poured fire into the beat, opium into the wine. For a long while the four stood amid the tumult.

Then they returned to their quiet table under the trees. The Armenian filled the cups with wine, stirred up doom, smiled brightly.

"Let us empty three hundred cups today," Klingsor sang. His sun-bleached hair glowed yellow, his laughter boomed. Melancholia knelt, a giant, upon his twitching heart. He held up his glass in a toast, he hailed doom, hailed the desire for death, the Tsing Tse key. The carousel music surged and roared. But inside his heart, dread lurked. The heart did not want to die. The heart hated death.

Suddenly more music assaulted the night, shrill, in-temperate, from the tavern. In the nook beside the chimney piece, whose shell was lined with neatly arranged wine bottles, a player-piano blazed, machine-gun fire, wild, hectoring, impetuous. Sorrow cried from discordant strings, steam-roller rhythm flattened groaning dissonances. There was a crowd here too, light, noise, young men and girls dancing, the lame waitress too, and Tu Fu. He danced with the blond little girl. Klingsor watched. Lightly, sweetly, her short summer dress whirled around the pretty skinny legs. Tu Fu's face smiled amiably, filled with love. The others sat at the chimney piece; they had come in from the garden, were close to the source of the music, in the very midst of it. Klingsor saw tones, heard colours. The magus took one and another bottle from the shelf, opened them, poured. His smile never wavered on his brown intelligent face. The music thumped fearfully in the low-ceilinged hall. Slowly the Armenian opened a breach in the row of old bottles on the mantle, like a temple robber removing, chalice by chalice, the precious utensils from an altar.

"You are a great artist," the astrologer whispered to Klingsor as he filled his cup. "You are one of the greatest artists of this age You are quite entitled to call yourself Li Po. But, Li Po, you are a poor, harried, tormented, and anxiety-ridden man. You have struck up the music of doom; you sit singing in your burning house, which you yourself have set afire, and you do not feel happy about it, Li Po, even if you empty three hundred cups every day and drink with the moon. You are not happy about it, you are very sorry about it, singer of doom. Won't you stop? Don't you want to live? Don't you want to continue?"

Klingsor drank and whispered back in his somewhat hoarse voice: "Can a man change fate? Is there freedom of the will? Can you, astrologer, guide my stars differently?"

"I cannot guide them, only interpret them. Only you yourself can guide. There is freedom of the will. It is the wisdom of the Magi."

"Why should I practice the wisdom of the Magi when I can practice art? Isn't art just as good?"

"Everything is good. Nothing is good. The wisdom of the Magi abolishes illusions. It abolishes that worst of illusions which we call 'time'."

"Doesn't art do that also?"

"It tries to. Is your painted July, which you have there in your portfolio, enough for you? Have you abolished time? Are you without fear of the autumn, of the winter?"

Klingsor sighed and fell silent. Silently, he drank. Silently, the magus filled his cup. Hectically, the unleashed mechanical piano rumbled. Angelically, Tu Fu's face floated among the dancers. July was over.

Klingsor toyed with the empty bottles on the table, arranging them in a circle.

"These are our cannon," he exclaimed. "With these cannon we shoot time to pieces, death to pieces, misery to pieces. I have also shot at death with paints, with fiery green and explosive vermilion and sweet scarlet lake. Often I have hit him on the head; I have driven white and blue into his eye. I have often sent him scurrying. I shall meet him often again, overcome him, outwit him. Look at the Armenian; he is opening another old bottle and the imprisoned sun of past summers shoots into our blood. The Armenian, too, helps us shoot at death; the Armenian, too, knows no other weapon against death."

The magus broke bread and ate.

"I need no weapon against death because there is no death. There is only one thing: dread of death. That can be cured; there is a weapon to use against that. It is a matter of an hour to overcome that dread. But Li Po does not want to. For Li loves death; he loves his dread of death, his melancholy, his misery. Only his dread has taught him all that he can do and all we love him for."

Mockingly, he raised his cup to Klingsor's; his teeth flashed, his face grew more and more jovial. Sorrow seemed alien to him. No one answered. Klingsor shot his wine cannon against death. Death loomed at the open doors of the tavern, which was swollen with people, wine, and dance music. Death loomed at the doors, softly shook the black acacia, lurked darkly in the garden. Everything outside was full of death, filled with death; only here in the crowded hall they still fought on, fought gloriously and bravely against the black besieger who whimpered at the windows.

Mockingly, the magus looked across the table; mockingly, he filled the cups. Klingsor had already broken many cups; the magus had given him new ones. The Armenian had also drunk a great many, but he sat as erect as Klingsor.

"Let us drink, Li," he said in low-voiced mockery. "You love death, you know, you want to be doomed, you are glad to die the death. Didn't you say so, or have I deceived myself - or have you after all deceived me and yourself? Let us drink, Li, let us be doomed."

Rage bubbled up in Klingsor. He stood up, stood erect and tall, the old sparrow hawk with his chiselled face, spat into the wine, hurled his full cup on the floor. The red wine splashed out into the hall; his friends paled, strangers laughed.

But smiling silently the magus fetched a new cup, smilingly filled it, smilingly offered it to Li Po. Then Li smiled, he too smiled. A smile flickered like moonlight over his distorted face.

"Friends," he cried out, "let this foreigner talk! The old fox knows a great deal; he has come out of a deep and hidden den. He knows a great deal, but he does not understand us. He is too old to understand children. He is too wise to understand fools. We who are about to die know more about death than he. We are men, not stars. See my hand, holding a small blue cup of wine! This hand, this brown hand, can do many things. It has painted with many brushes, has wrested fresh segments of the world from the darkness and. placed them before men's eyes. This brown hand has stroked many women under the chin and seduced many girls. Many have kissed it, tears have fallen on it, Tu Fu has written a poem to it. This dear hand, friends, will soon be full of earth and maggots; none of you would touch it then. Very well, that is the reason I love it. I love my hand, I love my eyes, I love my soft white belly; I love them with regret and with scorn and with great tenderness because they must all wither and decay so soon. Shadow, dark friend, old tin soldier on Andersen's grave, you too will meet the same fate, dear fellow. Drink with me: Three cheers for our limbs and guts! Long may they live!"

They drank the toast. The Shadow smiled darkly from his deep eye sockets - and suddenly something passed through the hall like a wind, like a spirit. Abruptly the music stopped, the dancers vanished, as if swallowed by the night, and half the lights went out. Klingsor looked at the black doors. Outside stood death. He saw death standing there. He smelled him. Like raindrops in the leaves by the highroad, that was how death smelled.

Then Li Po pushed the cup away, knocked back the chair, and walked slowly out of the hall into the dark garden and on, in the darkness, heat lightning flashing over his head, alone. His heart lay heavy in his breast like the stone upon a grave.

Appendix 11

From '**My Friend Henry Miller**' by Alfred Perles

AFTER the semi-isolation of Clichy, Miller became the centre of a number of new friends who surrounded him with a sort of vague aura. The inner circle remained unchanged, Anais Nin, Michael Fraenkel, Liane and, perhaps, myself, being his closest associates. Drifting in from the outside there were a few I should particularly like to mention. For one, Hans Reichel, the German painter who used a paint brush like a magic wand, who constantly and without transition went from one extreme to the other, from an alcoholic fit to the mystical interpretation of a marsh marigold. Another was David Edgar, the most lovable neurotic American ever pro-duced, who initiated Miller into the secrets of the Bhagavad Gita, the occult writings of Mme Blavatsky, the spirit of Zen and the doctrines of Rudolf Steiner. ...

A word about Edgar. While Reichel and I lived in the Impasse du Rouet out of dire necessity, Edgar, who could easily have afforded more luxurious quarters, lived there by choice. His squalid little room always seemed warm and cosy with the exhalations of his multiple neuroses which added spice to his quite remarkable intellect; there wasn't a thing David couldn't grasp with his head, but his knowledge didn't help him in smoothing out the vast complexities of his soul. Both Henry and I loved him dearly. I remember the first time I met him, at a bottle party in Montparnasse. Henry was there, too, and I vividly recall how we watched Edgar at a distance. He was explaining the fourth dimension to a small group of female American art students. According lo him, the fourth dimension was spatial time in relation to temporal space, a sub-abstraction of the abstraction, Eternity, which was the element of the subconscious universe. He spoke in an even seesaw voice as though he were dying to keep in rhythm with a metronome. His face had a curiously mild expression which never changed. What he said made absolutely no sense, but sounded highly convincing. Then he made a parenthetical comment on surrealism - he had it all pat: there was a fourth-dimensional quality about surrealism, too, but upon a different plane entirely. Surrealism, he said, was a phenomenon of metalepsis and definitely of traumatic origin. The fourth dimension *per se* was in the nature of an absolute, the actual thing of space and time on the supralapsarian plane. Thus he went on and on. His speech was full of words no one had ever heard, such as 'metempiricism', 'praecognitum', 'entropy', etc., over which he slid, unconcerned and nonchalant, like a neurotic eel. Women loved him; he was very charming with them, but love was too simple to excite him: any idiot can fall in love, his attitude seemed to imply, and almost any idiot can have a love affair. Whenever he did fall in love, it was usually with one of the more neurotic female art students.

He was a bizarre and lovable character, and completely lost. His eyes were pale blue, like schizophrenia, and his personality was split: not in two or three or seven, but into its component parts, each of them living a weird existence of its own, singly, in groups, collectively; there were so many of them he could never make up his mind. When it came to making a simple decision, such as selecting a tie at a haberdasher's or choosing a dish from among the items of a restaurant menu, he became completely paralysed. Who of him was to decide what he was going to wear, or eat? There were too many of him; he had to hold a referendum with himself, a sort of one-man plebiscite.

Fortunately for him, he had an income and did not have to work for a living. Or maybe that wasn't so fortunate after all. Had he been obliged to go out into the cold and hostile world to fend for himself, he wouldn't have had the leisure to indulge in the luxury of being such an accomplished neurotic. It is the lack of petty, everyday problems that lands nice fellows like David Edgar in the arms of neurosis. David had no small problems, only big ones—world problems, universal problems, cosmological, religious, historical, psychological, metaphysical, esoteric and occult problems—and being intelligent (not *too* intelligent), thought he could solve all these problems, which in the progress of his galloping neurosis became his own personal problems, by argument. Needless to say, he solved nothing. The more he thought about these problems—the more *intelligently* he thought about them—the more impenetrable and insoluble they seemed to become. What was the meaning of life? What was his—David's—role in life? Had he a mission to fulfill? Who was he? Whence did he come? Whither was he bound? And why? What was important and what wasn't? Was art Important? There were times when he thought it was; he had a thousand and one ideas on painting, and all he had painted in the last three years was a curious canvas representing the gnarled roots of a senile tree. The painting hung on the wall over his shaving mirror; he would stare at it uncomprehendingly: it was just another problem.

Edgar was a man drowning: he drowned gently, gracefully and continuously. He thought of abstractions in terms of abstractions—not like Fraenkel who saw in them a goal *per se,* but rather like a man drowning, looking desperately for a rope ladder that might lead him back to safety. He was very delicate about drowning; he began drowning about ten in the morning every day when he started shaving himself; he used brushless shaving cream and smiled a wan, gentle smile into the mirror that hung under the painting of the senescent tree: and communed with himself—his selves: every morning it was like a Cabinet meeting.

His friends liked him immensely. He had many lady friends, too, and they were all very fond of him. He seemed to have little, if any, sensuality—his sex requirements were moderate. As I've said before, he usually picked the slightly neurotic type, though he tried hard to avoid them. But the attraction was too strong, for *he* was so seldom in the majority. They were either sexually tainted, mild perverts, Lesbians, hopeless virgins, or, now and again, nymphomaniacs, but in the latter case he was on his guard: he used them as audience, sympathetic Samaritans, mothers, and at rare intervals, ephemeral lovers. They swirled around him like friendly electrons and neutrons rotating around a kindred atom; they were his satellites by virtue of some psycho-magnetic attraction.

His charm lay in his great helplessness. He was very gentle and generous, too, but it was his helplessness that endeared him to us, especially to Miller. The two became great friends, and the discussions they had together rivalled in length and esotericism those with Fraenkel. Henry was much more lenient with Edgar than he ever was with Fraenkel, probably because Edgar was the more interesting of the two; Edgar varied his subjects, a thing Fraenkel never did. His range was infinitely wider; there was nothing cut and dried about him. We often spent whole days or whole nights together, the three of us, in speculative talks on life, after-life, post-after-life, the Lemurian age, Atlantis, the meaning of myths and legends, occult powers and principalities, the relative spheres of influence of Lucifer and Ahriman, life in Devachan, and so on and so forth. We soon evolved a lingo of our own which must have sounded like a code language to any outsider listening in.

Oddly, enough, these long conversations always came about accidentally. Miller never made a date with Edgar, which would have been a deliberate waste of time. He would run into him in the street or see him sitting at a table at the terrace of the Cafe Zeyer, or we would bump into him on our way to Montparnasse. One innocent little word would lead to another, and before we knew what was happening, we would find ourselves sitting in some cafe drinking pernods or amer picons and discussing the planetary influences on plant life, or some such subject. It usually started with a book Edgar was just reading. You never met him without a book in his hand no matter where he was going; had he been in the habit of frequenting brothels he wouldn't have gone without a book. Sometimes he carried two books under his arm, sometimes half a dozen. Not all the books he read were good books but they were all on outlandish, recondite subjects. (I don't believe he ever read a novel in his whole life.) He had a habit of opening a book at random and reading a passage aloud. Henry was extremely wary of this technique of Edgar's which invariably constituted the opening gambit to one of these interminable sessions. But there was nothing Henry could do about it; you couldn't shut Edgar up like an ordinary bore; he was very sensitive and very thick-skinned at the same time; it was more painful not to listen to him than to listen to him. And after a while it struck you that whatever he was talking about was really interesting, absorbingly so, interesting to the exclusion of all else, although you had never before heard of the subject under discussion.

Miller confessed to me repeatedly that Edgar's desultory ending of passages from books he had picked up haphazardly led him to explore entirely new avenues of thought. It was Edgar who induced him, in his vicarious way, to take up a more profound study of Zen Buddhism. Miller had always been leaning toward Zen, but without knowing it. When Edgar introduced him to Alan Watts' *The Spirit of Zen* Miller realized that in his own way he had always been practising Zen (sometimes known as the philosophy of non-philosophy). In his neurotic babbling Edgar would sometimes drop an unfinished sentence which, to Miller's mind, hit the bull's eye; then even the Bhagavad Gita made sense. Was it chance that brought Edgar into Miller's life? Perhaps. But it is also possible that his advent at that particular time was planned, premeditated, by some pre-organized fate. The apprehension of truth comes in flashes, but only when one is ready to seize it. Henry was fast making ready for it and Edgar may, for all I know, have been but the instrumentality of some inscrutable force.

In the course of these pages I have mentioned that there Was an enigmatic power in Henry Miller which had a health-giving effect on those he came in contact with. This power no doubt derived from an inner source of crude religiosity of which he himself was only dimly aware, or perhaps not aware at all—very much like the owner of land in the sub-soil of which lie rich oil wells the existence of which is unsuspected. In order to extract the oil the wells have first to be drilled, and the crude oil has to be refined before it can be used. Miller never succeeded in exploiting this vague source of power but merely hovered over it, like a sort of human divining rod. Untapped and unrefined, this latent power nevertheless sufficed to alleviate the sufferings of some, restore the balance of others, and make a few whole again.

It didn't work with Edgar. Not that he was too far gone to be helped. True enough, he was rolling down the declivities of neurosis, but he was rolling down gently, gracefully, not at all like a man tumbling down a precipice; he could have been stopped and succoured had this kind of therapy been foreseen in the scheme of things. Edgar was not to be helped for two very valid reasons—firstly, because deep down in his good heart he refused to be helped; somehow subconsciously he sensed that the cure would deprive him of everything that made him so lovable to all: Edgar, cured, would have been just another American nincompoop and his heart resisted the prospect of contented mediocrity. The second, and to my thinking, chief reason of Miller's failure to help him was due to an occult conspiracy. This must sound fantastic to the reader, but I honestly believe that David Edgar was an emissary, a kind of unconscious messenger from a different realm, sent to deliver a message to Henry Miller, and he had to deliver it by hand, like a sort of subpoena. There was a quality of extraterritoriality about Edgar, and Henry could do nothing for him except love him.

Appendix - 12

From Henry Miller's
'BIG SUR AND THE ORANGES OF HIERONYMUS BOSCH'

I am led to speak of the "Millennium" because, receiving as many visitors as I do, and from all parts of the globe, I am constantly reminded that I am living in a virtual paradise. ("And how did you manage to find such a place?" is the usual exclamation. As if *I* had any part in it!) But what amazes me, and this is the point, is that so very few ever think on taking leave that they too might enjoy the fruits of paradise. Almost invariably the visitor will confess that he lacks the courage—imagination would be nearer the mark—to make the necessary break. "You're lucky," he will say—meaning, to be a writer—"you can do your work anywhere." He forgets what I have told him, arid most pointedly, about the other members of the community—the ones who really support the show—who are not writers, painters or artists of any sort, except in spirit. "Too late," he probably murmurs to himself, as he takes a last wistful glance about.

How illustrative, this attitude, of the woeful resignation men and women succumb to! Surely every one realizes, at some point along the way, that he is capable of living a far better life than the one he has chosen. What stays him, usually, is the fear of the sacrifices involved. (Even to relinquish his chains seems like a sacrifice.) Yet everyone knows that nothing is accomplished without sacrifice.

The longing for paradise, whether here on earth or in the beyond, has almost ceased to be. Instead of an *idee-force* it has become an *idee fixe.* From a potent myth it has degenerated into a taboo. Men will sacrifice their lives to bring about a better world—whatever that may mean— but they will not budge an inch to attain paradise. Nor will they struggle to create a bit of paradise in the hell they find themselves. It is so much easier, and gorier, to make revolution, which means, to put it simply, establishing another, a different, status quo. If paradise were realizable—this is the classic retort!— it would no longer be paradise.

What is one to say to a man who insists on making his own prison?

There is a type of individual who, after finding what he considers a paradise, proceeds to pick flaws in it. Eventually this man's paradise becomes even worse than the hell from which he had escaped.

Certainly paradise, whatever, wherever it be, contains flaws.(Paradisiacal flaws, if you like.) If it did not, it would be incapable of drawing the hearts of men *or* angels.

The windows of the soul are infinite, we are told. And it is through the eyes of the soul that paradise is visioned. If there are flaws in your paradise, open more windows! Vision is entirely a creative faculty: it uses the body and the mind as the navigator uses his instruments. Open and alert, it matters little whether one finds a supposed short cut to the Indies—or discovers a new world. Everything is begging to be discovered, not accidentally, but intuitively. Seeking intuitively, one's destination is never in a beyond of time or space but always here and now. If we are always arriving and departing, it is also true that we are eternally anchored. One's destination is never a place but rather a new way of looking at things. Which is to say that there are no limits to vision. Similarly, there are no limits to paradise. Any paradise worth the name can sustain all the flaws in creation and remain undiminished, untarnished.

If I have entered upon a vein which I must confess is one not frequently discussed here, I am nevertheless certain that it is one which secretly engages the minds of many members of the community.

Everyone who has come here in search of a new way of life has made a complete change-about in his daily routine. Nearly every one has come from afar, usually from a big city. It meant abandoning a job and a mode of life which was detestable and insufferable. To what degree each one has found "new life" can be estimated only by the efforts he or she put forth. Some, I suspect, would have found "it" even had they remained where they were.

The most important thing I have witnessed, since coming here, is the transformation people have wrought in their own being. Nowhere have I seen individuals work so earnestly and assiduously on themselves. Nor so successfully. Yet nothing is taught or preached here, at least overtly. Some have made the effort and failed. Happily for the rest of us, I should say. But even these who failed gained something. For one thing, their outlook on life was altered, enlarged if not "improved." And what could be better than for the teacher to become his own pupil, or the preacher his own convert?

In a paradise you don't preach or teach. You practice the perfect life—or you relapse.

There seems to be an unwritten law here which insists that you accept what you find and like it, profit by it, or you are cast out. Nobody does the rejecting, please understand. Nobody, no group here, would crave such authority. No, the place itself, the elements which make it, do that. It's the law, as I say. And it is a just law which works harm to no one. To the cynical-minded it may sound like the same old triumph of our dear status quo. But the enthusiast knows that it is precisely the fact that there is no status quo here which makes for its paradisiacal quality.

No, the law operates because that which makes for paradise can not and will not assimilate that which makes for hell. How often it is said that we make our own heaven and our own hell. And how little it is taken to heart! Yet the truth prevails, whether we believe in it or not.

Paradise or no paradise, I have the very definite impression that the people of this vicinity are striving to live up to the grandeur and nobility which is such an integral part of the setting. They behave as if it were a privilege to live here, as if it were by an act of grace they found themselves here. The place itself is so overwhelmingly bigger, greater, than anyone could hope to make it that it engenders a humility and reverence not frequently met with in Americans. There being nothing to improve on in the surroundings, the tendency is to set about improving oneself.

It is of course true that individuals have undergone tremendous changes, broadened their vision, altered their natures, in hideous, thwarting surroundings— prisons, ghettos, concentration camps, and so on. Only a very rare individual elects to *remain* in such places. The man who has seen the light follows the light. And the light usually leads him to the place where he can function most effectively, that is, where he will be of most use to his fellow-men. In this sense, it matters little whether it be darkest Africa or the Himalayan heights. God's work can be done anywhere, so to say. We have all met the soldier who has been overseas. And we all know that each one has a different story to relate. We are all like returned soldiers. We have all been somewhere, spiritually speaking, and we have either benefited by the experience or been worsted by it. One man says: "Never again!" Another says: "Let it come! I'm ready for anything!" Only the fool hopes to repeat an experience; the wise man knows that *every* experience is to be viewed as a blessing. Whatever we try to deny or reject is precisely what we have need of; it is our very need which often paralyzes us, prevents us from welcoming a (good or bad) experience.

I come back once again to those individuals who came here full of needs and who fled after a time because "it" was not what they hoped to find, or because "they" were not what they thought themselves to be. None of them, from what I have learned, has yet found it or himself. Some returned to their former masters in the manner of slaves unable to support the privileges and responsibilities of freedom. Some found their way into mental retreats. Some became derelicts. Others simply surrendered to the villainous status quo.

I speak as if they had been marked by the whip. I do not mean to be cruel or vindictive. What I wish to say quite simply is that none of them, in my humble opinion, is a whit happier, a whit better off, an inch advanced in any respect. They will all continue to talk about their Big Sur adventure for the rest of their lives— wistfully, regretfully, or elatedly, as occasion dictates. In the hearts of some. I know, is the profound hope that their children will display more courage, more perseverance, more integrity than they themselves did. But do they not overlook something? Are not their children, as the product of self-confessed failures, already condemned? Have they not been contaminated by the virus of 'security'?

The most difficult thing to adjust to, apparently, is peace and contentment. As long as there is something to fight, people seem able to brave all manner of hardships....

Appendix 13

On Colin Wilson's '*The Outsider*' by me
(written many years ago)

In 1955 Colin Wilson wrote a book called 'The Outsider' in which he examined the lives of some well-known historical figures. The people he chose were very different, both in character and in what they achieved. They included philosophers, artists, reformers and mystics; but most of them were writer-philosophers. In spite of their differences they had once thing in common: the characteristics of what Wilson called the 'Outsider'. The book, in spite of its publisher's doubts, turned out to cause something of a sensation, arousing a lot of media interest at the time, and Wilson himself became moderately famous. The book continues to sell after more than 50 years.

The subject Wilson was tackling was of the outsider in history, the problem of the outsider, and a search for a solution. It was, Wilson believed, the most pressing problem that mankind has ever had to face, and one which has always loomed in the background waiting to confront the 'thinking man' – and, I should add, the 'thinking woman'.

The sources Wilson draws upon range from Socrates through Blake to Dostoyevsky, Nietzsche, Hesse, Kafka, Sartre, Camus and others, including philosophers such as Kierkegaard, Shaw and Hulme. He investigates the Outsider problem as experienced by Van Gogh, Nijinsky and T E Lawrence, and finally explains the partial solutions of George Fox (founder of the Society of Friends – the Quakers), Gurdjieff (via accounts of his 'pupil' Ouspensky) and of other 'mystics'.

Of his nine chapters he dedicates more than one to Dostoyevsky, most predominantly to that culmination of his life's work '*The Brothers Karamazov*' in which, although unfinished at his death, he portrays in the three brothers the three aspects of the Outsider's dilemma, pointing towards a solution for each and laying the foundation upon which others could build. The three aspects were body, mind and spirit – or, in my own terminology: body, intellect and intuition.

Even more space is given to Nietzsche who 'lived' the problem of the Outsider as much as he wrote about it. In contrast to Dostoyevsky, who very much involved himself in the detail of practical living with all its upheavals and trivialities, Nietzsche was an idealist, unable to separate his Outsider ideas from his everyday life to the extent of eventually going insane. Unlike Dostoyevsky or Blake, for example, Nietzsche was completely alone. He did not have followers or the support of the devout wife.

In essence, and according to my own interpretation, the problem of the Outsider amounts simply to this: that regardless of material benefits, he has somehow acquired the recognition, a recognition apparently that eludes 'normal' men and women, of the utter futility and meaningless of life. For him there is no escape. 'belief' or faith, as is the remedy for many non-outsiders (and some of Wilson's), holds no sway; for an attempt to escape thus would amount to nothing more than cheating, sidestepping the issue - which leads the outsider precisely nowhere. The whole business of the outsider is to seek 'truth', not to delude himself - in fact he, unlike those others, is quite unable to knowingly succumb to delusion, however attractive, and finds himself with no choice but to look hard at the bewildering phenomenon of life, to face it squarely, head on, warts an' all. He has no interest in 'supernatural matters': such ideas belong to theology, belief and faith, and he vigorously rejects them. To the outsider the only important distinction is between existence and non-existence, life and death.

Mankind might be said to consist of several types. The most common perhaps are those who get on with their daily affairs without giving a moment's thought to why they exist, what is the meaning of their existence and how, even when taking into account the brevity and pettiness of their life, they should best use their allotted time. They prefer to avoid thinking along those lines, perhaps regarding that to do so is morbid and negative and leads nowhere anyway, except into depression. These include people who retain a certain naivety of youth - though not necessarily an open-mindedness - who live mainly for the material world around them and find fulfilment in acquiescing to social norms. Questions about existence are to them bizarre, and are as irrelevant to the substance of their everyday life as is the destiny of a discarded cigarette-end.

Then there are those who go about as if half in a dream, aware of some mysterious question but not sure what it is or even if there really is one; or if they are sure then how exactly to express it. This individual might sense that if he were to articulate his questions then the discovery that they were unresolved, unanswerable, even though they had been rigorously tackled by some of the greatest minds, would be too much to bear; and instead of risking such an outcome, he chooses to believe that there may be answers, but that they are hidden away in libraries or in the minds of intellectuals. This man is perplexed, not knowing where to look or how to make sense of his problem. He may not know how to represent it to himself in a way that is intelligible: what is the point of my existence? What is the point of anything? His self-expression may be impaired by the banality that such questions have come to acquire in recent years and which reduces them to a laughable absurdity. Laughable perhaps as a means of escaping them, of converting them by ridicule into an absurdity that makes the serious questioner appear absurd. And besides, aren't they the very questions asked by mere children?

From this state the individual might progress to one of 'letting go', partaking in extravagant entertainments or pastimes in which he is able to 'forget' the problem. He may become a workaholic, a prominent member of various groups or clubs, or he may even partake in dangerous sports.

Finally there remains beyond all the intermediary possibilities the path of the fully-fledged outsider, the path of impending gloom and isolation. This man is utterly disillusioned, destitute of all meaning and value in his life. For him life is a colossal confidence trick, a joke played accidentally by nature. Life is a phenomenon of the universe just as is the debris of space, and has no purpose whatever. He can either shrug, accept his lot and make the most of it, or he can cut his throat and be done with the entire charade.

But being tied as we are to our primitive needs, our inborn inclination to survive and to our attachments, few men ever reach this extreme outsider condition. Perhaps Van Gogh, T E Lawrence and Nietzsche are exceptions, but before they finally 'arrived' they engaged themselves in a lengthy period of investigation and introspection during which they lived, internally at least, as outsiders, not knowing which way to turn. These particular men, as we know, were perhaps unscrupulously honest and gave themselves no choice but to turn towards total negation. But before reaching that point is the stage of the man who ruminates, who circulates his thoughts in constant recurring reasoning, endlessly digging himself deeper and trapping himself in the increasing necessity and uncertain hope of finding a solution; and all to no avail.

When, sparing a moment from his thoughts, this man glances up to look at the world, 'all' he sees is everything just as it plainly is, and just as anyone can clearly see without any recourse to mysticism or metaphysical interpretation. The crucial word 'all' is what makes him different from the masses, who, he thinks, are in a constant state of delusion. Only he, and possibly a few others like him, has his eyes wide open; only he knows the real and despicable 'truth' behind existence. Indeed, even if he wanted to delude himself with all or any of the varieties and vagaries of 'wishful thinking', of the possibility of there being some kind of heaven or ulterior purpose, he would be immediately disabled, since the crux of his problem resides in the very fact that he must seek the genuine, objective 'truth', and nothing else will do. Nothing!

Any sort of attempt to placate the pessimism to which this leads, he finds at best pathetic, at worst abhorrent. He is as stuck with his bleak perception as he is stuck with the need to breathe, and he well knows how he can 'escape' both those obligations. But not yet, for there might, he thinks, assuming he retains an iota of hope, be a solution, or at least a partial solution. While any perception of the universe that involves 'belief' or faith is out of the question, there is only what is revealed by the senses, there is only 'This'! Or is there?

Now, the paradox that arises for the outsider is that he both accepts his condition and at the same time refuses to accept it. And it is clear from the examples referred to and quoted in Wilson's book that most of his Outsiders sort vehemently for a way out, a way that would not compromise the fundamental outlook and yet would give purpose and meaning to their lives. For all of them, except the mystics and those who 'cheated' by developing a faith of sorts, failed in their quest. And Wilson, while pointing the way to a method of 'escape', offers no 'truthful' solution - apart from asserting an extraordinary strength of will. His unvoiced conclusion might be wrapped up neatly in the first sentence of a quotation by Pirandello:

> 'Whoever understands the game can no longer fool themselves, but if you cannot fool yourself, you can no longer derive any pleasure or enjoyment from life. So it goes. My art is full of bitter compassion for all those who fool themselves. But this compassion cannot help but be succeeded by a ferocious derision of a destiny that condemns Man to deception. This, succinctly, is the reason for the bitterness of my art, and also my life.'

This suggests, as Wilson's conclusions seem to imply, that the only possible means of 'escape' so far envisaged is in fact to fool yourself. Yes, he might say, we're condemned to self-deceit; but so what? What's wrong with deception if it makes for contentment? This, clearly, is an old fable, and it breaks no ice with the authentic Outsider. In Wilson's terms, and there is no indication in his work that he saw it as 'deceit', the path to a solution is found by first of all resorting to the power of Will (as intimated by Nietzsche, and endorsed by others): to Will yourself into a certain state of awareness. This state I shall discuss later, but for the moment it is enough to recognise that so far in history a search in the outside world, the universe, has revealed nothing in answer to the problem; and therefore, as with the power of Will, our search has been redirected to encompass the inner world, the world of the intellect, the emotions and, if indeed it exists as something different from those two, the spirit.

Before attempting to clarify these terms as promised, most especially 'spirit', it would be appropriate here to offset Pirandello's apparent pessimism in the above quotation against his later statement that to some extent separates him from his art and creates a marginally less pessimistic, if vaguely ambiguous, insight into the problem of existence:

> *'For a long time I have been considered a pessimist... but I have been misunderstood. My art is free of that pessimism, which causes a lack of faith in my life. And I am not even a nihilist since, in the spiritual activity which torments me and animates my work, there is an incessant desire to create.'*

Although, like so many Outsiders, Pirandello sought meaning in life, as if his works were a route that might lead him to answers and to the relative contentment those answers might bring, a meaning continually eluded him. All he could find was absurdity:

> *'The taste for life! – that is never satisfied, because life, even as we are in the very act of living it, is so ravenously hungering after itself that it never lets itself be fully tasted. The taste for life comes to us from our past. From the memories that hold us bound, but bound to what? To this folly of ours, to this mass of vexations, to so many stupid illusions, to so many insipid occupations.'*

And this, avoiding for the moment the temptation to examine what he means by folly, vexations, illusions and occupations, takes us into the significance of memory: 'the memories that hold us bound' provides a key to what it is that prevents us all from becoming Outsiders, indeed, being born as Outsiders from the outset. But is he talking about instinct memory or about memory of learned attachments (whether essential artefacts of survival or the trinkets and baubles of 'civilisation')?

Perhaps he refers to all memories, whatever their source. For what are we but a collection of memories? What are we but a support mechanism and the instrument it supports in which all these memories are stored and which acts upon nothing but these memories (which might be a millisecond, or a million years old)? What else do we do but consult our memories at every step (either for amusement or to interpret and influence the present) and obey what they dictate for us to do?

Bearing in mind that compared to a bird, a snake, or a sea anemone, all Men, from a genetic point of view, are essentially identical, a question we might ask ourselves is whether our inherited memories are also essentially identical. And if they are then why do some men 'see' differently to others? Could it be that we all have the potential to 'see' as the Outsider 'sees', but that marginal differences (because we are in fact not quite identical) predispose some more than others to 'see' their existence in a different light; that is, if they bother in the first place to 'look' at it?

It may be, however, that what disposes a man to 'look' or to 'see' (though to look is one thing, and to see is something else entirely) is not so much his primordial memories, which after all have been established over millions of years of natural selection, but rather the influences in his upbringing. Whichever of these constitute the greatest influence is not strictly relevant to this discussion; it is sufficient for the moment to note the distinction. What concerns us here is that if a man thinks at all then what in fact does he think and where does he expect his thinking to lead him?

Alternatively, regardless of potential, perhaps we all do 'see' as the Outsider 'sees' if we care to 'look'; the difference between us being that most of us prefer not to 'look', or if we do 'look' – by accident, as it were – then we only glance and what we 'see' is so inherently horrifying that we turn swiftly away before we are 'hypnotised' into 'looking' deeper. To 'look' deeper into the abyss would be, perhaps, to 'see' that it is indeed bottomless instead of simply 'not there', nothing real. And this nothing, abyss, or whatever it is, is in any case of no importance: 'what do we care what it is, if indeed it exists, we're too busy living in the 'real' world to concern ourselves with such abstractions. Abyss? There's no such thing!' Or, with solemnity: 'It's no business of ours, abyss or no abyss.' – as if they somehow instinctively recognise it as 'forbidden' territory, to be observed at their peril – as some non-Outsiders probably suspect, at least subconsciously: that it is safer not to 'look', to stick with the dealt hand and make the most of it, for what it's worth, for once seen, a thing cannot be unseen. And now we have come full circle: both the Outsider and non-Outsider...

Appendix 14

From 'Never a Normal Man' by Dan Farson

Page 378

The great Caucasus range stretches from the Black Sea to the Caspian, dividing Europe from the East. There are twelve mountains higher than Mont Blanc, with Elbruz the highest at 18,784 ft- Between Elbruz and Mount Kazbek there are 125 miles of snowfields and glaciers, and seeing these from above it was easy to believe that some of the former tribes in their remote valleys could be reached only at certain times of year. It was this isolation which had made the Caucasus the refuge for the outlawed over the centuries, from Tsarist and Soviet oppression.

Your first approach to the Caucasus is something you never forget. I experienced a sudden, overwhelming sensation of happiness as irrational yet as powerful as if I were a young soldier returning home. The train crossed a countryside of lilac woods in heavy spring blossom, with headscarved women tending immaculate plots while others sunbathed on the green banks. When my father was in the mountains he felt that elation - '*It is seldom, as we get on, that one feels the sudden unaccountable, bubbling happiness of youth. But I had a burst of it*' - and so did I, even inside the rattling, overcrowded train. It is a sensation you are lucky to have a few times in your life, and it lasts for seconds, and there is nothing like it.

There is a moment in Tolstoy's The Cossacks, when the world-weary young officer Olenin, who has been posted to the Caucasus after his life has been tarnished by gambling debts and debauchery, sees the mountains for the first time:

> seeming to run along the horizon, their rosy rips gleaming in the rays of the rising sun. All his Moscow recollections, his shame and his regrets, all his trivial dreams of the

Caucasus, departed and never returned again. 'Now it has begun!' a sort of triumphant voice said to him.

My own approach by train could hardly have been more mundane, but I understood Olenin's emotion. Every mountain range is different: some are threatening, others have the softness of pillows, the Caucasus welcome you as if you belong.

Appendix – 15

Opening lines from a few great writers:

From '**Rock Springs**' by Richard Ford

ROCK SPRINGS

Edna and I had started down from Kalispell, heading for Tampa-St. Pete where I still had some friends from the old glory days who wouldn't turn me in to the police. I had managed to scrape with the law in Kalispell over several bad checks—which is a prison crime in Montana. And I knew Edna was already looking at her cards and thinking about a move, since it wasn't the first time I'd been in law scrapes in my life. She herself had already had her own troubles, losing her kids and keeping her ex-husband, Danny, from breaking in her house and stealing her things while she was at work, which was really why I had moved in in the first place, that and needing to give my little daughter, Cheryl, a better shake in things.

CHILDREN

Claude Phillips was a half-Blackfeet Indian, and his father, Sherman, was a full-blood, and in 1961 our families rented out farm houses from die bank in Great Falls—the homes of wheat farmers gone bust on the prairie east of Sunburst, Montana. People were going broke even then, and leaving. Claude Phillips and I were seventeen, and in a year from the day I am going to tell about, in May, I would be long gone from there myself, and so would Claude.

Where all of this took place was in that remote part of Montana near the Canada border and west of the Sweetgrass Hills. That is called the Hi-line, there, and it is an empty, lonely place if you are not a wheat farmer. I make this a point only because I have thought possibly it was the place itself, as

OPTIMISTS

All of this that I am about to tell happened when I was only fifteen years old, in 1959, the year my parents were divorced, the year when my father killed a man and went to prison for it, the year I left home and school, told a lie about my age to fool the Army, and then did not come back. The year, in other words, when life changed for all of us and forever—ended, really, in a way none of us could ever have imagined in our most brilliant dreams of life.

My father was named Roy Brinson, and he worked on the Great Northern Railway, in Great Falls, Montana. He was a switch-engine fireman, and when he could not hold that job on the seniority list, he worked the extra-board as a hostler, or as a hostler's helper, shunting engines through the yard, onto and off the freight trains that went south and east. He was

* * * * *

From '**Success Stories**' by Russell Banks:

MISTAKE

In the spring of 1960 I turned twenty. By June I'd be married, so I was working at a second job, selling women's shoes at a Thorn McAn's in a shopping center out in West St. Petersburg. Driving home late six nights a week in my shaky '48 Studebaker, I cast wary glances out the open window at the causeway that loped across the bay north to Tampa, a string of lights over dark water that somehow made me think of New York City, and for a few terrifying seconds each night I wondered if I was making the biggest mistake of my life.

Days I worked as a window trimmer for Webb's City, after I'd been let go at Maas Brothers. It was an early cut-rate department store parked on an invisible line that separated

291

the neighborhood where middle-class blacks lived from the neighborhood where poor whites lived. There were eight of us in the Display Department, as it was called—art school dropouts, alcoholic ex-stagehands, sign painters and me— and from the small warehouse on the edge of the Webb's City parking lot where we toiled through the long, hot Florida day building frames, cutting and stretching paper, carving Homosote, painting signs, repairing old mannequins, we

ADULTERY

By the time I was nineteen years old I had broken all but three of the Ten Commandments. I'd made no graven image, had killed no one and had not committed adultery. On the other hand, I lied, did not keep the Sabbath holy, did not honor my mother and father, especially my father, and I stole—not much, but enough to count as a violation. I'd done it as recently as last week, skimming a few bucks from the night's take at the Thorn McAn's out at the Pinellas Shopping Mall, where I worked nights. Selling shoes was a second job—I was saving a thousand dollars for my forthcoming marriage to Eleanor Hastings, an event I'd begun to imagine as capable somehow of washing me clean, like a baptism.
My marriage was going to be a Fresh Start. The new life would cancel the old life and create a new me, a youth who no longer coveted, like the old me, his neighbor's split-level house, his perky, dark wife who looked like Teresa Brewer, new Dodge car, boat, summer vacation, great angular height, Georgia accent. My neighbor was in fact my boss, Art, in the display department at Maas Brothers, where I worked days, a kindly, witty man who now rented the small,

* * * * *

From **New York Son** by Mike Feder

When I was about fifteen, I was possessed of a great many psychosomatic complaints. I'm sure a lot of this had to do with trying to compete, although fruitlessly, with my mother, who was always sick on a grand scale—mentally and physically. Nevertheless, I had, as a loving son, inherited a large number of her ailments and complaints, although I was probably much healthier than I thought I was.

I was very allergic in those days. I was allergic to cats, grass, trees, anything you could imagine. A lot of Jewish boys are familiar with this condition. The allergist I had to go to worked in Manhattan, which for a little wimp boy like myself was a long adventurous trip. It held a lot of terrors for me, one of which was that I had to get on the subway. I lived way out in Laurelton, Queens, near Nassau County—at the edge of the city. I had to take a bus to the subway and then the F train into Manhattan, get off, go to the allergist, and come back.

One morning, I was leaving my house to see the allergist and I was in my constant state of teenage depression because in those days my mother was sick all the time. She was sitting in her room moaning, or calling her mother to complain that she wished she had never had children, which was sort of a cheery way to start my day. Naturally, I did not enjoy going to the allergist, to say the least; it was not just because I had to go through all the dangers and terrors of the trip, but also because the damn guy stuck me with five or six needles every time. Besides all this, he was a turd, a real insensitive jerk. I did this twice a week for a couple of years.

I got the bus, and changed for the subway. I went downstairs and got the F train, somewhere out in Jamaica, Queens. Right away, I was scared. Now there's so much personal violence in the train, you have to watch out for the people. When I was a kid, there wasn't all that much violence. You didn't have teenagers wandering around eating people and throwing them on the tracks. What bothered me then was

* * * * *

From '**Good Rockin' Tomight**' by William Hauptman

KOZMIC BLUES

In the summer of 1967 I went to San Francisco, where I lived in a walk-in closet, six feet by four, on the second floor of a big gray house on Turk Street. Six blocks away was the Haight. Two blocks downhill was Fillmore Street, the heart of the black ghetto.

For a year, ever since graduating from college, I had been suffering from a strange depression. I was living alone in Austin, wondering what lo do with myself. I knew if I found a woman I would feel better, but I couldn't find one who understood me. Somehow I had to get it together—but I couldn't get it together until I found the right woman, and I couldn't find the right woman until I got it together.

My friends Larry and Cathy, who had gone out to San Francisco six months before, wrote and told me it was great. So one morning I threw my sleeping bag in the trunk of my old Chevrolet and drove out of Austin, hoping that in San Francisco I could find a woman who understood me. They said it was going to be the Summer of Love.

The trip there look three days. The desert was hot, but it was cold and foggy the night I drove across the Bay Bridge into San Francisco. I found Turk Street and followed it until I came lo the big gray house. I had known from their letters that they were hippies now, but it was still a shock when Larry opened the door, wearing an Air Force parka and love beads, his hair as long as Prince Valiant's. Cathy stood behind him, holding a cat. We sat on the floor, around a lamp that burned scented oil. The walls were covered with posters of Big Brother, The Sir Douglas Quintet, Country Joe and the Fish. I couldn't take my eyes off their faces: They were smooth and shining and seemed to have no muscles in them at all. "We've gone through a lot of changes," Larry told me, his eyes black as buttons, all pupil.

I asked them if they weren't afraid of getting busted—in Austin, you couldn't have gone around looking the way they did without attracting the attention of the cops,

"We've lost all our paranoia," Larry said. "And once you lose your paranoia, it's impossible lo get busted." He told me how, when they'd first gotten here, they'd been afraid they were taking too many drugs, burning out their brains or something. "Then one day," he said, "we went up on Mount Tam and took this tremendous dose of acid, that's when we saw the Clear White Light."

"What's that?"

"Leary describes it in *The Tibetan Book of the Dead.* You lose your ego, and then these waves of while lights start going through you."

"The acid out here is very pure," Cathy said.

"After that, we just stopped worrying and started dropping acid every day. We've probably taken it a hundred times by now."

"Everybody in this house is into acid," Cathy said. "Even the cats. She stroked the cat sitting on her lap. "Zero here's taken more than anybody. We gave him two thousand mikes."

"You've got to try some of this acid," Larry said "We're going to open up your third eye and get you spiritual."

I didn't tell them I'd stopped taking drugs. I couldn't even smoke grass — it gave me the horrors, spells of paranoia so strong I couldn't move.

"I don't know how long I can stay," I said. "I haven't got much money."

"Don't worry about that." he said. "Pretty soon, money 's going to be no problem."

I thought he meant money was going to be no problem because love would soon replace it. But it turned out he meant that he and his partner Angel were cooking up a batch of good mescaline. It was a solid deal, and I could get in on it if I wanted.

The next morning Angel showed up, a dude from Galveston who claimed to have a degree in chemistry. With him was his wife Nova, eight months pregnant. We got in my car and followed them across the Golden Gate to Fairfax, where we parked in front of a little white frame house just off the freeway. I thought I could feel the neighbors staring at us as we got out of our cars. The kitchen was full of jars of chemicals and laboratory glassware, all of which could be seen through the window in the back door. In the bathtub, a hundred pounds of peyote buttons were cooking down to a green soup that smelled like dirty socks.

I mentioned the window and Angel said, "Yeah I caught the landlady snooping around here the other day."

"What did you do?" Larry said.

"Told her to get fucked."

Angel lit a joint and they talked about the underground economy. Angel had read an article about a hippie who had walked into a showroom and bought a Rolls-Royce right off the floor, with cash. Larry said our parents wouldn't understand, but there was really nothing wrong with what we were doing. People wanted to get spiritual, and we could help them do it. And it was going to be righteous mescaline, with no meth in it.

My paranoia was coming in waves. I lifted a blind and looked out the window. Parked down the block was a Pacific Bell panel truck, the favorite vehicle of narcs on stake-out. I pointed this out to Larry.

"Yeah," he said. "It was there yesterday, too."

Angel asked me what was wrong.

"He's got bad vibes," Larry said.

Angel shrugged and passed me the joint, the remedy for all paranoia. I could see I was making everyone uptight, so I told them I was going back to the city.

It was dark when I got back to the house on Turk Street. The moment I walked into the apartment, the telephone rang.

Larry had once been a disc jockey on the campus radio station. Now he spoke in a clear, factual voice, as it he was giving the news. "We got busted," he said. "Right after you left. This is my phone call. I want you to clean out the apartment. Do you understand?" I told him I did. He told me to come to the Marin County Courthouse tomorrow morning and hung up. . ,

This was a role I had never played before, but I found myself performing it effortlessly. I gave the apartment a thorough search. In the closet I found a brick of grass and a bag full of acid tabs. I dropped them in a shopping bag and went down to my car. Then I drove in the bus station, put it in a locker, and pocketed the key. It was still early, so I walked around North Beach for a while. I went to the City Lights bookstore and bought a couple of books, then went to an all-nite cafeteria and ate chow mein. Later I drove to the beach below the Golden Gate and took my sleeping bag out of the trunk. The foghorns were blowing and a lighthouse beam flashed overhead. I scooped a hollow out of the sand for my hips, got in my bag, and lay there for the rest of the night, listening to the waves roll in.

I was no longer depressed. In fact, I fell better than I had for months. In Austin, I had sometimes spent days sitting in my apartment, wondering what to do with myself. But once I found some action to take, some role to play, I forgot myself and my depression. If only there could be a bust every night, everything would be fine.

* * * * *

From **Twenty-six Men and a Girl** by Maxim Gorky

There were twenty-six of us-twenty-six living machines-incarcerated from morning to night in a damp basement-room, making dough for pretzels and cracknels. The -windows of this room gave out on to a large pit sunk into the ground and lined with bricks which had grown green from mould; the window frames were barred on the outside with dose-meshed metal grilles and the sunlight was unable to penetrate the flour-covered glass. Our boss had barred off the windows to prevent us giving any of his bread to the beggars and those comrades of ours who were unemployed and starving. He called us crooks and gave us putrid offal instead of meat for dinner.

Life in this stone box with its low, heavy ceiling, covered In cobwebs and blackened from smoke, was stifling and cramped. Within these thick, dirt-stained walls, rotten with mildew, we led a wretched and miserable existence. We got up at five in the morning, still tired, and by sis o'clock, dulled and indifferent, we were sitting at the table making pretzels from dough which others had been preparing while we were asleep. And the whole day, until ten in the evening, some of us sat at the table untwisting the soft dough and swaying backwards and forwards to prevent stiffness, while the others mixed the flour and water. All day long the boiling water in the cauldron where the pretzels were cooked bubbled away to itself in sorrowful meditation, and the baker's shovel rasped in hasty anger against the bottom of the oven, as he tossed the slippery pieces of boiled dough on to the hot bricks. From morning till night the wood burnt in one section of the oven, the red flames casting a flickering shadow onto the wall of the bakery, as if in silent mockery of its inhabitants. The huge oven was like the misshapen head of some mythical monster, seemingly rising out of the floor and opening its huge fiery jaws, exhaling flames and viewing our endless toil through the two sunken air-vents in its forehead. These two deep hollows were like eyes - a monster's pitiless, dispassionate eyes with a persistently veiled expression, as if they had grown tired of looking at slaves, despising them with the cold scorn of wisdom and expecting nothing human from them.

Day in, day out, covered with flour dust and the dirt which we brought in on our boots, in the fetid, suffocating atmosphere we untwisted dough and made pretzels, moistening them with the sweat of our brows, and we hated our work with a deep loathing. We never ate anything that we ourselves had made, preferring black bread to the pretzels. Sitting at a long table opposite each other - nine against nine - we worked mechanically away with our fingers and hands for hours on end, and we had grown so used to our work that we no longer even watched what we were doing. We knew each other's faces so well that every wrinkle was familiar. There was nothing to talk about and we had become accustomed to the silence, broken only by the sound of cursing, for you can always find a reason to curse someone, especially if he is a mate. But this didn't happen very often; how can someone be to blame if he's half-dead, turned to stone, his feelings crushed by the burden of work? But silence *is* painful and terrifying only for those who have already said everything and who have nothing left to say; but to those who have not yet begun to talk, silence comes easily and simply...

* * * * *

CONTENTS page of the book of Russian short stories the above story is from:

THE THIRD SON - *Andrey Platonov (1899-1951)*
SPRING IN FIALTA - *Vladimir Nabokov (1899-1977)*
STREAMS WHERE TROUT PLAY - *Kenstantin Paustovskj (1892-1968)*
THE WINTER OAK - *Yuty Nagibin (1920-   )*
ON THE ISLAND - *Yury Kazakov (1927-   )*
ZAKHAR-THE-POUCH - *Alexander Solzhenitsyn (1918-   )*

INDEX of names

Printed in Great Britain
by Amazon